JOHN STOSSEL

NO,
THEY CAN'T

Why Government Fails—But Individuals Succeed

THRESHOLD EDITIONS

NEW YORK   LONDON   TORONTO   SYDNEY   NEW DELHI

THRESHOLD EDITIONS
A Division of Simon & Schuster, Inc.
1230 Avenue of the Americas
New York, NY 10020

Copyright © 2012 by JFS Productions, Inc.

First Threshold Editions hardcover edition April 2012

THRESHOLD EDITIONS and colophon are trademarks of Simon & Schuster, Inc.

For information about special discounts for bulk purchases,
please contact Simon & Schuster Special Sales
at 1-866-506-1949 or business@simonandschuster.com.

The Simon & Schuster Speakers Bureau can bring authors to your live event. For more information or to book an event, contact the Simon & Schuster Speakers Bureau at 1-866-248-3049 or visit our website at www.simonspeakers.com.

Designed by Ruth Lee-Mui

Manufactured in the United States of America

1   3   5   7   9   10   8   6   4   2

Library of Congress Cataloging-in-Publication Data
Stossel, John.
No, they can't : why government fails—but individuals succeed / John Stossel.
        p.   cm.
Includes bibliographical references.
1. United States—Social policy—1993–   2. United States—Economic policy—2009–   3. Free enterprise—United States.   4. Social control—United States.   I. Title.
HN59.2.S765 2012
320.60973—dc23   2011047605

ISBN 978-1-4516-4094-6
ISBN 978-1-4516-4096-0 (ebook)

CONTENTS

NO,
THEY CAN'T

INTRODUCTION

Is There Anything Government Can't Do? Well . . .

I'm a skeptic. I'm suspicious of superstitions, like, say astrology. Or that "green jobs will fix the environment and the economy." I understand the appeal of such beliefs. People crave simple answers that give us the impression that some higher power determines our fates.

The worst superstition—the most socially destructive of all—is the intuitively appealing belief that when there is a problem, government action is the best way to solve it.

Opinion polls suggest that Americans are dissatisfied with government. As I write this, Congress has only a 12 percent approval rating. Government planners failed in the Soviet Union, in Cuba, in America's public school system, and at the U.S. Postal Service. Yet for all this failure and the resultant public dissatisfaction, whenever another crisis hits, the natural human instinct is to say, "Why doesn't the government *do* something?"

What government usually does is make the problem worse and leave us deeper in debt. Why don't we ever learn?

Because there are always problems that must be solved! And

1

there are always politicians pretending to be problem solvers. They are so interested in our welfare that it's all they talk about. Some of them even went to Harvard, so they must be smart. So we believe them when they say, "Yes, we can!"

At first, when Obama's supporters shouted, "Yes, we can!" they spoke as individuals eager to work toward common goals: they wanted to elect Obama, fire Bush, help the poor, invent better medicines, etc. Individuals can actually do those things.

But the Obama frenzy soon turned into the people expressing faith in the power of *government* to solve those problems. Some acted as if Obama was a magical politician whose election would end poverty and inequality and bring us to "the moment when the rise of the oceans began to slow and our planet began to heal," as he said in a famous campaign speech.

The oceans, somehow, did not slow, and at least now people have come to understand that presidents—including this president—can't do all that. But it's harder to grasp that a free people probably can. That's a counterintuitive idea. To most people, it seems intuitive to think that an elite group of central planners can accomplish more than free people pursuing their own interests. Those people need a better understanding of economics. In 1988, just before European communism collapsed, Nobel Prize–winning libertarian economist Friedrich Hayek wrote in *The Fatal Conceit* that "the curious task of economics is to demonstrate to men how little they really know about what they imagine they can design."

I often begin my Fox Business Network TV show by doing "man on the street" interviews. Once I asked people, "What do you want your government to do?" No one said that they'd like 1) predictable rules, 2) to be kept safe, and 3) to be left alone. People said things like "provide jobs" or "provide better jobs."

Why would anyone think that the government is capable of giving them a "better job"?

It's usually a mistake for me to ask people what they want government to do. Each time I do, I invite them to assume that politicians can figure out how 300 million Americans should organize their lives.

Most people are humble. They struggle to run their own lives. They're grateful to politicians who want to take charge. But this is always a bad bargain. History is filled with examples of how the rules politicians make create new problems without solving the old ones.

WHAT INTUITION TEMPTS US TO BELIEVE:

When there's a problem, government should act.

WHAT REALITY TAUGHT ME:

Individuals should act, not government.

I never went to journalism school. I learned on the job.

It didn't take me long to understand—first in my years at local TV stations and then at ABC'S *20/20*—that almost every "news" story should draw attention to some terrible problem: homelessness, illegitimacy, the crack cocaine epidemic, people spending too much time on the Internet, poor people not spending *enough* time on the Internet. Whatever the problem, there was almost always just one answer: "Government should *do* something." (Sounds better than doing nothing, right?) "The government should pass a law"—after a while, it just seemed like common sense.

But that intuition is flawed. People vastly overestimate the ability of central planners to improve upon the independent action of diverse individuals. What I've learned watching regulators try to improve the lot of consumers is that they almost always make things worse. For each new problem that regulators imagine they've solved, they invariably create new ones. If the regulators did nothing, the miraculous self-correcting mechanisms of the market would mitigate most problems with more finesse. And less cost.

But people don't get that. People instinctively say, "There ought to be a law."

If Americans keep voting for politicians who want to spend more money and pass more laws, the result will not be a country with fewer problems but a country that is governed by piecemeal socialism. We can debate the meaning of the term, but there should be no doubt that socialism leaves us less prosperous and less free.

Economists tend to focus on the "prosperous" part of that statement. They use statistics to gauge how average incomes or the gross domestic product of one country compare with another's. But the "free" part, which sounds vague, is just as important. Individuals matter, and individuals' choices matter. Objecting to restrictions on individual choice is not just an arbitrary cultural attitude. It's a moral objection. If control over our own lives is diminished—if we cannot tell the mob, or even just our neighbors, to leave us alone—something changes in our character. We become passive, and that is tragic.

Every time we call for the government to fix some social or economic problem we accelerate the growth of government. If we do not change the way we think about problems, we will end up socialists by default, even if no one calls us that.

President Obama was called a socialist for saying that government can solve our economic problems with massive spending—and for increasing the government's control over banks, the auto industry, housing, health care, and more. Shortly after he took office, *Newsweek* ran a cover story declaring, "We are all socialists now!" But calling Obama a socialist is probably unfair. After all, he hasn't called for government ownership of the means of production. But what he has done is move toward more government control of the economy. That's been his first answer to every problem. And, in the end, that's pretty close to socialism.

But then, surprise! The Tea Party movement emerged and challenged the welfare-state politicians. Now Republican presidential candidates talk about the private sector. That's progress. People say the success of the Tea Party shows that Americans want less central planning.

Maybe. But what scares me is that, contrary to what some Tea Party activists tell you, Obama today is not all that out of step with the way *most* Americans think.

- The president saw a faltering economy and thought: "Government should spend more to increase economic activity." Judging by the initial enthusiasm for programs like Cash for Clunkers and "shovel-ready" stimulus jobs, so did most Americans.
- He saw automakers on the verge of bankruptcy and thought: "We can't let GM or Chrysler go bankrupt—too many jobs would be lost." Most Americans, and George W. Bush, agreed.
- He saw people out of work and moved to extend unemployment benefits to almost two years, saying, "We've got a responsibility to help them make ends meet." Many Americans agree.

- He saw the banking sector implode and thought: "Regulation could prevent that." Most Americans still believe that today. Both Bush and Obama said government had to bail out the banks to prevent "systemic collapse." Most Americans agreed.

Consider your own political instincts. If you are on the right, do you think that government ought to be in the business of promoting good things (maybe marriage, or religious charities) and discouraging bad things (perhaps porn, pot smoking, and violent video games)?

But if government is in the business of promoting what is good and suppressing the bad, that is a license for it to stick its nose into virtually every human activity.

Politicians—and we voters—can dream of guaranteed incomes, world peace, or green energy. But reality puts limits on our political fantasies. The mature response to cries of "Yes, we can!" should be "No, we can't—not when 'we' means government. Government cannot, and it shouldn't try!" Saying "no" will not win you many cheers, but we should be realistic about what government cannot do. And being realistic sometimes means fighting what our instincts tell us.

WHAT INTUITION TEMPTS US TO BELIEVE:

Someone needs to plan, and the central planners know best.

WHAT REALITY TAUGHT ME:

No one knows enough to plan a society.

Pity us poor humans. Our brains really weren't designed to do economic reasoning any more than they were designed to do particle physics. We evolved to hunt, seek mates, and keep track of our allies and enemies. Your ancestors were pretty good at those activities. If they were not, you would not be alive to read this.

Those evolved skills still govern humans' favorite activities (modernized versions include game playing, dating, gossiping). We're hardwired to smash foes, turn on the charisma, and form political coalitions of friends. We're not wired to reason out how impersonal market forces arrive at solutions. But it's mostly those impersonal forces—say, the pursuit of profit by some pharmaceutical company—that give us better lives.

Learning to think economically—and to resist the pro-central planning impulse—is our only hope of rescuing America from a diminished future.

Hayek argued in *The Fatal Conceit* that one of humanity's biggest problems is that we use instincts that evolved when we lived in small tribes and extended families to make decisions about how to run the far more complex "extended order" of a modern economy. This creates a "Father knows best" approach that doesn't work well outside the family or tribe.

It's natural to trust the elites in Washington. After all, their very eagerness to address the "public good" shows that they have "enlightened values." Such arguments strike an emotional chord—but shouldn't. The days when society was an extended family—when you were likely to starve in the cold unless you heeded the village elders—left us with instincts that make us feel safer when the elders call the shots. But we should resist those instincts. Ancient societies weren't safe by our standards—people lived perpetually on the brink of starvation.

In a world where millions of people make complex economic decisions, often what "feels right" makes for bad policy. It leads us to think that politicians can manage our lives as easily as the head of a simple village used to decide when it's time to harvest more fruit.

As long as Americans—and perhaps all human brains—leap to the intuitive *yet false* conclusion that governments solve problems, we're in big trouble. That's why we keep increasing government power: it seems like the obvious solution. Yet such "solutions" inevitably generate more problems for government to "solve."

Here are just a few examples:

- *We can revitalize the neighborhood with a big project like, say, a new sports arena!* The big government–subsidized sports arenas and stadiums never achieve their promised goals, and their costs—usually paid by taxpayers—suck the life out of the local economy.
- *We must guarantee workers a "living" wage!* Simple intuition seems to tell us that such laws help the working poor. It takes some thinking to realize that a law can't make a $5 worker worth $10—if it could, we might as well set the minimum wage at $100 an hour. Living-wage laws have nearly eliminated ushers, gas station attendants, grocery store baggers, and other entry-level jobs that used to give people vital early employment experience.
- *Home ownership is good, so government can and should create more of it!* The left wanted to subsidize home buying to help poor people escape greedy landlords. The right wanted to promote "family values" and an "ownership society." Politicians on both sides coveted housing subsidies because they won applause from lobbyists.

But subsidies rewarded irresponsible risk taking and punished thrift. They created the housing bubble, gutted retirement accounts, and screwed the taxpayer.

- *We can steer America toward cleaner forms of energy. If Congress jump-starts the research, the country that sent men to the moon will invent an alternative to oil!* The market didn't arbitrarily pick oil as the dominant source of energy. It really is an efficient way to generate power. No matter how much we love windmills, solar panels, or fields of biofuel, we can't get nearly as much energy out of them as we do out of oil—and we have to pay substantially more for what little energy we do get. Government's "green" subsidies suck money away from far more useful activities. They kill more good things than they create.

WHAT INTUITION TEMPTS US TO BELIEVE:

The important thing is to have heroic leaders.

WHAT REALITY TAUGHT ME:

Real heroes don't control other people's lives.

We give politicians *far* too much credit. Harris Interactive Polls asks people who their heroes are. In 2001, Jesus Christ topped the list. In 2009, it was Barack Obama, followed closely by Ronald Reagan and George W. Bush. When people think of "heroes," they think about politicians.

Sixteen years ago, Senator Edmund Muskie died. Newspapers ran long stories about his life. To reporters, this politician was very important. He was a Democratic presidential contender.

"Generations to come will benefit" from his work, the *New York Times* quoted Bill Clinton as saying.

On the same day, the papers also ran a much smaller obituary for David Packard, founder of the Hewlett-Packard Company. Laser printers, 60 million PCs, hundreds of useful products, and thousands of jobs exist because of David Packard. His management style changed lives. He deemphasized rank and privilege and gave everyone from the chairman on down a doorless office. Ideas like "profit sharing" and "flex time" started at Hewlett-Packard. These are things that make *all* our lives better.

But to the media, Ed Muskie was the hero—Packard was just a businessman.

Likewise, when Ted Kennedy died in 2009, the media talked about him for days. Presidents attended his funeral. The *New York Times* ran a long obituary on its front page.

Norman Borlaug died that same year. You probably don't even know who he was. Borlaug was an American scientist who invented a type of wheat that makes it possible to grow much more food on less land. When he won the Nobel Prize the prize committee wrote, "More than any other single person of this age, he helped to provide bread for a hungry world."

Borlaug saved millions of lives. Senator Kennedy . . . well, I won't go there. Borlaug is a hero, but it's politicians who get celebrated in the media. Something is wrong with this picture.

We long for villains in the same foolish way we long for heroes. After the financial crisis started in earnest in 2008, candidate Senator Barack Obama favored bailouts (President Bush had launched us down that disastrous road) and increased regulation. But the response of his opponent, Senator John McCain, was just as bad. McCain dismissed the complications of regulation and economics altogether—admitting at one point that he'd "never really understood" economics—and said he would find the bad guys on Wall Street whose "greed" got us into the mess. "I've taken on tougher guys than this," McCain bragged in one campaign ad. He implied that a few villainous traders had simply run off with bags of dollars.

That kind of oversimplification is appealing. We've evolved to spot—and become outraged by—cheaters and thieves, not to sift through decades of bad investment decisions, regulatory changes, and legalese trying to figure out whether *de*regulation might prevent similar disasters. It's more satisfying to just say, "Punish the bad guys!"

I attended college at the height of the hippie era, when so many of us were convinced that bad guys in the Establishment caused our problems. One of my heroes at Princeton was someone especially good at pegging established businesspeople as villains: consumer activist Ralph Nader. In books like *Unsafe at Any Speed*, which claimed that the Chevrolet Corvair was prone to roll over, Nader confirmed our assumption that we were being ripped off, if not killed, by callous corporations in pursuit of a quick buck. New regulations, he said, would fix that.

My intuition told me that made sense. Instinct told me to watch people's motivations. What motivates corporations? They want to make money. They don't care about me. They aren't part of my tribe or family. Besides, after Nader wrote about the Corvair, General Motors had Nader followed. Creepy. Not hard to spot the villains here.

Nader's efforts didn't inspire just me. They inspired countless activist lawyers and "consumer" groups like the Public Interest Research Group, which at many colleges now gets an automatic cut of student tuition money—even when the students don't agree with its goals and don't know who Ralph Nader is.

Few of us paid attention when government scientists later concluded that the Corvair was just as safe as other cars. By then Nader had moved on to an ever-widening crusade against chemicals in food, dangerous toys, air pollution, and more. Egged on by a compliant media and political class that instinctively favor central planning, Nader's "raiders" created thousands of freedom-killing regulations.

When I started work as a consumer reporter, those regulations made sense to me. I could see the injured consumers and the scams perfect for exposing on TV. With Nader-inspired zeal, I wrote about shoddy products and greedy businessmen. My colleagues and I demanded "reforms."

I barely noticed as the number of regulations mushroomed. During the 1960s, the *Federal Register*, which publishes new regulations, doubled in size. The *Code of Federal Regulations*, which contains all the final regulatory rules under which we live, is now 160,000 pages long. Do you comply with all 160,000 pages of federal law? Every year, Congress adds several thousand new pages.

I was too busy winning Emmy Awards for bashing corporations to notice that there are a million subtle, unintended effects of all this "protection." When companies are forced to redesign products, prices rise. That alone makes life less safe. Tougher airline safety rules lead to higher ticket prices, which lead more people to drive to Grandma's house. I call that statistical murder.

• • •

Lately, Nader has moved on to denouncing the entire American political system as a corrupt tool of corporations.

But what exactly do these evil corporations do to me? Mostly, they try to sell me stuff, and they hope I'll like it so they can sell me more stuff. The way capitalists get really rich is to serve their customers *well*. If they rip me off, word gets out, their reputation takes a hit, and they lose business. The free market is ruthless at ferreting out and punishing inferior products and services.

Yet progressives tell us that companies are a menace. "Corporate power lies behind nearly every major problem we face—from stagnant wages and unaffordable health care to overconsumption and global warming," warn columnists in the political magazine *Yes*. Progressives always fear the "power" of business, rather than the power of government. But government has a power no business has: force. If we refuse to do "business" with government, government will fine us—jail us. I can rudely tell Microsoft that I refuse to buy its products—but I can't tell the Internal Revenue Service to take a hike when it orders me to pay for the Department of Energy, foreign wars, monuments, bailouts, and everything else the government does, no matter how dissatisfied I am with its results.

The more power we give government to control businesses, the more businesses seek to control government. Instead of obsessing about inventing better products, they obsess about getting cozy with politicians and regulators. They "invest" in people who are clever at manipulating rules. This distracts them from real entrepreneurship.

It's no coincidence that one of the greatest wealth creators in history, the computer business, blossomed in the two metropolitan areas farthest from Washington, D.C.—Silicon Valley and Seattle. For years, Microsoft created great wealth by hiring engineers and programmers. They employed no lobbyists. Then government sued

Microsoft, claiming antitrust-law violations. Now the company spends millions on lobbying and even uses its Washington connections to attack rivals.

This is not a good trend.

It's one more reason that we're better off keeping government small—and laws simple enough that businesses have little to lobby about. The smaller the government, the less the need to manipulate politicians.

WHAT INTUITION TEMPTS US TO BELIEVE:

Big business runs the media, so the media support business.

WHAT REALITY TAUGHT ME:

The media hate business.

This libertarian view of the proper scope of government (namely, small and limited) wasn't popular at Princeton, nor in any newsroom where I worked. Economists like Hayek and Milton Friedman won Nobel Prizes, but for years their words didn't reach me. Only twenty years into my career, after I discovered *Reason* magazine, did libertarian ideas begin to inform my reporting.

My first serious attempt to express them on TV was a piece that *20/20* let me run in 1989 called "Relaxing the Rules." I covered some unexpected consumer benefits that had come from deregulation. Remarkably, this deregulation—something that most intellectuals and media opposed—began under President Carter's reign. Regulators freed natural gas prices, eliminated the Interstate Commerce Commission and its control of trucking prices, and eliminated the

Civil Aeronautics Board and its stranglehold on airlines' decision making. Politicians and reporters predicted disaster.

When natural gas prices were deregulated, they wailed that prices "would skyrocket." The opposite happened. More fluid markets meant more competition, and prices dropped.

Airlines, once limited to a handful of big carriers, suddenly faced competition from upstart local airlines. Prices dropped sharply. True, planes and airports got more crowded, but flights went from something reserved for the rich to transportation for the masses.

Once trucking companies were allowed to set their own prices, shipping costs dropped, and almost every product became a little cheaper. This saved Americans billions, but most people didn't notice. The media barely paid attention.

Hugh Downs was a little shocked when I said these things on *20/20*. "Really, John, I had no idea," he said.

I then set out to learn more about free markets and to do as much reporting about economics and regulation as I could. ABC News wasn't thrilled about that. But I was good at producing TV programs, so they kept me on and reluctantly agreed to let me do three hour-long prime-time specials.

When I proposed my first one, on risk, *Are We Scaring Ourselves to Death?*, my bosses resisted. Alan Wurtzel, ABC's research director at the time (he's now at NBC), said: "A show on risk? You should do something on diet or breast implants—we know people will watch that." My bosses delayed the show for two years. But I give ABC credit. After bitter arguments, they ran it. Although my bosses often disagreed with my point of view, they usually let me air it.

Two producers quit rather than work on the hour. They said a show about the negative side effects of regulation was "conservative dogma—not journalism." ABC flashed the disclaimer "perspective" on the screen, and the hour had to be followed by a "town meeting" segment, where people could rebut the program's assertions. ABC executives were surprised when the special got big ratings and praise from scientists.

Despite that special's success, each new one was a battle. European communism was collapsing because of the failure of central government planning, but saying "let the market decide" was still heresy at ABC.

I fought the lawyers and liberal producers for twenty years. I tried to ignore their sneers and skepticism. After all, ABC paid me well, and I got to give millions of viewers a take on markets that they didn't generally get. But finally, two decades later, I gave up.

Just as the choice-in-education movement blossomed, *20/20* rejected my request to update my prime-time special *Stupid in America*, even though the initial broadcast got great ratings (see chapter 9 for more on education). Then, in 2009, the big story became Barack Obama and his health-care plans. The media quickly agreed that Obama's ideas were brilliant.

I knew better. I had already done a TV special on government-run health care in Great Britain and Canada. I'd confronted Michael Moore about the claims he made in *Sicko* (see chapter 5). I had cool video of the rare Canadian medical patients who got cutting-edge treatment (dogs and cats).

I was excited to be ahead of the media curve. With ObamaCare in play, I knew that ABC would be eager to update my special. *20/20*'s executive producer said he would run it shortly after ABC aired a "town hall" meeting that Barack Obama held at the White House. My special would help balance the discussion.

But then my report was "delayed." Michael Jackson died, and I was told that *20/20* obviously needed to do the entire hour on that. The following week, *20/20* aired an interview with Michael Jackson's sister. The following weeks, *20/20* covered his drug use, his music, his friends, his influence on America, where his money went, and so on.

ABC never found time to run my hour on the downside of ObamaCare.

I saw the writing on the wall. Network ratings were down. ABC wanted to cut costs. My politics were wrong. I would be among the first to go when my contract was up. I jumped before I was fired.

I phoned Fox News and said, "Please, hire me!" Fortunately, they did.

I never thought I'd be a weekly show for Fox Business Network (FBN), in addition to fighting with Bill O'Reilly on Tuesday nights and producing documentaries. I'd always done stories that I carefully edited. I'd obsess for hours over a few seconds of videotape. Now I do shows live! This was a shock. There were many shocks.

Arthur Brooks, president of the American Enterprise Institute, warned me that it takes eighteen months to get comfortable in a new job. He was right.

I struggled at first. I'm scared of *live*. I'm a stutterer. I feared that I'd humiliate myself on live TV. In elevators, people asked how I was doing. I told them that it was difficult—that I wasn't used to so much unedited television, let alone *live* TV. Eventually one person told me, "Y'know, when people say 'How are you?' they don't really need to hear how you are. You can just say 'Fine.'"

Now I'm doing better. As I write this, just past my eighteenth-month mark, I'm actually having fun. Fox makes it easy. The company is better run than ABC. Being nonunion probably helps. So does the fact that people are very busy. At ABC there were endless meetings—lots of waiting around. Not at Fox. You do the work. They put it on the air.

My Fox Business Network show has a smaller audience than *20/20*'s, but my best work now reaches 12 million high school students. A nonprofit, Stossel in the Classroom, gives free copies to teachers, along with teacher guides. Today thousands of teachers use my DVDs to introduce students to free markets. An ABC executive had tried to kill that project. She sneered, "We don't want libertarian activists associated with ABC!" Fox, being more open-minded, allows Stossel in the Classroom to use the videos. Now, to my great satisfaction, more Americans watch them than watch *20/20*.

Also, Fox runs my edited specials several times, and then I reach an audience equal to *American Idol*'s. Really. One show, *Freeloaders*, was seen by 15 million people.

Even if I had fewer viewers, the job change was worth it just for the improvement in my working climate. At ABC News, when Peter Jennings saw me in the hall, he abruptly turned the other way. Others rolled their eyes. Politically hostile lawyers and producers combed though my scripts, demanding extra documentation if I said something positive about markets, asking me to "take this out" or "tone that down." Usually I could persuade them to let me say most of what I wanted to say, as long as I "softened" some of it. But too many stories I thought were important—like government land theft called eminent domain, or the FDA actually endangering people's lives by withholding lifesaving drugs—were not aired. At Fox, they let me speak.

I'm so glad I made the switch. At FBN, business reporters

actually understand free markets. They don't sneer when I offer ideas that seem counterintuitive.

Many at Fox disagree with some of these ideas. But the big difference—and joy—is that at Fox, difference is respected. They believe different ideas deserve to be heard. If I get into a political argument—like my fights with Sean Hannity and Bill O'Reilly about drug legalization—the people arguing usually understand that they have a political position. At ABC, my colleagues denied that ideology influenced their reporting. Many acted as if the only person in the building with political views was . . . me. When I once suggested that politicians' love of socialism kept India poor, Peter Jennings said my "bias" was "an embarrassment" to ABC and demanded that I be fired. At least ABC executives ignored his demand.

Of course everyone has biases—even ABC reporters. They just don't think they do. I know that my brain is full of biases and misperceptions, but at least I am aware of the problem—and of a few of the important ways the human brain routinely goes wrong. That, as well as my ignorance, keeps me humble when people ask me questions like "Don't you think we should abolish the Fed?"

I mention my ignorance because plenty of people know more than I do. My scientist brother is smarter than I am. So are most people who work at FBN. Milton Friedman once called me "that rare creature, a TV commentator who understands economics, in all its subtlety." I loved that quote. But it's one of the few things Milton got wrong.

After forty years of consumer reporting, I do have an understanding of the subtleties of markets and government's incompetence at improving on them. But I don't understand economics.

I was a college psychology major. I think I've learned a thing or two—with help from great minds who came before me: Hayek, Sowell, Friedman, Murray, and others—but there is so much that I don't understand.

What I *have* learned, though, may be the most important thing: that even if I were an economic genius, that wouldn't mean I could be trusted to manage the economy. No one can be trusted to manage the economy. I began this introduction with criticism of President Obama, but I don't assume that Republicans would be better. Both parties share the fatal conceit of believing that their grandiose plan will solve America's problems. Neither plan will.

But cheer up: saying that government is not the way to solve problems is not saying that humanity cannot solve its problems. What I've finally learned is this: despite the obstacles created by governments, voluntary networks of private individuals solve all sorts of challenges. Government offers guarantees on paper, promises in speeches, new rights to replace old ones (and often undermine old ones, like property rights). But government doesn't deliver. Individuals do. Markets do.

Markets aren't perfect. But they allow for a world where prudence is rewarded and recklessness punished—a world in which people are more likely to take risks and innovate—one where more people prosper. That includes the poor. It's said that "the poor will always be with us," but if free markets were unleashed, that would be much less true. The future could be one so rich—so filled with technology and wonders—that my grandchildren would need to read about poverty to know what it was.

To get to that sort of world, though, we need to discard a lot of appealing ideas. We need to retrain our brains. It took me twenty years to retrain mine.

1

"FIXING" THE ECONOMY

We spend too much time waiting for orders—and money—from Washington.

This happens because people think "something must be done" (by government) whenever bad things happen. When the housing bubble burst and stock prices tanked, President Obama told us: "The consensus is this: We have to do whatever it takes to get this economy moving again—we're going to have to spend money now to stimulate the economy. . . ."

The idea, always implicit in the government's thinking, but made explicit in the past few years, was that whatever the government spends money on will create a "multiplier effect"—that is, each dollar spent by the government will somehow generate more than a dollar's worth of economic activity. That activity will create jobs.

The recession gave politicians a license to do what they wanted to do all along: spend. The usual checks on extravagance, weak as they are, were washed away. Budgets? We'll worry about that later. Inflation? We'll worry about that later.

WHAT INTUITION TEMPTS US TO BELIEVE:

Government can "get the economy moving again."

WHAT REALITY TAUGHT ME:

Government does not spend money better than individuals do.

A true free market doesn't require much. It needs property rights, so no one can take your stuff. Then, people trade property to their mutual advantage, life never being perfect, but generally improving with each trade. Resources move around without the need for a central, coercive government telling people which resources should go where—or telling them that they must get permission to do what they think advantageous.

Ever see the website that tells the story of the guy who starts with a paper clip and trades his way up to a house? It was just a stunt, but that's roughly what happens when the market is left alone. People combine resources in new ways to create wealth—and, in the process, jobs.

When President Obama took office, he promised to "save or create" 3.5 million jobs. Should we credit him for saving any jobs? He says that unemployment would be worse without his stimulus. But how can we know? I assume his spending on expensive government jobs crowded out better, more sustainable jobs.

If the economy recovers and President Obama claims he caused that, it wouldn't be the first time a "leader" ran in front of a crowd and claimed to have led the way. But politicians don't deserve credit for what free people do.

Given time, an economy, unless crippled by government intervention, will regenerate *itself.* The Keynesians in the administration said government had to "jump-start" the economy because businesses weren't hiring. But an economy is not a machine that needs jump-starting. The economy is people who have objectives they want to achieve.

For now, the big-government media are baffled that big spending hasn't paid off. "Companies are sitting on billions of dollars of cash. And still, they've yet to amp up hiring or make major investment," wrote the *Washington Post.*

C'mon, *Post,* don't blame the companies. CEOs don't just wake up one day and decide not to hire. They hold back, quite reasonably, because they don't know what obstacles they'll face next. Will activist government prop up housing prices? Impose a new health-care mandate? Forbid me to move to South Carolina?

When rules are unpredictable or unintelligible (is the investment firm you use in compliance with the 2,300-page Dodd-Frank finance regulatory act?), then businesses hesitate to hire. When new employees are threats because byzantine Labor Department regulations make it impossible to fire them, businesses hesitate to hire. When tax increases lie ahead, businesses hesitate to hire. I don't blame them.

Nothing more effectively freezes business than what historian Robert Higgs calls "regime uncertainty."

WHAT INTUITION TEMPTS US TO BELIEVE:

Government creates good things.

WHAT REALITY TAUGHT ME:

We see what government creates—but don't
see what might have existed instead.

Despite politicians' talk of "giving" money to this or that (remember those tax rebate checks with President George W. Bush's name emblazoned on them?), government has no money of its own. It has to take it from the private sector. Grabbing those scarce resources stifles the real economy.

One of the most important questions in politics *should* be: "Would the private sector have done better things with that money?" (And we should ask a similar question about the decision-making authority government takes from us every time it regulates.)

A healthy economy does not just create jobs-of-any-kind, it creates *productive* jobs. The pharaohs of ancient Egypt created plenty of jobs building pyramids, but who knows how much better the lives of ancient Egyptians (especially the slaves) might have been had they been free to engage in other work? They would all have had better housing, more food, or snazzier headdresses. Even as smart a person as economist John Maynard Keynes seemed to forget about that when he wrote in his *General Theory* back in 1936, "Pyramid-building, earthquakes, even wars may serve to increase wealth."

By that logic, government could create full employment tomorrow by outlawing machines. Think of all the work there'd be to do then! Or government could hire people to dig holes and then fill them up (sadly, some government work resembles that).

Think about the two other methods to "increase wealth" that Keynes lumped in with pyramid-building: earthquakes and war. Now, sure, after a war or earthquake, there's plenty of construction to be done. After the Haitian earthquake, Nancy Pelosi actually said, "I think that this can be an opportunity for a real boom economy in Haiti." *New York Times* columnist Paul Krugman made a similar error. On CNN, he said if "space aliens were planning to attack and we needed a massive buildup to counter the space alien threat . . . this slump would be over in eighteen months." Before that, he'd said the 9/11 attacks would be good for the economy.

This is Keynesian cluelessness at its worst. Sure, rebuilding after 9/11 or a Mars invasion would be good for the economy—but only if you ignore the fact that the same money and effort *could* have been used to make Crock-Pots, save for college, invest in Apple, or for countless other things.

Isn't it obvious that those same workers could have done more productive work—with the resulting overall standard of living higher as a result? Does anyone really wish for earthquakes? There is something very wrong with mainstream politics and economics if some of its most respected practitioners overlook this point.

The economic philosopher Frédéric Bastiat called their mistake the "broken window fallacy." If I break your window, it's easy to see that I've given work to a glass-maker. But what we don't see or think about is this: you would have done something else with the money you paid the glass-maker. That money would have created different jobs.

Reporters get confused by this. We favor government projects because we cover what is *seen*, not the *unseen*. The beneficiaries of the politicians' conceit are visible. We see the windmills, solar farms, and housing subdivisions. The media see workers who got a raise from the new minimum wage. But we cannot see what *didn't* happen because politicians acted. I cannot photograph the store that didn't open because taxes went to homebuilders and solar farms. I cannot interview the worker never offered a job because the minimum wage priced him out of the market. I don't even know who he is.

Creating jobs is not difficult for government. What is difficult is creating jobs that produce wealth.

As I write this, the *New York Times* reports that the Dodd-Frank regulation has been "a boon" to lawyers and corporate accountants. The article actually calls the regulations an "unofficial jobs creation act."

Give me a break. Pyramids, broken windows, and extra accounting work do not produce wealth.

Under President Obama's "stimulus" plan, jobs were created to weatherize buildings, build wind turbines, and repair roads. Politicians claimed these were valuable projects. But outside the market process, there is no way to know whether those were better uses of scarce capital than what would have been produced had the money been left in the private economy.

Since government services are funded through the compulsion of taxes, they have no market price. Without market prices, *we have no way of knowing the importance that free people place on those services*. We cannot calculate how much wealth we lose when politicians allocate resources.

Underlying President Obama's (and Paul Krugman's) call for more "stimulus" spending is the largely unexamined assumption that government spending will be more productive than spending by you and me.

But we don't just throw our money off a cliff. We buy things. We invest, give to charity, save for college, save for retirement. All that is useful. Individuals do all kinds of things the government pretends that only it can do.

Krugman seems to think we're all just goofing off here in the private sector, whereas the president and his wise advisers will steer money to truly productive uses, just as John Maynard Keynes believed back in Franklin D. Roosevelt's day. Progressives say that FDR helped pull America out of the Great Depression. But his programs probably lengthened the Depression, even generating a depression within the Depression in 1937. Roosevelt's Treasury secretary did complain: "After eight years of this administration we have just as much unemployment as when we started." Sound familiar?

Amity Shlaes shows in her book *The Forgotten Man* that the New Deal failed because it interfered with the market's natural regenerative processes. By creating uncertainty about what government would do next, government made businesses afraid to invest and hire. Again, sound familiar? Why expand if you fear new taxes? If you can't even understand the rules?

WHAT INTUITION TEMPTS US TO BELIEVE:

It's good for government to encourage home ownership.

WHAT REALITY TAUGHT ME:

When government interferes in a market . . . bad things happen.

U.S. politicians want to "support" the housing market. They've created housing subsidies, mortgage-backing Fannie Mae and Freddie Mac, the Federal Housing Administration, and zero down payments. What great ideas! The subsidies and loan guarantees would help more people buy homes, and since homeowners are more responsible citizens, everything will be better.

You've seen the result.

By the way, Canada has no Fannie, Freddie, FHA, or zero down payment loans, yet Canadians have a higher rate of home ownership than we.

The U.S. housing bubble was *created* by subsidies and regulations—including laws encouraging subprime mortgages and increased lending in neighborhoods with high loan default rates. Far from needing government to step in and "fix" the economy, housing is a mess precisely because of earlier government interference. Easy mortgage terms and guarantees contrived a housing boom that could not be sustained.

The media didn't help. We interviewed people who said home values would always go up.

At *20/20*, at the peak of the boom, I was embarrassed to anchor shows that my boss called "real estate porn." Porn, because people love to look at elegant houses and fantasize. These shows rated well. In one, a promoter gave advice like "You can't get rich if you're a renter . . . even if you have credit card debt, the banks will loan you money." *20/20*'s producer introduced him to a couple who, sensibly, worried about "getting in over their heads." The so-called expert said "no problem" and steered them toward a mortgage and home ownership.

I didn't protest, but I should have. I chickened out because my ideas already made me something of an outcast at ABC. I had to pick my battles. And of course, maybe I was wrong. Maybe housing prices would rise forever. At the time, people said they would.

Then came the bust.

Now the FHA has taxpayers on the hook for almost a trillion dollars in home loan guarantees, the Federal Reserve has bought a trillion dollars' worth of dubious mortgage securities, and taxpayers have already given Fannie and Freddie a $125 billion bailout, with Congress promising "unlimited" further assistance. Remember when Fannie CEO Franklin Raines told us: "It is private capital that is at risk, not the taxpayer's. . . . We do not receive a nickel of federal money"?

When the housing bubble burst, President Obama insisted that the subsequent turmoil was "a stark reminder of the failures of . . . an economic philosophy that sees any regulation at all as unwise and unnecessary." In other words, George W. Bush, who spent more money on regulation and hired more new regulators than any president before him, was somehow a deregulator? Then capitalists ran amok because benevolent government wasn't there to mind the store?

Nonsense. The real culprits were politicians of both parties, who for years relieved big companies of the responsibility that market discipline imposes. The promise—explicit or implicit—to bail out companies deemed "too big to fail" destroys market discipline. That invites recklessness. Home ownership, all else being equal, is a good thing. But when government lumbers into the market and subsidizes folly, that's a very bad thing.

WHAT INTUITION TEMPTS US TO BELIEVE:

Some institutions are too big to fail.

WHAT REALITY TAUGHT ME:

Failure makes markets work.

After the fall of Lehman Brothers in September 2008, everybody said we *had* to bail out American International Group (AIG) and the banks. Even the *Wall Street Journal* editorial page said so. So did those brilliant investment bankers. They must be brilliant, I thought, because they're so rich; they probably understand markets in ways that I don't.

When I was skeptical about bailouts, they scoffed. There was no doubt, they said, that our leaders had to "create liquidity, restore confidence, give banks time to get their balance sheets in order."

It still seemed wrong to me. Businesses that make bad decisions *should* fail. That's how capitalism works. Economists call it "creative destruction." That allows markets to adjust to real price signals. If housing prices crash, so be it. They had risen so fast. Probably they were ridiculously high. Now maybe prices are back to realistic levels. I don't know. The media don't know. The Fed doesn't know. Only the market knows.

A price is neither good nor bad; it is simply information—it tells buyers and sellers how much people value a particular product. No good comes from manipulating prices. That only deceives the market.

The media portrayed falling home prices as a tragedy. Why? There were winners and losers. Speculators lost, but renters who saved responsibly could now afford homes.

If some banks fail, some investors lose big, but that's how markets work. America has a safety net to protect the truly needy. Bank deposits are insured up to $250,000. If you lost millions, that's sad for you, but your losses will remind you, and others, to diversify next time.

So why the eagerness to bail out banks?

I confronted economist Steve Moore of the editorial board of the

Wall Street Journal. I told him I didn't understand why the *Journal* ran pro-bailout columns with titles like "Secretary Paulson Makes the Right Call." He said something about a need to "calm the markets." But he didn't sound convinced. Months later, he said he was embarrassed that he supported the bailouts. "I want to apologize," he said. "I drank the Kool-Aid."

Panic produces that Kool-Aid. The *Journal*'s editors live and work among people who are at the center of the storm. The editors' judgment is right about almost everything, but when Lehman fails and the market dives, friends call them to shriek, "It's terrible! We're losing *everything*! There's going to be a global depression. Washington has to *do* something!"

I was relieved when the *Journal* ran an op-ed by George Mason University economist Russ Roberts with the headline "Don't Just Do Something, Stand There." Roberts correctly argued that politicians can't wisely spend the trillions they commit, "even if they want to. . . . It is time to let the imprudent fail and the prudent pick up the bargains."

But most of the media were in the center of the "do-something" panic. Our 401(k)s had been clobbered. The financial "experts" said government "had" to act.

Experts often believe government "has" to act. During the Y2K panic, "technology experts" said government "had" to act. The global warming scientists said the same thing during the global warming hysteria, as did the swine flu doctors, AIDS activists, flesh-eating-bacteria scientists, terrorism gurus, and so on. People close to a problem want big-government action. Many believe that if we don't get it, disaster will happen. They don't fake panic just to get government funds (well, maybe some, but most are genuinely superscared). But the flesh-eating-bacteria scientists and global warming alarmists don't have the power to seize and spend *trillions* of your dollars. Treasury secretaries Hank Paulson and Tim Geithner did.

Both say that the world would now be in worse shape had they not thrown your money around. Again, *how do we know*? What if the government cut loose GM, Citigroup, and the others, forcing them to do what other businesses do in hard times: renegotiate with creditors and revalue assets? Wouldn't prices have found a more solid floor? Wouldn't scarce resources have flowed to more valuable uses? We'll never know.

What we've got from the bailouts is worse than a temporary "systemic collapse." We have big taxpayer losses, artificially propped-up prices, and Fannie and Freddie and the FHA putting taxpayers further at risk by continuing to subsidize big loans. We also have the moral hazard (the decreased pressure to avoid reckless behavior) and economic distortion created by declaring some institutions "too big to fail." Those banks today, by the way, are even bigger than they were before the bailouts. Dodd-Frank didn't even address that problem. In fact, the bailouts gave "too big" banks an *advantage* over smaller competitors because people prefer to park their money in a bank that's "too big to fail."

Jim Rogers, the successful investor and author, puts it well: "Why are 300 million Americans having to pay for Citibank's mistakes? The way the system is supposed to work [is this]: People fail. And then the competent people take over the assets from the failed people, and then you start again with a new stronger base. What we're doing this time is . . . taking the assets from the competent people, giving them to the incompetent people, and saying, 'OK, now you can compete with the competent people.' So everybody's weakened: The whole nation is weakened."

. . .

Had I been working at Fox Business when the bailouts began, I could have at least reported on it. I could have asked Hank Paulson or his colleagues about the moral hazard. I could have asked about panicky phone calls he got from his former coworkers at Goldman Sachs. I could have asked why AIG deserved my money but Lehman didn't, and what right he had to force healthy banks to take bailout money. I would have tried to ask Tim Geithner why, if taxing the rich is so good, he didn't pay thirty-five thousand dollars of his own taxes.

But I couldn't do any of it because I was still at *20/20*. My bosses had no interest in my asking whether it was smart for government to try to micromanage the economy. The same week that the House approved the stimulus plan and jobless claims hit an all-time high, *20/20* devoted our whole show to "Seduction: Why Him? Why Her?"

After Obama was elected, my colleagues seemed even *less* interested in criticizing government. When federal spending increased to a degree that I hadn't even thought possible, my colleagues believed that this "stimulus" would "create jobs." But most didn't have much time to think about it. They were busy reporting on claims of sexual harassment at Starbucks.

When the millions of new jobs didn't appear, Paul Krugman said that the initial plan to spend $500 billion was too small, and that even Franklin Roosevelt had been too timid: "the reason for FDR's limited short-run success, which almost undid his whole program, was the fact that his economic policies were too cautious."

Cautious? FDR began the modern transformation of the United States from an individualistic society with relatively little government bureaucracy into the society we have today, which takes for granted that the most important things in life—health, retirement, education, science, safety, poverty relief, and more—will be largely run and subsidized by government. This was enormous.

The stimulus was not timid, either.

President Obama said, "There is no disagreement that we need action by our government, a recovery plan that will help to jump-start the economy." But there was plenty of disagreement. The Cato Institute ran a full-page newspaper ad signed by more than two hundred economists, including Nobel laureates, stating: "We the undersigned do not believe that more government spending is a way to improve economic performance. More government spending by Hoover and Roosevelt did not pull the United States economy out of the Great Depression in the 1930s. More government spending did not solve Japan's 'lost decade' in the 1990s. . . . Lower tax rates and a reduction in the burden of government are the best ways of using fiscal policy to boost growth."

Many economists thought the stimulus spending was a terrible mistake. But the mainstream media weren't interested.

WHAT INTUITION TEMPTS US TO BELIEVE:
Government officials act with the public good at heart.

WHAT REALITY TAUGHT ME:
Government officials act in their self-interest just like the
rest of us—but when *they* do, it's a bigger problem because
government's customers cannot take their business elsewhere.

So far I've referred to the hypothetical case in which well-intended government tries to create useful economic activity (but fails to allocate resources as efficiently as the private sector would). But let's not pretend that political processes are devoid of, well, politics.

After Obama took office, a little window company in California, Serious Materials, got a lot of media attention. *Fortune* magazine said Serious was "booming." *Inc.* magazine did a cover story, titled "How to Build a Great Company," that said Serious was "on a roll."

The company sure seemed to be. Vice President Joe Biden turned up at the opening of a Serious plant to say: "You are not just churning out windows; you are making some of the most energy-efficient windows in the world. I would argue the most energy-efficient windows in the world." Biden laid it on pretty thick.

And why do I mention only the *vice* president? President Obama himself singled the company out: "Serious Materials . . . will now have a new mission: producing some of the most energy-efficient windows in the world." How many companies get endorsed by the president and the vice president of the United States?

Rachel Maddow, usually not a big promoter of business, gushed that Serious was an example of "stimulus working."

When Obama announced a new set of tax credits for so-called green companies, one window company was on the list: Serious Materials. Why? Serious's products are not particularly special. Other companies make similar windows.

But Serious had one thing that definitely made it special: connections. Its executives gave money to Obama's campaign. Of course, many companies did that. But the Freedom Foundation of Minnesota pointed out something else: Cathy Zoi, an Energy Department official who oversaw $16.8 billion in stimulus funds—much of it for weatherization programs that benefit Serious—happened to be the wife of Robin Roy, vice president of "policy" at Serious Materials.

Of all the window companies in America, maybe it's a coincidence that the one that gets presidential and vice presidential attention and a special tax credit is one whose executives give thousands of dollars to the Obama campaign and one where the policy officer is married to the Energy Department's weatherization boss.

Or maybe not.

As far as I know, there's nothing illegal about this. Zoi (who now works for George Soros) disclosed her marriage and said, "I will not participate . . . in any particular matter that has a direct and predictable effect on [my financial interests]." But it sure seems wrong to me.

When we asked Serious Materials about all this, a spokeswoman said that my story was "full of lies." But she wouldn't say what those lies were.

On its website, Serious Materials said it did not get a taxpayer subsidy. But that's just playing with terms. What it got was a tax credit, an opportunity that its competitors did not get: to keep money it would have paid in taxes. Let's not be misled.

If government wants job creation, it would simplify regulations and cut taxes across the board. They wouldn't single out certain companies for special treatment. Why should there be favoritism?

Because politicians like it. Big, complicated government gives them opportunities to do favors for their friends.

WHAT INTUITION TEMPTS US TO BELIEVE:
Capitalism is corrupt because big companies use
their influence to manipulate the system.

WHAT REALITY TAUGHT ME:
That's not capitalism. That's crapitalism.

Crony capitalism—some call it "crapitalism"—is the economic system in which the marketplace is substantially shaped by a cozy relationship between government and business. Think Serious Materials. Under crony capitalism, government bestows privileges on some companies: import restrictions, bailouts, subsidies, loan guarantees, etc. In a true free market, a business has no more power to use government to gain advantage over competitors than you have to restrict your neighbors from throwing more-entertaining parties than yours.

Crony capitalism is as old as the republic itself. Congress's first act in 1789—on July 4, no less—was a tariff on foreign goods passed to protect influential American businesses, like cotton growers.

Since then, American capitalism has become more perverted by special deals. One of President George W. Bush's first acts upon entering office was to increase tariffs on steel to help out the steel industry. *Crapitalism.*

Crony capitalism, in the form of government bailouts, saved (temporarily?) General Motors and Chrysler. Legislators shouted, "These companies are too big to let them fail!" President Obama's cronies, the United Auto Workers, got preferential treatment over other creditors. (This was even more outrageous because the union's rigid work rules and fat pension deals helped bankrupt the companies.) If free-market capitalism is a private profit-and-loss system, crony capitalism is a private-profit and public-loss system. Companies keep profits but use government to stick the taxpayer with losses. Clever trick.

The public has become suspicious of bailouts, but the role that regulation plays in crapitalism is unappreciated. People assume that regulation tames corporations. That's the intent, but regulation soon becomes a way for some businesses to gain advantage. It's why Philip Morris joined the "war on tobacco" and General Motors pushes for clean-air legislation.

As economist Bruce Yandle writes in his famous article "Bootleggers and Baptists," just as bootleggers loved alcohol prohibition because the law made them rich, "[i]ndustry support of regulation is not rare at all; indeed it is the norm."

Heavy regulation helps bigger businesses crush competitors who might offer us better deals. Ask yourself which are more likely to be hampered by vigorous regulatory standards: entrenched corporations, with their big legal and accounting departments, or start-ups? When government decides to set "standards" for an industry, to whom will it turn for expertise? Brilliant newcomers? No, government doesn't even know who they are. The older, lazier, bigger, arthritic businesses suggest the rules and make sure that *their* way is the only legal way.

This kills innovation. It's hard to build a better mousetrap if regulations decree that only the existing one fits the codes.

WHAT INTUITION TEMPTS US TO BELIEVE:

Government should use the tax code to reward good behavior.

WHAT REALITY TAUGHT ME:

Show me a tax break, and I will show you results that
even the program's advocates wouldn't like.

Our emotions tell us to watch for politicians' motives. If they give pretty speeches that sound compassionate, surely their policies will be helpful.

But even the most well-intended policies have unintended

consequences. For example, in the abstract, creating tax incentives to support "family-based agriculture" sounds nice. But such incentives distort markets in nasty ways.

Twenty-five years ago, there were about 150 alpacas in America. Now there are probably 150,000. One website advertises: "Have Uncle Sam Help You Buy Your Alpacas."

Rose Mogerman raises alpacas in New Jersey. When I met her, dozens of alpacas were in her backyard. She told me that without the tax break, "I might have had two."

Alpacas are cute. Rose sells fiber made from their fleece. But selling fleece doesn't explain the growth in alpaca raising. At one auction, half-ownership of one male alpaca sold for $750,000. Economists at the University of California, Davis call the alpaca boom a speculative bubble. "Values wildly in excess of even the most optimistic scenarios," wrote Tina L. Saitone and Richard J. Sexton in an article titled "Alpaca Lies? Speculative Bubbles in Agriculture." They argue that "current prices are not supportable by economic fundamentals and, thus, are not sustainable."

In other words, tax breaks led people to overinvest, bid up prices, and produce more animals than their fleece would demand. Kind of like the housing bubble. Alpaca breeders wrote me angry emails when I said that on TV, but recently on an alpaca Web forum others posted comments like these:

"I'm getting few hits and zero sales on quality girls. I've been lucky to sell a couple of males for $250 each."

"I am so glad we did not purchase on borrowed money [the way] some folks did."

Big government builds bubbles.

Another example: Electric vehicles are touted as "green" technology. So Congressman Charles Rangel pushed through a tax credit for electric vehicles. Ironically, the National Research Council points out that electric cars—because ultimately they plug into coal-fired plants—may be *worse* for the environment. But that didn't deter Congress.

My Fox colleague Mike Huckabee and I were unintended beneficiaries of Rangel's dumb law. When a golf cart dealer advertised that his $6,000 carts were "free" because of the $6,000 tax credit, Huckabee and I promptly bought carts. A friend of his bought seven. (I gave mine to the charity that helps manage Central Park.)

It's possible that the credits led to a gain in electric car research, but I doubt it. It's definite that the deal diverted resources that might have gone to solve real pollution problems, cure cancer, or—well, we'll never know how those resources might have been used. What we do know is that the credit helped the golf cart industry. My dealer sold ten thousand.

At least the golf cart credit expired. Most government handouts *never* go away. If people propose cutting them, those benefiting from the deal, no matter how absurd it is, scream louder than the rest of us. After all, we're busy dealing with our own lives. Most of us don't even know that we're being fleeced.

WHAT INTUITION TEMPTS US TO BELIEVE:
If auto companies are in trouble, government
should encourage the purchase of new cars.

WHAT REALITY TAUGHT ME:
Wealth will be destroyed, and poor people will be hurt.

Cash for Clunkers was another program that impressed the economic illiterates. Congress said the program would "stimulate the economy" and "green the world" by giving people $3,000 to junk their old car and buy a new one. Good for consumers—good for car businesses! Greening the world was a bonus.

As usual, the program was judged only by its first and most visible consequences, violating Bastiat's broken window fallacy, which Henry Hazlitt adapts in his classic book *Economics in One Lesson*: "The art of economics consists in looking not merely at the immediate but at the longer effects of any act or policy; it consists in tracing the consequences of that policy not merely for one group but for all groups."

Cash for Clunkers did give the auto industry a boost. "Manufacturing plants have added shifts!" bragged Secretary of Transportation Ray LaHood. "Moribund showrooms were brought back to life, and consumers bought fuel-efficient cars that will save them money and improve the environment!"

It would be more accurate to say *some* consumers and workers benefited, but most of us lost, and the environment didn't notice.

Let's start at the beginning: The government paid car owners $3 billion to trade in old cars. But the government doesn't have $3 billion to hand out. It borrows the money, which reduces the amount of money available for other investments. Moreover, the government must either raise taxes in the future to pay back the principal and interest—or the Federal Reserve will monetize the debt through inflation. Either way, we pay.

That isn't all. Those car buyers were either going to trade in their used cars soon or they weren't. If they were, Cash for Clunkers simply billed taxpayers for what car buyers would have funded. In the case of buyers who planned to keep their cars longer, the program imposed less visible costs: Without government's bribe, car consumers would have bought other things—computers, washing machines, televisions. Sellers of those products *lost* those sales.

Mechanics who would have serviced the used cars lost business. Nor should we forget low-income people who depend on the used car market. Cash for Clunkers destroyed so many used cars that the average price of used cars rose $1,800. And politicians claim they help the poor.

And there is something revolting about the government subsidizing the destruction of useful things. It's like the New Deal policy of killing piglets and pouring milk down sewers to keep food prices up. Leave it to politicians to think we can prosper by obliterating wealth.

Why are we stupid enough to believe such benefits can be pulled out of a hat? For the same reason we fall for magic tricks: our brains are not designed to think thoroughly—when the story right before our eyes looks so appealingly simple.

WHAT INTUITION TEMPTS US TO BELIEVE:

A new stadium will act as a giant jobs program.

WHAT REALITY TAUGHT ME:

The central planners always say that, and
they're almost always wrong.

Politicians love shiny new projects like sports stadiums. They get a big, easily photographed, and heavily reported ribbon-cutting ceremony. They give reporters "fact" sheets about how many jobs will be created. The fact sheets are prepared by consultants loyal to sports tycoons and the politicians. They make optimistic promises. The actual stadiums don't pay the taxpayers back. Many make neighborhoods poorer.

Reporters focus on what they see: the new stadium. They ignore the smaller businesses that were taxed—sometimes condemned and bulldozed—to fund the project. A baseball stadium brings in fans only eighty-one days per year (only forty-one home games for basketball, just eight for football). There are also a few concerts and special events, but most days the stadium is empty. Neighborhood business owners who were conned into thinking that the new stadium would help them are surprised and poorer. The sports tycoons are richer. The politicians move on to their next boondoggle.

In the 1990s, economically ailing Cleveland built two new sports facilities. They were supposed to revitalize the economy. But $275 million worth of taxes later, neighborhoods near the new stadium look like slums.

The Florida Marlins asked Miami-Dade County to build them a new ballpark. The team claimed they were not profitable (later, leaked documents showed that the Marlins were profitable), and so taxpayers paid for 70 percent of a beautiful $500 million stadium.

Don't you wish *you* could bill taxpayers to build your business?

But at least now there is hope. People aren't endlessly stupid. When I first reported on the stadium scams, taxpayers routinely paid. Lately, more refuse. In New York City, we voted down a new football stadium. When we did, then-governor George Pataki complained: "It's extraordinarily disappointing that people have said 'no' to over a billion dollars of private investments, said 'no' to thousands of construction jobs, said 'no' to thousands of hotel and restaurant convention center jobs, have said 'no' to the Olympics!"

Actually, George, it's smart when the public says "no" to dubious promises like that.

WHAT INTUITION TEMPTS US TO BELIEVE:

If we just elect the *right* politicians, we can
reinvent government and balance its books.

WHAT REALITY TAUGHT ME:

It's not about electing the right people. It's
about narrowing their responsibilities.

Obama is hardly the first president to say he would "go line by line through the federal budget and eliminate wasteful and ineffective programs." It's not like no one thought of this before.

But it never happens. Every piece of pork has well-connected advocates who swear the money is vital to the national interest. They line up to testify. Even if they didn't grease the palms of lobbyists and congressmen, their cries would be hard to resist: "This program will keep this poor woman, your constituent, alive! Would you be so cold as to deny her that?"

Congress appropriates the money, and then the permanent bureaucracy fights forever to preserve it. After all, its very life depends on it.

It's not that people in government aren't as decent or competent as those in the private sector (though the longer they stay, the worse they get). The difference lies in the feedback they face. Bureaucracies have no bottom line, no market prices for their "output," fewer rewards for excellence. What they have is an incentive to keep their heads down and to spend all the money budgeted (or lose it next year).

It is absurd to think the humongous constellation of federal bureaucracies is going to identify and root out "waste" in any significant way. It's just not in the nature of the beast. It doesn't matter which party is in power. No one spends other people's money as carefully as he spends his own.

You can't change those incentives by electing a different president or a different Congress. The only way to do it is to switch from the noncompetitive, parasitic incentive structure of politics to the competitive, efficiency-seeking incentives of the free market. Good government has to mean less government.

Far from "fixing" the economy, President Obama's "bold" actions diminished our freedom and exacerbated the troubles they were supposed to cure. In 2010, the United States fell to eighth place in the annual *Wall Street Journal*/Heritage Foundation ranking of nations called the Economic Freedom Index. In 2011, we fell to ninth. This year, we fell to tenth. Bill Beach, director of the Heritage Foundation's Center for Data Analysis, came on my show to deliver the bad news: for the first time, "the United States fell from the 'totally free' to 'mostly free' group. That's a terrible development."

Terrible because each demotion in economic freedom makes prosperity harder to achieve. The lesson is clear: the more government intervenes in an economy, the worse people live. You see that looking at the countries at the bottom of the freedom list: Burma, Eritrea, Cuba, Zimbabwe, and North Korea.

Why did the United States fall on the list? "Our spending has been excessive," said Beach. "We have the highest corporate tax rate in the world. [Government] takeovers of industries, subsidizing industries . . . these are the kinds of moves that happen in Third World countries."

In other words, rule of law declined when the Obama

administration declared contracts void, like when GM bondholders were forced to the back of the creditor line. And there's more regulation of business, such as the Dodd-Frank law.

The laws of man cannot change the laws of economics. We cannot raise wages or create jobs or eliminate poverty by executive order. We do so by freeing people to save and invest and accumulate capital.

There are only two ways to get people to do things: force or persuasion. Government is brute force. If you doubt that, try ignoring your tax bill or some Environmental Protection Agency rule. Men with guns will soon appear to force you to obey. By contrast, the private sector—whether nonprofit or greedy business—must work through persuasion and consent. No matter how rich Bill Gates gets, he cannot force us to buy his software.

Government uses force in an attempt to defy economic logic, to make the square peg of political desires fit into the round hole of available resources and inevitable trade-offs. That's why the consequences of government action are frequently different from those intended. Cash for Clunkers raised used car prices. The brand-new stadiums suck money from surrounding neighborhoods.

Politicians give speeches about how things *ought* to be—and it's tempting to judge them by those speeches. But high hopes can't alter reality. Ludwig von Mises wrote that understanding this is liberating: once people realized that they must adjust to economic forces "in precisely the same way as they must take into account the laws of nature, [that led to] policies of liberalism [classical liberalism, that is, what we today call libertarianism] and thus unleashed human powers that, under capitalism, have transformed the world."

Libertarianism is liberating—but is it fair?

2

MAKING LIFE FAIR

WHAT INTUITION TEMPTS US TO BELIEVE:
Individuals are selfish, so we need government to
"level the playing field" and make life "fair."

WHAT REALITY TAUGHT ME:
When government "makes life fair," that
brings stagnation and poverty.

All right, maybe I convinced you in the last chapter that the market is more efficient, but you care more about "fairness." My wife used to complain that libertarian reasoning is coldhearted. Since markets produce winners and losers—and many losers did nothing wrong—market competition is cruel.

One of America's most influential modern liberal philosophers, John Rawls, constructed "a theory of justice" based on the idea that we have an innate sense of fairness that is offended when some people fare better than others. Our close relatives the chimpanzees freak out when one chimp gets more than his fair share, so zookeepers are careful about food portions. Chimps are hardwired to get angry when they think they've been cheated—and so are we.

Filmmaker Michael Moore took this thinking to its intuitive conclusion during an interview with Laura Flanders of GRITtv, saying of rich people's fortunes, "That's not theirs! That's a national resource, that's ours!"

Moore thinks that government should dominate the economy. In his documentary *Capitalism: A Love Story*, he praises Barack Obama for promising to "spread the wealth."

Moore's movie suggests that capitalism is evil, but he's never clear about what "capitalism" means. Considering how much time he spends documenting the cozy relationship between business and government, I thought he might mean "state capitalism." But then he uses the term "free market" to describe the same thing.

Bailouts and cozy deals with Congress have nothing to do with capitalism or free markets.

What does Moore want instead of "capitalism"? He's coy about that. At his movie's premiere, he wouldn't directly answer questions from one audience member about whether he endorsed communism. Moore does say that the public became more curious about socialism once Obama was accused of favoring it, and in his documentary he goes to the only self-described socialist in Congress, Senator Bernie Sanders (whose staff says he will not talk to me under any circumstances), to ask for a definition. Socialism, Sanders tells Moore, means "the government represents the middle class and working class, not the wealth."

Huh? That's socialism? It's not government ownership of the means of production? By Senator Sanders's definition, I'm a socialist. I want government to represent the middle and working classes. But government does that best when it guards our safety and then leaves us free.

Moore makes a grand visit to the National Archives to confirm that—aha!—the Constitution does not establish capitalism as the country's economic system. He sees the words "people," "union," and "welfare" in the document and says, "Sounds like that other *ism*." Like a lot of things Michael Moore says, that's cute, but ludicrously superficial. The Constitution limits government's power to interfere with the people and their property. The Constitution is on the side of the free market, not activist government. But Moore—and the many disgruntled leftists who think in the same sloppy way he does—isn't just joking about wanting to get free markets and limited government out of the American system. Toward the end of the movie, Moore says capitalism is irredeemably evil and "has to be replaced." With what? I thought he'd say "socialism." Instead his answer is "democracy." That's a crowd-pleaser but so vague that it's meaningless.

Moore rails against reckless banks and government bailouts but never once mentions that government colluded for decades with the real estate and construction industries to divert resources in the name of home ownership—even for people who couldn't afford it. You'd never know from *Capitalism* that Fannie Mae and Freddie Mac are privileged *government-sponsored* enterprises that encouraged shaky loans and created the conditions for the housing bust.

The fact that America doesn't have a genuinely free market is the unnoticed elephant in Moore's room. To the anticapitalist mind, all economic problems are caused by excessive reliance on the market, and all hope of rescue emanates from government.

Bad idea.

While a free market doesn't produce equal outcomes, it produces better outcomes. There's truth to the saying that a rising tide lifts all boats. Even "losers" in a free market system do pretty well, since there is profit in providing services to everyone, including the poor.

A more astute observer than Moore might show that government intervention—licenses, taxes, regulations—makes it harder for the average worker to start his own business, harder to go from being a "little guy" to owning the means of production. Fewer regulations would mean that a worker who wants to be an entrepreneur doesn't have to pay corporate lawyers just to navigate the rules. Then he would have an easier time moving up and out of poverty. Most new businesses fail, but running your own business is the best route to prosperity, and—surveys suggest—happiness, too.

Why don't more Americans try it? Because big government makes it hard. It raises what economists call "barriers to entry."

I once opened a dinky business called "The Stossel Store." I embarrassed myself hawking hats, books, and other goodies on the street. Bizarrely, it was hard to open this business. I needed help from Fox's lawyers to get the permits. We chose Delaware because it's supposedly the state that makes opening a business easiest, but "easiest" didn't mean "easy." It still required help from a lawyer and took a week to get the permits. In New York City, it would have taken much longer. In Europe, it can take months. In Iraq, more than two months, according to the World Bank.

By contrast, in Hong Kong I started a business in one day. Hong Kong's limited government makes it easy for people to try things, and that has allowed poor people to prosper. People in Hong Kong were once as poor as those in the rest of China. I suppose leftists would call that fair—everyone was *equally* poor. Today residents of Hong Kong are almost as wealthy as Americans.

Even poor people in Hong Kong have pretty good lives. It's the little guys who benefit most from economic freedom.

What makes it hard for most people to dismiss anticapitalist zealots is that the zealots, with their talk of Americans pulling together to take care of each other, remind us of the coziness of village life. Instinct tells us that's where we'll find trust and fairness.

But our intuition fools us. We think that since family and village life feel most natural, government models that institutionalize that sort of living must be good. In practice, assuming that government can foster togetherness better than voluntary associations, businesses, and private charities leads to coziness of the bad kind: backdoor dealings between the well connected and government.

This point is important because of that far-flung, impersonal "extended market order" that economist Friedrich Hayek talked about. If we're going to have a large-scale, modern society, we need relatively simple rules that can be applied to all sorts of new situations without having to put global commerce on hold until the hypothetical village elders come up with a plan.

Since most human beings still lived as farmers two centuries ago, the idea of doing without the village elders is still novel. It was only around the eighteenth and nineteenth centuries that the ideas we now think of as classical liberalism, libertarianism, anarchism, and laissez-faire capitalism began to be articulated. As Westerners became accustomed to living without the rule of kings and aristocrats, they began, for the first time since the dawn of writing, to imagine living ungoverned lives.

But the Michael Moore method assumes that the best way to take care of everyone is to treat all our property as if it's held in common, and each time there's a decision to be made, get everyone together in the main hut (or town hall or Congress) and decide what's best. To a primitive part of our brains, that sounds fair. Letting some people make big profits sounds unfair, like letting one villager grab all the berries. But today we aren't just collecting berries. We create vast amounts of new wealth largely because we don't have to ask permission every time we want to try something new.

WHAT INTUITION TEMPTS US TO BELIEVE:

Government makes life fairer.

WHAT REALITY TAUGHT ME:

Life is fairer when individuals are free
to make their own decisions.

Americans rightly celebrate democracy and majority rule, but majority rule means that some people are forced to do things they don't want to do. Fifty-one percent of the voters get to boss the other 49 percent around.

By contrast, capitalism allows every individual to make his own choices.

Think about what occurs when you buy a cup of coffee. You give the clerk a dollar. She gives you the coffee. Then you *both* say,

"Thank you." Why the odd double thank-you moment? Because it's a mutually beneficial exchange (the store wants your money more than it wants coffee, whereas you want the coffee more than the cash).

Marxists and the watered-down Marxists of today's left tell us that one party in that exchange exploited the other. Today, if you stopped and asked the customer and the shopkeeper, since they've heard the same left-wing economic claptrap the rest of us have, they might even say that's true—the shopkeeper exploits you or you exploit the shopkeeper. Yet somehow that almost instinctual "thank you" tells us the truth about the relationship. It's fair—not because the two parties are "equals" but rather because each party thinks he came out ahead. You wanted the coffee more than you wanted the buck. The shopkeeper wanted your money more than the coffee. Under genuine capitalism, everybody wins or the trade never happens. That's because business is voluntary. The free market is voluntary. Government is force.

Voluntary is better.

Everyone loses when government prevents trades or forces us to make exchanges we would not make voluntarily—telling people they can hire only "licensed" cabs, buy certain lightbulbs, or pay a "minimum" wage.

Progressives tend to think, like FDR, that fairness means being "willing to sacrifice for the good of a common discipline." They think the way to make sure that everyone gets his fair share is to make sure we're all yoked together. President Obama echoes that when he promotes higher taxes on the wealthy by saying, "I want to live in a society that's fair."

This idea of fairness means forcing us to put the politicians' vision of society's needs before our own. To them, this is as intuitive as telling children, "Everyone should share." Sharing is good. But when government *requires* sharing, bad things happen.

WHAT INTUITION TEMPTS US TO BELIEVE:

Government steering resources to the

"common good" helps everyone.

WHAT REALITY TAUGHT ME:

It leads to the "tragedy of the commons."

Had today's political class been in power in 1623, Thanksgiving would be called "Starvation Day." Many of us wouldn't be alive to celebrate it.

Schoolchildren are lectured about the beauty of "sharing." Teachers portray Thanksgiving as a big group hug. But the first Thanksgiving almost didn't happen, because the Pilgrims' leaders dictated a group hug by force.

Plymouth Colony organized their first farm economy along communal lines that would have pleased Michael Moore: Everyone got an equal share of what the community produced. Such sharing seemed fair. But because of it, the Pilgrims nearly starved. When workers can get an equal return for less effort, workers make less effort. Plymouth settlers often faked illness rather than work the common property. Some stole, despite their Puritan convictions. Total production was too meager to support the population. This went on for two years.

"It well appeared that famine must still ensue the next year," Governor William Bradford wrote in his diary. So the colonists argued about how they might "obtain a better crop than they had done, that they might not still thus languish in misery. At length after much debate . . . [we decided] that they should set corn every man *for his own particular*, and in that regard trust to themselves. And so assigned to every family a parcel of land."

Once each colonist had his own land, the results were dramatic. "This had very good success," wrote Bradford, "for it made all hands very industrious, so as much more corn was planted than otherwise would have been. By this time harvest was come, and instead of famine, now God gave them plenty, and the face of things was changed, to the rejoicing of the hearts of many."

In other words, the people of Plymouth prospered because they moved from socialism to private property. Because of the change, the first Thanksgiving could be held in 1623. What Plymouth suffered under communalism was what economists today call "the tragedy of the commons." The problem has been known since ancient Greece. As Aristotle noted, "That which is common to the greatest number has the least care bestowed upon it."

If individuals can take from a common pot regardless of how much they put in, then each person has an incentive to be a "free rider"—to do as little as possible and take as much as possible because what one fails to take will be taken by someone else. Soon the pot is empty.

What private property does—as the Pilgrims discovered—is *connect effort to reward*, creating an incentive for people to produce. Then, when there's a free market, people trade their surpluses to others for things they lack. Mutual voluntary exchange for mutual benefit makes the community richer.

Ironically—and tragically—the U.S. government has yet to learn this lesson. It even imposes the socialism that nearly killed the Pilgrims on the very people the Pilgrims conquered.

The government holds most Indian land "in trust" for Indians.

As a result, individuals aren't free to improve land as they choose, or use it as collateral. This stifles initiative.

"Drive through western reservations," says economist Terry Anderson, executive director of the Property & Environment Research Center. "You see on one side cultivated fields, irrigation, and on the other side, overgrazed run-down pastures and homes. One is a simple commons; the other side is private property."

That needless contrast between poverty and wealth seems to me the ultimate unfairness. The irony is that by claiming to "care" for Indians, the government kills their spirit. Indians who live on communal, government-managed lands suffer greater poverty, more alcoholism, and earlier deaths. But this is so counterintuitive that tragically, tribal leaders often think the solution to the poverty on reservations is *more* government involvement. Like most people, when asked what should be done about the problems government causes, they say, "More of the same."

They would benefit from rediscovering the lost lesson of Thanksgiving: Secure property rights are key. Property rights leave individuals the freedom to use their possessions and bodies in the most diverse ways imaginable. Like a personal force field, property lays down guidelines that allow an infinite number of voluntary arrangements.

WHAT INTUITION TEMPTS US TO BELIEVE:

If we want nice public spaces, government must create them.

WHAT REALITY TAUGHT ME:

The nicest public spaces escaped government control.

Dan Biederman understands the benefits of private property better than most. He rescued the park outside my office.

America is filled with parks that are filthy and badly maintained. Governments in charge say: We can't help it. Our budgets were slashed.

Manhattan's Bryant Park was one of those parks—until Biederman essentially privatized it. With permission from frustrated officials who'd watched government fail to improve a park that was barren, and mostly used by drug dealers and vagrants, Biederman raised funds from local businesses and landlords. "We have not asked the city government for a single dollar." Today the park is beautiful and used by thousands of tourists and office workers having lunch.

Sounds good to me. But not to "community activist" Shirley Kressel. I asked her what's wrong with what Biederman does.

"There's commercial revenue from renting it out to businesses! He keeps all that money!" she complained.

So what? I don't care if money goes to Biederman or to visitors from Mars. The park is nice, and taxpayers no longer pay for it. Sure, the park is more "commercial" now. Some booths sell food and gifts. But park users seem to like that.

Now Biederman wants to apply his skills to the Boston Common, America's oldest park. Like many parks, it's largely a barren field. It resembles what Central Park used to look like before a private charity called the Central Park Conservancy took control. I know something about Central Park, because I'm now on that charity's board. When government managed the park, it was a filthy crime zone. Now it's wonderful. People volunteered to donate most of the money that renovated it.

For the Boston Common, Biederman wants to combine the Bryant Park and Central Park models. He'd raise money from both businesses and residences.

Shirley Kressel says she'll fight him.

"[W]e don't need . . . to teach our next generation of children that the only way they can get a public realm is as the charity ward of rich people and corporations," she said. "That's government's job."

"What's wrong with the Central Park model?" I asked.

"Because these people, the moneybags, get to decide how the park is used and who goes there and who the desirables are and who are the undesirables. . . . Homeless people have to be somewhere."

Biederman had a ready answer: "We have the same number of homeless people in Bryant Park today as we had when it was viewed by everyone as horrible in the early 1980s. What we didn't have then—and we have now—is four thousand other people. The ratio of nonhomeless to homeless is 4,000 to 13 instead of 250 to 13. So any female walking into Bryant Park who might have in the past been concerned about her security says, 'This doesn't look like a homeless hangout to me.' The homeless people are welcomed if they follow the rules. And those same thirteen people are there almost every day. We know their names."

Once again, creative minds of the private sector invent solutions that never occur to government bureaucrats. If government would just get out of the way, entrepreneurship, stimulated by the profit motive, will make our lives better and fairer. But first the assumption that profit is unfair—and that communal is better than private—has to be overcome. It is intuitive to think *public* is better than *private*, but next time someone tells you that, tell them to think about this: public toilets.

FIVE UTOPIAN EXPERIMENTS THAT GAVE UP ON COMMUNISM

Catholicism: Sir Thomas More, executed for opposing Henry VIII's separation of the Anglican Church from the Catholic Church, was in some sense the grandfather of socialism, since his political essay *Utopia* helped promote the idea that abolishing private property is the key to solving social ills. The idea appealed to many Catholics, until they came to realize that socialist plans to confiscate private property almost always began by confiscating *church* property.

New Harmony, Indiana: The Welsh utopian writer and social reformer Robert Owen acquired land in Indiana on which to found a utopian society in 1825. He banned money and private property. By 1829, the community was dissolved amid constant quarrels.

Brook Farm, Massachusetts: Unitarian minister George Ripley, inspired partly by the quasi-mathematical commune designs of utopian socialist Charles Fourier, created a farming community in 1841 based on collective agriculture. It never achieved financial stability and was abandoned within six years.

Oneida Community: Begun in 1848, Oneida was a religious commune in upstate New York based on the belief that Christ had returned to earth in the year 70 A.D. and thus that heavenly living in this life was possible. They expressed heavenly living through communal property and group marriages. By 1881, all branches of the Oneida Community had dissolved except for one. That was their privately managed and highly profitable silverware company, which endures to this day.

Israeli Kibbutzim: These equal-labor-oriented communities were beacons of hope to egalitarians around the world for the first years of their existence. Then they began to stagnate. Now most kibbutzim embrace some degree of privatization, and the people living there often support themselves with off-kibbutz careers.

The Pilgrims' experience should have taught us that individualism solves problems that collectivism cannot. But we're slow learners.

The crucial distinction between government and private decision making is that government threatens to put people in jail if they do not comply. Private sector plans are ones you can opt out of, even if thousands of other people are involved. Letting people decide voluntarily on what basis they interact with each other is the fairest rule of all. That means a large group of people can try banding together to try living or farming communally—but they don't get to regulate competitors out of business or tax their neighbors when their experiment fails.

WHAT INTUITION TEMPTS US TO BELIEVE:

Communities need planning.

WHAT REALITY TAUGHT ME:

They do, but they don't need government planning.

Nobel Prize committees are, well, committees, and people who join committees tend to think like socialists. So it was reassuring to see that the 2009 Nobel Prize in economics was shared by Elinor Ostrom, whose life's work demonstrates that politicians and bureaucrats are not nearly as good at solving problems as regular people. Based on numerous studies of fish stocks, pastures, woods, lakes, and groundwater basins, Ostrom concludes that when the people using the common resources make the rules, the outcomes are better. "[R]esource-users frequently develop sophisticated mechanisms for decision-making and rule enforcement to handle conflicts" is how the Nobel committee put it.

Ostrom's research was largely a response to the "free-rider problem." Similar to the tragedy of the commons, the free-rider problem is the tendency for people to freeload—to try to be a nonpaying beneficiary of a service that others fund. The free-rider problem is often cited as the reason why "government must step in and force everyone to contribute." Few scholars actually venture into the field to see what people actually do when faced with free-rider problems. Ostrom did.

It turns out that free people are not as helpless as the theorists believed. Ostrom writes in her 1990 book, *Governing the Commons*, that there is no shortage of real-world examples of "a self-governed common-property arrangement in which the rules have been devised and modified by the participants." Even in the absence of clear legal rules about property, farmers in Africa worked out rules for determining when different farmers could use pastures, and villages in Nepal made agreements that avoided overuse of water.

In other words, free people work things out on their own.

I was amused to see the lengths to which the *New York Times* went to spin Ostrom's selection in an anti-free-market direction. Reporter Louis Uchitelle wrote, "Neither Ms. Ostrom nor [co-winner] Mr. [Oliver E.] Williamson has argued against regulation. Quite the contrary, their work found that people in business adopt for themselves numerous forms of regulation and rules of behavior."

Please. Rules of behavior adopted by businesses are not what the *New York Times* means when it calls for "regulation." Advocates of regulation don't devise rules that leave politicians out of the picture. They think only intervention from *above* brings order out of chaos. Ostrom shows they are wrong. Top-down planning screws things up because planners are ignorant of local customs.

Jim Scott's book *Seeing like a State* lists examples like the massive social engineering under apartheid in South Africa, the modernization plans of the shah of Iran, Stalin's collectivization of Soviet agriculture, villagization in Vietnam, and some I hadn't known about, including "Tanzania's attempt to permanently settle most of the country's population in villages, of which the layouts, housing designs, and local economies were planned, partly or wholly, by officials of the central government. . . . Five million Tanzanians were relocated. The campaign was undertaken largely as a development and welfare project, not ethnic cleansing or military security. . . . Like Soviet collectives, ujamaa villages were economic and ecological failures."

Sometimes the unintended consequences are subtler. Scott shows how urban planners' schemes can suck the life out of a city:

> In parts of Europe, State authorities endeavored to map complex, old cities in a way that would facilitate policing and control. But that created unintended consequences like absence of a dense street life, loss of the spatial irregularities that foster coziness, gathering places for informal recreation, and neighborhood feeling. . . .
>
> To illustrate the diversity of urban life (the type of local adaptations and idiosyncrasies which are inevitably missed by top down planning), Jane Jacobs lists more than a dozen uses which have been served over the years by the center for the arts in Louisville: stable, school, theater, bar, athletic club, blacksmith's forge, factory, warehouse, artists' studio. She then asks, rhetorically, "Who could anticipate or provide for such a succession of hopes and services?" Her answer is simple: "Only an unimaginative man would think he could; only an arrogant man would want to."

There is no reason to believe that bureaucrats and politicians, even when their intentions are good, are better at solving problems than the locals, who have the strongest incentive to get the solution right and who, unlike bureaucrats, bear the costs of their mistakes.

We libertarians aren't against rules—we are against top-down rules. Lately, Republican anti-ObamaCare talking points about "death panels" include the complaint that "unelected bureaucrats" will decide which treatments we get. After Karl Rove said that to Bill O'Reilly, I shouted across the greenroom at him, "What's with the 'unelected bureaucrats' stuff? 'Elected' bureaucrats are no better!" He rolled his eyes.

Rove knows good talking points, but decrying "unelected bureaucrats" misses the larger point. "Unelected" isn't the problem. *Top-down*—allowing a few people to force rules on millions of different people—that's the problem.

People generate fairer rules when the state leaves us alone. From bird-watching societies to private clubs to soccer leagues, when rules are freely, privately adopted, they work better. They can be assumed to hold some advantage for all participants. Not so when the participants act mostly out of fear of a government that can put them in jail. In the marketplace, if you think you're being treated unfairly, you can change the stores you shop in, the clothes you wear, the long-distance phone service you use.

But politicians limit your choices. You cannot decide to stop funding, say, the Department of Transportation, foreign wars, the National Endowment for the Arts, or poverty programs that don't work. That, I would say, is truly unfair. "Fair" means leaving people the right to opt out.

Still, even if you accept the idea that capitalism creates greater opportunity than socialism, your intuition probably *still* tells you not to trust businesspeople. And why should you? Corporations are out to make a buck. That's their job. Surely, then, says your intuition, government is needed to check the power of corporations.

That intuition is wrong, too.

3

KEEPING BUSINESS HONEST

WHAT INTUITION TEMPTS US TO BELIEVE:

Businesses only care about the bottom line, so consumers
need protection—government regulation.

WHAT REALITY TAUGHT ME:

Reputation, not regulation, protects consumers better.

Our brains are always on the lookout for other people's motives. We
need to know whom we can trust and whom we can't. We're especially skeptical of business because we know what business wants:
our money.

It took me too long to understand that business's desire for profit is a *good* thing. To get our money (to create that "thank you/ thank you" moment), businesses need to give us what we want—and do it better than the competition.

WHAT INTUITION TEMPTS US TO BELIEVE:

Groups working to rein in greedy business are selfless and noble.

WHAT REALITY TAUGHT ME:

Those groups (mostly politicians, bureaucrats, and labor
unions) are also in it for themselves—and their behavior is
worse because they're not accountable to paying customers.

Once we label businesses greedy (fair enough), it is natural to assume that groups that butt heads with business—government regulators and labor unions—are motivated by concern for others. Regulators protect consumers. Unions protect workers. Together, they help us by keeping business "honest."

Let's take these groups one at a time:

It's intuitive to assume that unions are altruistic protectors of the working class, but I have to wonder whether people who think unions are altruistic have ever met actual labor leaders. Few will come on my show, but one who did was John Samuelsen, president of Transport Workers Union Local 100, a union that represents thirty-eight thousand workers who run subways and buses that get millions of New Yorkers (myself included) to work every day.

Is the union boss concerned about those millions of commuters? Not that I could tell.

Samuelsen's concern, naturally, is the happiness of his dues-paying members—and growing their numbers. Recently some entrepreneurs started offering van service on roads that are also serviced by city buses. "Dollar vans" offer commuters an alternative. Commuters like that. They wouldn't pay the fare if they didn't prefer the vans to the buses that Samuelsen's union workers drive. Van customers told me, "The vans are more convenient," "faster," and the "drivers are friendlier."

The van owners are "greedy" in the sense that they want to make more money, and they offer customers an appealing alternative precisely *because* they are greedy. The greedier they are, the harder they work. Desire for money gives them an incentive to keep their vans relatively clean, figure out what routes are most useful to most commuters, and drive in a way that pleases their customers.

Samuelsen wants them out of business. His union would be better off without the competition. Of course, he couldn't come right out and say so. He told me, "Dollar vans undermine the essential service called mass transit." By "undermine," he means: compete. Unions don't like non-union-dues-paying entrepreneurs competing with them for commuters whom they consider "their" customers.

Now, in a free market, there would be a fair fight. City buses and dollar vans would duke it out for customers. Both would try to offer the most appealing service for the cheapest price. Some would innovate—one might offer wireless service while another offered free coffee. I don't know. But I do know that when government unions are involved, that's not what happens. Instead, the unions go to their cronies in government to get protection from competition.

Politicians and regulators are much cozier with unions than with immigrant entrepreneurs. Members of New York's City Council get most of their campaign money from unions. When new van drivers applied for permits, the council turned down 98 percent of the applications. When a court put a stop to that, the council insisted on regulations that forbid vans to work roads served by city buses, and forbade them to pick up passengers who wait on street corners. Passengers are supposed to *call* and make an appointment. Such rules, if they were obeyed (they aren't), would kill the dollar vans.

"The MTA's unions work in conjunction with local politicians to eliminate the vans," Hector Ricketts, who runs one van service, told me. Ricketts started his business because he saw firsthand how "public" transit underserved poor black neighborhoods. "We live in a community where the unemployment rate is upwards of eighteen percent. We are putting people to work by taking people to work. We provide a service that people have chosen to use."

Not allowed, say the unions and their political friends. Having the vans compete with a government service would mean that government had to compete in the free market—can't have that!

Union workers certainly don't want to compete by taking a pay cut or working harder, and Samuelsen won't please his members if he proposes that. They might not reelect him. So Samuelsen even defends bus drivers who do things like take an average sixty-four days of paid sick leave if they are spat on. One claimed that he had to take off a year and a half.

The Metropolitan Transit Authority, the government body that is supposedly Samuelsen's boss, also doesn't try very hard to compete. Because of ancient government civil service rules, demanded by "progressive reformers" years ago, the MTA cannot hire the best people, fire the worst, or change much of anything. New York City's deputy mayor told me, "Even asking employees for their ideas can be against the rules."

When the dollar vans appeared and improved on the MTA's service, I naïvely thought that politicians would see them as innovation—a new form of carpooling that would save taxpayers money, create jobs, reduce congestion, and give commuters new ways to get to work. I thought Mayor Bloomberg would celebrate the van drivers as an example of immigrants embracing the American entrepreneurial spirit.

As I said, I was naïve.

And yet people think of government bureaucrats and union reps as protectors of the little guy. It's not intuitive to think that profit-seeking businesses would do a better job. Progressives always tell me how we need government because the private sector won't provide "public goods" like mass transit. "There's just no profit taking poor people to work," they say. "That's why government had to build the subways."

They are shocked when I tell them that most of our subways were built, not by government, but by private companies. In New York City, it was the private sector that dug the tunnels and ran things pretty well until the government, as it so often does, decided to get in on the action. When the private company proposed raising the subway fare to five cents, the politicians said, "Outrageous!" They forbade the increase and took over the subways.

They promised to improve service and hold down fares. They did neither. Despite raising the fare to what is now $2.25, they still manage to lose money every year. Taxpayers fund them with billions in subsidies. If New York City had left the trains in private hands, maybe our subway would be more like Hong Kong's clean, efficient, and profitable one.

Yes. The world's only profitable mass transit is privately run.

WHAT INTUITION TEMPTS US TO BELIEVE:

Some "public goods" are best regulated by government
to prevent "destructive" competition.

WHAT REALITY TAUGHT ME:

Competition works better than regulation.

When cable TV first appeared, local governments rushed to sign exclusive contracts with cable companies. They reasoned that cable was a "natural monopoly." It was wasteful to have several companies dig up streets or string duplicate overhead wires, so granting a monopoly license to one company seemed like the way to go. The contract would guarantee that the whole town gets wired and that cable service would be sold at a "fair" price.

Of course, it would also mean that the politicians get lobbied, if not bribed, by companies that want that one monopoly license. Politicians like that. They get wined and dined and flattered. They get campaign contributions. They feel important.

Licensing delayed hundred-channel television for years, because every cable company had to jump through political hoops to get started, and once they got a license, they had no incentive to spend more to offer you more channels. Why bother? They had no competition in that town.

This was bad for you, but great for me. It increased my salary. I worked for the big, signals-sent-to-your-antenna "broadcast" networks—first NBC, then CBS, then ABC. Because most Americans received just those three channels, plus a couple of independent stations and PBS, we had a semicaptive audience. My TV specials were watched by as many as 17 million people. Advertisers eagerly paid to reach that many eyeballs. My employers and I thrived.

Decades later, with the numerous choices available to TV viewers, it all seems ridiculous. Your town's politicians, in the name of *protecting* you and saving you money, limited your choices and forced you to pay *more*. As economist Thomas DiLorenzo notes: "[I]n those cities where there are competing cable companies prices are about 23 percent below those of monopolistic cable operators. Cablevision of Central Florida, for example, reduced its basic prices from $12.95 to $6.50 per month in 'duopoly' areas in order to compete."

WHAT INTUITION TEMPTS US TO BELIEVE:

Consumers are manipulated by brand names.

WHAT REALITY TAUGHT ME:

We are, and that's fine.

Some people are incensed by branding. One harsh critic of capitalism, Canadian journalist Naomi Klein, wrote a book titled *No Logo*, decrying "superbrands." Leftist college professors have students read her book to teach kids that they are brainwashed by brand names and lured into spending their money on trash.

But brands are good things. Recognizable logos tell customers what to expect. And those expectations have to be good to get customers to come back. We hear about heartless companies, but think how heartless we consumers are. None of us thinks twice about switching brands. Nor should we. If we get shoddy merchandise even once from a company, we flee. So how does a company maintain the value of its brand? It must constantly innovate and work to hold prices down.

Major food chains—McDonald's, Starbucks, Chili's, whatever—employ "secret diners" who go to their own restaurants and act like customers to test whether their franchises maintain quality.

They also take extra steps to keep food safe.

When anyone proposes to cut government, pundits claim that cuts will kill people. "Hello, E. Coli," said a *New Republic* headline about budget cuts.

But it's not government that keeps *E. coli* to a minimum; it's food producers' concern about their brand's reputation. That, and insurance premiums incentivize food producers to be even more careful than government requires them to be. Tyson Foods, McDonald's, and others have brands to maintain—and millions of customers to lose. So while the stodgy U.S. Department of Agriculture merely has an army of union inspectors eyeballing birds for visible abnormalities, food producers run much more sophisticated tests.

One executive told me that they employ 2,300 more safety inspectors than the government requires: "Every flock of birds is tested for avian flu, pesticides and antibiotics. . . . To kill pathogens, beef carcasses are hit with a 185-degree steam rinse . . . production facilities are monitored for sanitation with microbiological swab testing." I asked if that meant that they run Q-tips over surfaces and send the cotton to labs. "Dead-on," she answered. "A technician inserts the swab into a tube containing Luciferase (named after Lucifer) that glows (same chemical reaction that makes a firefly's tail light up) if dirt is detected. . . . If this is the case, we re-clean the equipment, resample it, conduct corrective actions which may include retraining, discipline for the person assigned cleaning duties, or finding a new way to clean. . . . Equipment is routinely taken completely apart to be swab tested."

None of that testing is required by government. Companies do it to protect their brands. Brands protects us better than regulators do.

We do need protection from reckless businessmen. But there is only one sure way to provide that: market discipline. That means no privileges and no bailouts. That applies equally to chicken, housing, banks, and every business. That's very different from what we've got now.

It was once assumed that if a bank had a prestigious name it must have done a good job serving customers. Their *name* meant something. Protecting that name's reputation made banks careful about overextending themselves. Maintaining their brand was a check on their behavior. But when government steps in and bails out banks—faltering and not-so-faltering alike—that makes reputations for fiscal stability irrelevant.

Citigroup and AIG continue to exist, but they shouldn't. We would be better off if reckless businesses went bankrupt—painful as that would be in the short term—so that customers and investors could know what to expect. The public would learn to be wary of debt, and wary of "growth" companies with high leverage. Market signals would tell us which institutions were prudent, and companies would compete to win that reputation. That's capitalism.

WHAT INTUITION TEMPTS US TO BELIEVE:

Licensing protects consumers.

WHAT REALITY TAUGHT ME:

Licensing ends up protecting politically connected businesses from fair competition.

Intuition tells us to be wary of newcomers. Newcomers are, by definition, less experienced. Maybe they'll do something unsafe or dishonest! We don't want government to stop them from doing business—we just want consumers *protected*! Governments claim to do that by making sure a business is licensed.

People like the idea of "licensing." We license drivers. We license dogs. It seems prudent. People naïvely think this government seal of approval makes us safer.

This naïveté is used to justify all sorts of licensing arrangements that kill competition. It's not (usually) that politicians mean to kill competition. Most believe their rules will provide safety or an orderly marketplace. Even established businesses that collude with politicians often mean well. They want to maintain "high standards."

Las Vegas regulators require anyone who wants to start a limousine business to prove that there is a need for his new business, and, worse, that it will not "adversely affect other carriers." But that's absurd. Every new business intends to beat its competitors. That's the point. That competition is good for consumers. Businesses must serve customers well—or die. Las Vegas's anticompetitive licensing rules mean limo consumers pay more. In a similar case in Nashville, regulators ruled it illegal to charge less than forty-five dollars a ride. One entrepreneur had won customers by charging half that, but the new regulations mean the established car service businesses no longer have to worry about him.

Perhaps Nashville's and Vegas's regulators really believe "this is an area where the free market doesn't work," as the manager of the Nevada Transportation Services Authority put it. But it's fishy that charging big fees for licenses just happens to be a very effective shakedown operation. Vegas cab and limousine businesses give "substantial" donations to Vegas-area political candidates, according to the *Las Vegas Sun*.

Our big government has justified its existence (ever since the Progressive Era) by claiming it is a "countervailing influence" to corporate power—when it is, in fact, incestuously entwined with corporations.

The list of business activities that government insists on licensing, supposedly for our sake, is ridiculous:

- In Mississippi, a hair braider was told she needed a cosmetology license. Getting one requires thousands of hours of expensive cosmetology training.

  The braider, Melony Armstrong, had hundreds of satisfied customers. No customer complained about her work. It was a competing business that filed a complaint. On my show, Armstrong braided an audience member's hair and told me that Mississippi demanded that she take a 1,200-hour course on haircutting, and then, because she employed others, "I would then need to get an instructor's license, which would have been another two thousand hours." Neither course dealt with the braiding service she provided. The state also said that after she took the useless and expensive courses, she'd have to work for three years as an apprentice before she could reopen her business.

  Fortunately, a public interest law firm, the Institute for Justice (IJ), is around to challenge such anticompetitive licensing rules in court. "One of the most fundamental tenets of the American dream is the right to earn an honest living without arbitrary government interference," says IJ president

Chip Mellor. IJ helped Armstrong take Mississippi's stupid rules to court and got the law changed. Now she can practice capitalism in peace. At least—until regulators strike again.

- In Louisiana, monks who've made simple wooden caskets for a hundred years were threatened with jail time.

A casket is just a wooden box. But Louisiana officials decreed that no one should be allowed to sell that box without a funeral director's license. Getting the license would force the monks to turn their monastery into a full-fledged funeral home—complete with embalming facilities—and to take a one-year course on funeral procedures. Who sits on the state board that requires such absurd things? Surprise! Established funeral directors.

When I accused David Tatman of the Louisiana Funeral Directors Association of "trying to hog all the business," he responded with exasperation. "Great. So you and I, for one hundred and ten dollars, could set up the Stossel-Tatman Casket Company—got some glue and some wood boxes and went out on the street corner. . . . What if that casket doesn't fit in that crypt? What if it doesn't fit in that vault? What does the family do then?"

He doesn't understand that the free market solves such problems. A casket business that disappoints customers does not stay in business. But understanding that the market protects consumers is not intuitive.

Also, most funeral directors want to maintain what they consider to be high standards. A competitor who doesn't do exactly what they do must be . . . cheating. There ought to be a law!

- Regulators in Louisiana "protect" people not only from unlicensed caskets, but also from, of all things, unlicensed florists. No one may sell flower arrangements without permission from the government. How do you get permission? You must pass a test that is graded by florists *who already have licenses.* They rarely welcome the competition.

  Their test requires knowledge of techniques that florists don't even use anymore. The Louisiana test asks the name of the state's agriculture commissioner—as though you can't be a good florist without knowing that piece of vital information.

  When I confronted the head of the licensing board about his test, he said that it's necessary "to ensure the quality of the actual flower." Then he said that he was confident licensing made sense because Louisiana surveyed *existing* flower shops and "eighty-six percent liked the license." Well, duh.

  Sadly, other states are considering adopting Louisiana's licensing law. Government always grows.
- In Virginia, you need a license to be a yoga instructor.
- Florida demands that interior designers get licenses.
- Established businesses have always tried to use government to handcuff competition. When margarine was first developed, the dairy industry got Wisconsin legislators to pass a law making margarine illegal. Several states ruled that margarine was "deceptive," since it might be mistaken for butter. Some required that a bright pink dye be added to make margarine look different. An "oleomargarine bootlegger" was thrown in Leavenworth Federal Penitentiary.

When supermarkets were invented, small grocers tried to ban them. "A&P will dominate the grocery business and destroy Main Street," the grocers claimed. Minnesota legislators responded by passing a law that forbade supermarkets to put food "on sale."

Established capitalists can be capitalism's biggest enemies.

WHAT INTUITION TEMPTS US TO BELIEVE:

Okay, Stossel, maybe licensing florists and
restricting supermarkets is stupid, but licensing is
essential for *really* important jobs like law.

WHAT REALITY TAUGHT ME:

Licensing hurts consumers by limiting competition.

I used to believe that licensing people like doctors and lawyers was needed consumer protection, but now I realize that licensing is always an expensive restraint of trade.

David Price spent six months in a Kansas jail because he wrote a letter on behalf of a man who was wrongly accused of practicing architecture without a license. Because Price had no law degree, he was charged with "unauthorized practice of law" and threatened with jail time unless he promised never to "practice law" again. When he refused, a judge sent him to jail.

All Price did was write a letter. He didn't misrepresent his credentials. In fact, he saved a man from paying three thousand dollars to a lawyer. Perhaps that was his real offense.

Some of the most famous lawyers in American history, like Thomas Jefferson and Abraham Lincoln, had no licenses. Their customers decided whether they were worthy of being hired.

Competition and reputation are better protection against shoddy work than government licenses. Consider this: When you move to a new community, do you choose new doctors, dentists, and mechanics by checking their license? No. You ask neighbors or colleagues for recommendations. You ask because you know that even with licensing laws, there is a wide range of quality and outright quackery. You know that licensing doesn't really protect you.

That's why instead of relying on regulation—and the false sense of security it creates—smart consumers turn to ratings by private organizations like Underwriters Laboratory, Consumer Reports, Angie's List, etc.

Licensing is unnecessary. It creates a false sense of security, raises costs, stifles innovation, and takes away consumer choice.

It could be worse. In Europe, a rule called the precautionary principle declares that government will allow no one to sell new foods, medicines, or anything risky until sound science shows no harm will result.

That sounds reasonable. Better safe than sorry. At least it sounds reasonable until you realize that it also means, as *Reason* magazine's Ron Bailey pointed out, "Never do anything for the first time."

FOUR RIDICULOUS BUSINESS REGULATIONS

- Philadelphia instituted a $300 licensing fee for all bloggers. One woman who earned $11 from her blog was prosecuted.
- Antitrust law forbids "predatory pricing." "Predatory" turns out *not* to mean high prices, but charging prices low enough to drive your competitors out of business. (In theory, such pricing leads to a monopoly. In practice, monopolies almost never happen and consumers benefit from "predatory" pricing.)

- In Milwaukee, you must purchase a license to go *out* of business.
- Giving an unlicensed tour of Washington, D.C.—a town that takes tours very seriously—could get you ninety days in jail.

WHAT INTUITION TEMPTS US TO BELIEVE:

Without government, there would be no reliable safety standards.

WHAT REALITY TAUGHT ME:

Reputation and insurance companies create the best standards.

Government's regulations often give businesses completely irrelevant things to worry about. Joseph Brennan, who worked as a commercial pilot—and ran unsuccessfully for mayor of New York City on the Libertarian Party ticket—recounts regulations that required him to report the status of his plane's pontoons, even when he flew planes that had no pontoons. Does that mean he would have preferred having no rules, no safety checks? On the contrary, he says other rules required him to do perfectly reasonable safety checks—for fuel levels, icing on the wings, and so forth—but these rules weren't generated by regulation. Where did they come from? Insurance companies.

Businesses take out insurance. Insurance companies demand higher premiums from people who behave recklessly. Lindsay Lohan has to pay more for car insurance.

Businesses and insurance companies, precisely because their own money is at stake, have a much bigger incentive to make smart rules about safety than do distant politicians, who play around with other people's money or simply do what sounds right—or worse, what sounds impressive in a press release: "Senator X demands larger airbags in cars!"

Insurance actuarial tables—statistics on how likely it is that different sorts of customers will have accidents—are probably the most rational, unbiased forms of information about human behavior ever devised. Your intuition tells you that flying is more dangerous than driving—but actuaries crunch the numbers and give you the real odds.

If we want businesses to be smart about protecting us, we are better off letting them be guided by these sorts of calculations, rather than by regulations that result from a moving speech on the floor of Congress after a child falls into a well.

I don't deny that there is fraud in business. I won Emmys for exposing it. Fraud is one of three crimes that must be prevented for the market to function (theft and physical assault are the others). Fraud should be policed and punished. Once that's done, however, honesty pretty much takes care of itself.

No law prevents a restaurant from charging you fifteen dollars and then serving you a tiny portion of lasagna. "Consumer advocates" assume that businesses can't wait to pull such scams and are kept from such rapacious behavior (followed by maniacal laughter) only by some unseen government watchdog. But it's not true.

The reason the restaurant won't give you a minuscule portion is a simple, purely free-market phenomenon: repeat business. Even a roadside diner in the middle of nowhere knows that if they do a lousy job, word gets around. They may get a black mark in a tourist guide. That's why good companies grow and bad ones atrophy. Free competition protects consumers best.

Not only does it protect consumers, but if we don't screw it up, it will create the growth that we absolutely need to pay for the crushing entitlement debt that looms ahead. Let the market work!

But wait, you say. The market works for customers and business owners, but not for workers. Workers will be abused by bosses unless government is around to protect them. Senator Sherrod Brown of Ohio believes that. A free market for labor, he claims, would lead to "a race to the bottom." Workers would be underpaid, unsafe, and treated badly.

But it's not true.

4

IMPROVING LIFE FOR WORKERS

WHAT INTUITION TEMPTS US TO BELIEVE:
Without the intervention of labor unions and
government, business will treat workers like dogs.

WHAT REALITY TAUGHT ME:
When unions buddy up with their friends in government, it's bad
for customers, taxpayers, and ultimately, even union members.

It seems intuitive that the vicious competition of the marketplace
will lead to lower wages. Employers, desperate to cut costs, will pay
workers less and less, ship jobs to China, and dodge safety measures.

It's a reason that progressives say government must protect

workers. So America now has thousands of rules that do things like outlaw any wage below $7.25 an hour, restrict unpaid internships, forbid employers to make anti-union arguments, limit the right to fire, and so on. These rules appear to help workers. But they don't.

Take OSHA. The Occupational Safety and Health Administration was created to reduce the number of workplace injuries. It is certainly true that after OSHA's rules were created, accidents dropped. President Clinton's OSHA boss was fond of showing people the following graph.

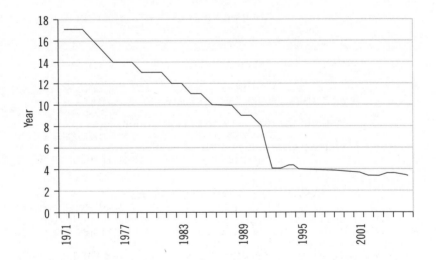

Impressive, isn't it? What could be a clearer example of cause and effect? Deaths dropped steadily after OSHA began its work.

But then someone bothered to produce this chart, showing the years before OSHA.

Workplace fatalities per 100,000 workers

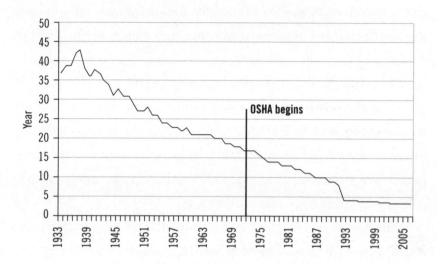

Before regulation, deaths dropped just as fast. OSHA made no difference.

As people get richer and smarter, life gets better. Government is like someone who gets in front of a parade and pretends to lead it. The *bigger* truth is that OSHA's rules saved some workers but killed others. OSHA's byzantine bureaucracy sometimes diminishes safety because it discourages companies from creating their *own*, more innovative safety improvements.

As the research on group rule-making by Nobel Prize winner Elinor Ostrom demonstrated, rules are better when vested players in an industry make them. (Progressives say this is like the fox guarding the henhouse—but politicians and bureaucrats are simply not as good at solving industry's problems as people in industry are.) Even ruthless employers want to protect workers, in part because it's expensive to hire and train new ones. In a free society, things get better without government intervention!

• • •

I once surprised Arianna Huffington with that second OSHA graph. Her reply was an emotionally appealing one: "If you were the husband of one of the women who died recently because OSHA regulations were not sufficiently implemented, you would not be so cavalier about the speed at which things get better!"

Similarly, when I argued that welfare reform was, on balance, a good thing because millions of people left the welfare rolls and in most cases, went to work, Huffington acknowledged that some people are better off—but added: "We have over thirty million Americans living below the poverty line!"

Like most advocates for big government, Huffington didn't give much thought to ways in which limiting welfare made things better. She immediately thought of problems still out there that she believed government should address.

When well-meaning people observe suffering, they overlook the gradual, piecemeal improvement that markets make. Accustomed to government's promise of once-and-for-all solutions (promises that rarely lead to actual solutions), they miss how free markets gradually help humanity solve problems.

Economic historian Robert Higgs joked that it will always be easier to rally politically inclined people behind unrealistic, revolutionary causes than to rally them around subtle economic progress, because no crowd of activists marches behind a banner proclaiming, "Toward a Marginally Improved Society!" Even as life gets safer, longer, and richer, people clamor for new regulations every time a child falls down a well.

I'm called coldhearted because I say new regulations are the wrong response—that we're better off thinking like statisticians instead of wringing our hands over the child, and that economic freedom does much more for workers than protests and legislation crafted in workers' names.

President Reagan once said that he'd like to take Soviet president Gorbachev on a helicopter flight over an American city and point down at all the swimming pools. Then he could remind Gorbachev that all those nice swimming pools belong to "the workers." Reagan had the right idea.

WHAT INTUITION TEMPTS US TO BELIEVE:
"Collective bargaining" is a "right."

WHAT REALITY TAUGHT ME:
If workers choose to band together and "collectively bargain" with an employer who is free to hire someone else, fine—but often, choice is not allowed.

"Collective bargaining" sounds good. Collective bargaining "rights" sound even better. Employers are more sophisticated about job negotiations than an individual employee is. So why shouldn't workers be able to join together to bargain?

They should. What galls me is that in much of America, labor laws grant unions an effective monopoly on certain jobs, and *force* workers to join. When I got a job offer from CBS, I was told that I *had* to join AFTRA, the American Federation of Television and Radio Artists. I didn't want to join AFTRA. I don't consider myself an "artist." I didn't want to pay dues to a union that didn't appear to do much. But I had no choice. If I wanted to work (for CBS and later ABC), I had to join.

Laws that force workers to join unions end up treating millions of diverse people, most of whom want very different things, as undifferentiated collectives. That makes it impossible for innovators to go their own way. It also means that good workers get punished.

Here's what one union member wrote on my blog: "I thought unions were great—until at Chrysler, the union steward started screaming at me. Working at an unhurried pace, I'd exceeded 'production' for that job."

That comment matched my experience. When I was at ABC and CBS, no one *ordered* me to slow down, but union culture slowed all of us down. Sometimes a camera crew took five minutes just to get out of the car. One union cameraman slept through interviews.

In the private sector, such sloth is tempered by competition. If Steve Jobs had given in to a union's demand for rigid work rules or expensive contracts, he would have had less money to put into research. Or his products would have cost more. After all, money for fat benefits comes from *somewhere*. Bosses don't simply shout "Curses!" and dip into the pots of gold littered about their mansions, then fork over money to the "common man." Unions' gains come at others' expense.

Steve Jobs couldn't abuse his employees without consequences. Because American workers have choices. Private employers have an incentive to maintain good relationships with employees—a relationship that keeps them reasonably loyal—because they can always quit and go work for the competition.

WHAT INTUITION TEMPTS US TO BELIEVE:

Corporations are beyond our control, but

government serves the people.

WHAT REALITY TAUGHT ME:
Private institutions face more pressure to
serve the public than "public" ones do.

Governments, unlike private employers, don't face competition.

Well, every two or four years, politicians face some competition, sort of. But bosses in the private sector face competition every minute.

Maybe I shouldn't use the phrase "private sector." It suggests the choice is between serving *private* interests versus the *public*. That belies the fact that businesses (and charities) do much more for the public than most government agencies do. "Public" also suggests that the facilities are open to the public. But it's much easier for people to enter a supermarket or church than to enter many "public" buildings. Try walking into a public school without permission. You might get arrested. Let's stop calling them "public buildings" and "public sector" workers. They're government buildings and government workers.

Some government workers don't even face competition every two or four years. Bureaucrats have a job for life and gerrymandering ensures that most politicians get reelected year after year, regardless of how they perform. In some places, public sector unions are so good at getting out the vote that the union basically elects its "bosses." The bosses then reward the people who voted them in. So politicians give workers the raises they demand, and in return, workers campaign for the politicians. It's a money pump. Money goes from the taxpayers to the public employee's salary, to dues to the union, then from the union to the candidate who promised to do more for the union.

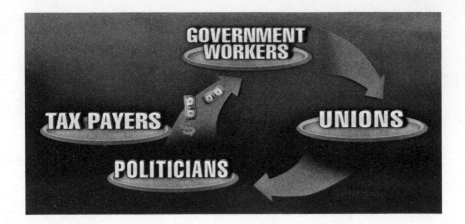

Round and round it goes, with a rapidly rising amount of your money involved. This has led to government pension deals that are unsustainable.

WHAT INTUITION TEMPTS US TO BELIEVE:

If collective bargaining is good for the private

sector, it's good for government workers, too.

WHAT REALITY TAUGHT ME:

Government workers are *special*.

Government work was once a trade-off: you got paid less, but you got job security and early retirement. Now government workers get job security, early retirement, and more money too.

When free-market advocates finally got the media to acknowledge that, progressive groups quickly came out with studies claiming that government workers don't earn more. The studies were cleverly deceitful. A "Federal Salary Council" said federal workers earn 24 percent less. When my researcher checked that out, we learned that the Federal Salary Council is just nine people, most of them labor reps, like the secretary-treasurer of the National Federation of Federal Employees. Their "study" ignored pensions and medical benefits. That's big because government pensions and benefits are much better than private sector benefits.

A Heritage Foundation study concluded that federal employees earn 30 percent to 40 percent more. Chris Edwards of the Cato Institute says, "Their wages are roughly comparable to private sector workers', but their benefit packages are much more generous." Unions countered by claiming that government work requires more skill.

It's possible, I suppose. But *USA Today* did a comparison of jobs like cook, janitor, and landscape architect:

	Govt.	Private
Cook	$38,400	$23,279
Janitor	$30,110	$24,188
Landscape architect	$80,830	$58,380

I doubt that government janitors are more skilled than private sector janitors.

Why do government workers get paid more? Because they negotiate with bosses who don't pay the bills. Politicians care less about balancing future budgets than they care about pleasing this year's voters. They don't want the bad press of a strike. Their incentive is to get a deal done.

It's often long after that politician leaves office when taxpayers discover that they are liable for his promises. The result, says Steven Malanga, senior policy analyst at the Manhattan Institute, is that the states' $3 trillion in pension promises to government workers "is squeezing out all other spending. . . . [Government workers are] allowed to retire at 58 and the rest of us are retiring at 65 and 67. . . . [I]t's crazy. The public sector is the version of the European welfare state—which in Europe, they're actually rolling back!"

When I report on such things, I get hate mail: "Stossel's take on unions is nothing but appalling. According to him, workers have no rights." "Workers are the ones who make a company profitable, not CEOs." "Are you really this stupid? Do you really want to lower American workers' standards to that of Honduras and China, where democratic unions do not exist? Would you like for us to go back to a time before we had unions? When children worked in factories for fourteen-hour days and health and safety standards simply did not exist?"

These are popular views. But they are wrong.

Factories are safer because of the prosperity created by markets, not because of unions. CEO decisions *are* largely responsible for whether a company is profitable. Ninety-five percent of American workers make *more* than the minimum wage. That's not because companies are generous, not because of laws or unions, but because competition forces companies to offer higher wages or better working conditions to attract good workers. They may move jobs overseas if U.S. wages get too high for them to compete (or because of U.S. taxes and regulations), but they clearly prefer to keep jobs here, close to their headquarters, suppliers, and customers.

Unions once helped advance working conditions, but now union work rules hurt workers because they stifle growth by making companies less flexible. When I first arrived at CBS, I was stunned to discover that I couldn't even watch a video in a tape player without risking a grievance being filed by a union editor, saying I'd encroached upon his job. Work ground to a halt while we waited for a union specialist to do something as simple as press the "on" button. ABC and CBS, being private businesses that had to compete, eventually got rid of some of those rules. But it took years.

Fox News, thankfully, is nonunion. It makes a difference in ways I didn't expect. Studio crews have a better attitude. They pay attention. They make suggestions. Some even seem to have fun. That was rare at ABC and CBS. At the unionized networks, grumpy crews acted like work was an imposition. Union rules create attitudes like that. Over time, the "protections" in the union contract send the message: Don't try anything new, don't shake the boat; work is something to be minimized—not an opportunity—certainly not something to get excited about.

Unions suck the joy out of work.

Many workers understand this. It's a reason why union membership has fallen to only 8 percent of private sector jobs. A bigger reason is that unionized companies atrophy. Nonunion Toyota grew, while GM shrank. Southwest Airlines became the largest airline in the United States, and JetBlue, founded in 1999, now takes in nearly $100 million a year, while unionized TWA and Pan Am went out of business. Union rules "protect" workers all the way to the unemployment line.

WHAT INTUITION TEMPTS US TO BELIEVE:

Free trade leads to a "race to the bottom."

WHAT REALITY TAUGHT ME:

Free trade helps more than it hurts.

Many, if not most, Americans view international trade (in both goods and labor) as a threat to jobs. Labor unions, far-left anti-globalization protesters, and even Pat Buchanan–style right-wingers agree: Foreign goods and foreign companies threaten American workers. An NBC poll found that even 61 percent of Tea Party sympathizers believe free trade has hurt the United States.

It seems logical. Intuition—and fear—tell us that American businesses will close as companies flock to places where they can find the world's lowest-paid workers. As Senator Byron Dorgan of North Dakota put it, "If you can't compete against thirty-cents-an-hour labor in some other country, you lose your job."

That seems logical. Why would I employ someone in New York City when I could find workers who will do the job for thirty cents an hour in the third world? If only we could erect some sort of wall around the United States, one preventing jobs from going overseas, America would thrive! That's why we need tariffs! Trade barriers! Rules against "exporting American jobs"!

Of course, if the race-to-the-bottom argument is true, it's puzzling that all New York's work isn't exported to Alabama, where wages are lower.

Economist Don Boudreaux points out that "[i]t's no more natural or unnatural—no more good or bad—for an Alabamian to trade with a Virginian than for that same Alabamian to trade with a Canadian or a Singaporean." We trade with other people in distant places because there are things those people can do more efficiently than we can, and vice versa. If we forbid those interactions, we miss out on all the gains from the comparative advantages of different regions.

Trade is good whether it's trade in products or labor. The efficiencies gained lead to better prices for American consumers and savings for American businesses; that allows those businesses to hire more people here. Politicians scream about American companies that "outsource" jobs. But a study at Dartmouth's Tuck School of Business discovered that American companies that outsourced jobs also hired more people *in* America. The wealth and efficiency created by outsourcing enabled companies to expand domestically. New jobs replaced the outsourced ones.

Poor countries make economic progress by building old-fashioned factories. People in America leave factories and move on to better jobs as Web designers, architects, and health-care aides. The dynamism of trade eventually creates more work than it destroys. Today's lamentations about America's disappearing manufacturing jobs should be accompanied by cheers for all the far-more-pleasant jobs we've created.

Of course, some Americans lose jobs and don't find comparable work. That's tragic for them. But unemployment would be worse without globalization. Last year, even with unusually high unemployment, America still created more than a million new jobs. Joblessness stayed high only because population growth was even greater.

Politicians and the mainstream media rarely understand that trade is win-win. My former employer did a series on its evening news called "Made in America" (anchored by Diane Sawyer) about the supposed tragedy of Americans buying foreign-made products. President Obama signed a "Buy American" provision of the stimulus bill. It mandated the use of domestic manufactured goods even if imports are cheaper (before him, President George W. Bush placed tariffs on imported steel). When presidents, the media, CEOs, and labor union leaders agree that foreign goods are unwanted, it's hard to be the voice speaking up for the little guy, saying, "Let those cheap foreign goods in, please—I may want to buy them—and I may want to work for a foreign-owned company too." But someone should say it. Trade has given us much of the prosperity that we have.

Obama's "Buy American" provision made our trading partners nervous. Obama seemed at first to recognize the problem, saying on Fox News, "I think it would be a mistake . . . for us to start sending a message that somehow we're just looking after ourselves and not concerned with world trade."

But some members of his party were elected on protectionist platforms. They didn't want Obama to blow this chance to reward their union and industrial constituencies. So Obama did what politicians do: he tried to have it both ways. He said he'd "see what kind of language we can work on this issue."

The Senate then added a line saying that the "Buy American" section must be applied in a manner "consistent with U.S. obligations under international agreements." Good luck to any company, foreign or domestic, that had to figure out what that meant. The Senate's addition was a good thing. But even diluted, protectionism is poison.

Protectionism does save some American jobs—often temporarily. But it destroys jobs in two ways. First, when foreigners lose sales here, they invest less in the U.S. economy. Second, when foreign nations retaliate and put tariffs on our exports, more jobs are destroyed.

As my college economics professor, Burton G. Malkiel, puts it, "Beggar-thy-neighbor policies create more beggars and hostile neighbors."

We should know this by now. In 1929–30, President Herbert Hoover and Congress helped turn a depression into the Great

Depression by enacting the infamous Smoot-Hawley Tariff on twenty thousand goods. Hoover's mere announcement that he would sign the bill drove the stock market into the tank. Hoover and Congress then made their bad tariff decision worse by approving a "Buy America Act," which required federal projects to use only American supplies. Other countries retaliated, and exports fell by 64 percent. Unemployment climbed above 20 percent.

Trade is not war—though governments often turn it into one by threatening tariffs, sanctions, and embargoes. Absent these threats, trade between nations is a win-win just like trade between individuals. It makes most everyone richer because different people can focus on doing what they do best.

Economists call it comparative advantage.

As the Cato Institute's Tom Palmer puts it: "Just like the case of you buying coffee. You could have made your own coffee. But your time might have been better spent doing something else. So you outsourced your coffee production. You made yourself better off. And that young lady who sold you the coffee made herself better off. . . . It's what we do on a one-to-one basis every hour of every day, if the politicians just leave us alone."

But the politicians don't leave us alone.

WHAT INTUITION TEMPTS US TO BELIEVE:
Businesses care more about profit than workers,
so they must be forced to provide benefits.

WHAT REALITY TAUGHT ME:
Where labor markets are free, businesses must
treat workers well in order to make a profit.

It's natural to think that corporations' drive for profit means that they will drive workers relentlessly. Certainly, they won't give them extra time off to raise children. That's why it seems humane to have a law that requires companies not to discriminate against pregnant women.

Sales consultant Holly Waters worked for Novartis, the drug maker. Shortly before she went on maternity leave, she was fired. "I was seven-and-a-half months pregnant," she told me. "There was no way I was going to be able to go out and find a job at this point." But Waters knew that she could punish Novartis. The Pregnancy Discrimination Act makes it illegal to fire, or not hire, a woman because she is pregnant. The government even warns employers that in a job interview, you must never even ask questions like "Might you start a family?"

Holly Waters's lawyer, David Sanford, sued Novartis. He told me his $200 million class-action lawsuit would teach all companies not to discriminate.

My ABC colleagues thought it obvious that women like Waters deserved special legal protection, so I found a working mother who would go on TV to defend freedom of contract.

Carrie Lukas, vice president of the Independent Women's Forum, said, "Laws that are intended to help women like me actually end up hurting women like me. All of a sudden, a potential employer looks at me thinking, 'She just might turn around and sue us.' That makes it less likely that I'm going to get hired. You raise the cost of hiring a woman like me."

And while some pregnant women work as hard as any man, "let's be honest," she said. "Most pregnant workers impose costs. Responsibilities are shifted each time I go to a doctor's appointment. One of my colleagues has to pick up the slack."

Free-market economists teach that there's a way to resolve such conflicts: voluntary exchange for mutual benefit. Companies like Novartis have an incentive to treat women well. They need good workers, even if some become pregnant.

Novartis wouldn't agree to an interview. Frightened corporate lawyers routinely say "no" when TV reporters call. But how bad could Novartis be? *Working Mother* magazine named Novartis one of "America's 100 best companies for women." I can't know what really led to Waters's firing, but it's generally not legal threats that persuade companies like Novartis to treat employees—including pregnant ones—well. The company's desire to protect its reputation in an open labor market does that all by itself.

Class-action lawyer Sanford won his lawsuit. The jurors ordered Novartis to pay Sanford and his "victims" $250 million! Novartis appealed, but then settled for $175 million.

I told Sanford that his lawsuits harm women because companies are reluctant to hire people whom they view as potential lawsuit bombs. He was unfazed: "If they do take that position, they'd be violating the law. If companies lose money because of it—and they may—that's not necessarily a bad thing from a societal perspective."

But it is a very bad thing. That $175 million might have been spent on medical research. Sanford's victory discourages companies from hiring women who might get pregnant. A free and open labor market is what benefits society most. But that is not intuitive. Viewers wrote angry emails:

- "What in the heck is wrong with you, John Stossel? This kind of backwards thinking only exists in third world countries."
- "Fire Stossel."
- "Without discrimination laws, who would hire pregnant women?"

"Plenty of employers," said Carrie Lukas. "Women are incredibly productive members of the workforce. . . . If an employer is going to discriminate against enough people, it's going to be bad for them in the long run."

Lukas works for an organization that's small enough to be exempt from the Pregnancy Discrimination Act. That meant that she and her boss could make their own deal—one that suits both of them. When she's pregnant, she works fewer hours and earns less money. She lets the company "discriminate" against her. Win-win. Freedom of contract is the best way to protect women, she says. "You don't have to hire me, and I don't have to work for you."

If companies are sexist or racist, the free market will punish them. Suppose a sexist company won't hire women, or pays men more. A nonsexist competitor who hires those women now has a comparative advantage. The nonsexist company's wage differential allows that company to sell goods at lower prices. The inclusive company thrives, and the sexist one dies. The market *usually* punishes bad behavior. We don't need so many laws.

When big government decrees a single solution to a problem, it overrides all the diverse solutions that increasingly educated and independent women, increasingly flexible businesses, and more enlightened males work out.

Some family-values conservatives are economically illiterate on this topic, arguing that government should show concern for families by requiring companies to provide more maternity leave. These conservatives are as guilty as feminists of thinking that government can create one rule that will strike just the right balance. No one will ever find a formula everyone agrees on.

But we can have 100 million different arrangements if lawmakers leave life to the experiments of the free market.

WHAT INTUITION TEMPTS US TO BELIEVE:

Disabled people need government protection.

WHAT REALITY TAUGHT ME:

Such protection hurts the disabled.

In 1990, Congress passed the Americans with Disabilities Act (ADA). President George H. W. Bush signed the law and announced that its antidiscrimination provision meant that more disabled Americans would get jobs. But the opposite happened. When the ADA became law, 59.8 percent of disabled men were employed. After the ADA passed, that number dropped to 48.9.

That didn't surprise me. When Congress creates a "protected group," some employers avoid hiring members of that group.

Steven Lonegan, owner of a cabinet-making company, is blind. He told me, "Had that law been in place when I was a kid, I don't know where I would be today. . . . Everybody who's classified with a so-called disability is a walking lawsuit to any possible employer. So when you go in to get a job, the employer, rather than thinking, what can he bring to my business, the first question is, what are you going to cost me? Are you going to be a burden on my business? It actually puts people at a disadvantage."

I'm a ticking lawsuit time bomb myself, since I'm a stutterer. I once stuttered so much that my TV station ran out of time and cut me off the air. Sometimes at my old job at *20/20*, Barbara Walters and I had to retape a segment because I stuttered. But at least *20/20* wasn't live. Fox programs usually are. What if I stutter now? If Fox responds by firing me, should I pull out the ADA card and demand compensation? Should I demand that Fox tape every program that includes me? That might be within my "rights of accommodation" under the ADA.

If I did that, I wouldn't blame Fox for wishing that they'd never hired me.

The disabled—or rather, lawyers who claim to represent them—now feed off the ADA. They sue businesses that fail to obey every ADA rule. They sued Chipotle Mexican Grill, saying that its counters were too high for people in wheelchairs. Chipotle didn't want to rebuild every counter, so it offered to bring samples of every dish to every handicapped person. A judge ruled that wasn't good enough. So Chipotle had to spend millions to retrofit its restaurants. Isn't the ADA grand?

Some lawyers file thousands of such suits, complaining of trivial violations of ADA specs—like paper towel racks that are an inch too high. Walter Olson of Overlawyered.com points out that the cost goes beyond retrofitting workspaces. "It's not just paying to move the paper towel rack, it's also paying the lawyer to drop the case." The legal fees run into the tens of thousands of dollars. Those costs kill many good things.

Basketball Town, in Rancho Cordova, California, was threatened with a lawsuit when a boy booked a birthday party upstairs and one guest showed up in a wheelchair. Basketball Town offered to move the party to the first floor, but the ADA lawyer said that wasn't good enough.

Even though the suit was dropped, Basketball Town still had to pay one hundred thousand dollars to lawyers, the only real winners in these cases. Basketball Town then went out of business. Children now have one less place to play.

All such regulation has unintended consequences. As Hayek understood, no government planner can anticipate most of them.

The ADA has even made it harder to go to the bathroom in my town. Many European cities have wonderful, self-cleaning, public toilets. A French company planned to build one hundred of them in New York City, but disability activists said that the ADA required that the toilets be bigger, to accommodate wheelchairs. *New York* magazine called the ensuing controversy "the Toilet Wars." The problem is that bigger toilets cost more to make, drug users use them to get high, and hookers use them for sex. The French company gave up on America, and we New Yorkers have to "hold it."

Another unintended side effect of worker protection laws: we no longer have honest job interviews. Employers don't even know what they're allowed to ask. The government's enforcer, the Equal Employment Opportunity Commission, tells employers that not only must they never ask a woman if she plans to start a family, but if a disabled person comes in for a job interview, they may not ask:

- Do you have a disability that would interfere with your ability to perform the job?
- How many days were you sick last year?

The law also sends a destructive message to the disabled: You always need special treatment.

On my show, Greg Perry said, "I walk around on an artificial leg most of the time. I've been confined to a wheelchair several times."

You might think he'd support the ADA, but he doesn't.

"I am so glad I was born before the ADA was passed. If the ADA had been passed before I was born . . . I would be a loser today because I was a typical lazy teenager. I would have been as disabled as possible."

What if the ADA had been law when I started out? As a stutterer, would I have been "accommodated," put in jobs that required no public speaking? That wouldn't have been good for my career—or my psyche. I would have spent energy worrying about accommodation instead of trying to become a more fluent speaker.

The grand schemes of the social engineers almost always go wrong. And they never even say sorry.

WHAT INTUITION TEMPTS US TO BELIEVE:

If it weren't for minimum wage laws, business

would pay workers next to nothing.

WHAT REALITY TAUGHT ME:

A minimum wage law makes it harder for

low-wage workers to get a job.

Even people who are skeptical of government regulation tend to like minimum wage laws. Nearly all Democrats support them—and in 2010, 51 percent of Republican voters favored increasing the minimum wage.

The media don't even bother trying to sound impartial (or economically literate): "Workers got a raise on Friday when the federal minimum wage was hiked 70 cents to $7.25 an hour," reported the *Christian Science Monitor*. "They'll be shouting, Olé!"

Maybe the 2 percent of American workers who earn the minimum will shout "Olé!" But workers who lose jobs—or never find jobs because now employers can't afford to hire them—will shout something else.

People assume that if politicians declare that workers should get a raise, they will actually get it. But the idea that government helps people by increasing wages by decree rests on an economic fallacy: the belief that employers set wages arbitrarily. By this logic, if wages are low, it must be that employers are stingy.

Actually, employers *are* stingy—they want to pay as little as possible, just as workers want to earn as much as possible—but in a market, even a government-hampered market like ours, employers' wishes are tempered by the reality of competition. An employer who offers low wages loses employees to competitors who pay market wages.

As economist Don Boudreaux puts it, "Even a casual glance at reality reveals that worker compensation is determined by the supply of, and demand for, workers, and that pay does not fall to any legally allowed minimum. If [it did], then physicians, accountants, morticians—even supermodels, rock stars, and labor-union officials—would be paid minimum wages. But 97.7 percent of American workers are paid wages above the federally mandated minimum. Most are paid multiples of this amount. Heck, to get someone to watch our child, my wife and I must pay even babysitters close to twice the minimum wage!"

Some clueless politicians say the current minimum of $7.25 an hour is too low. They want to "help" workers further by requiring a "living" wage. After all, it's hard to live on $7.25 an hour. Several years ago, the city council of Santa Monica, California, decided to make Santa Monica a workers' paradise by passing a union-backed law requiring everyone to be paid at least $12.25 an hour.

Restaurant owner Jeff King complained to me that that law

would "dry up the entry-level jobs for just the people they're trying to help." He was right. The minimum wage is why gas stations no longer hire teenagers to clean your windshield—why construction companies no longer let teenagers learn on the job. Wage minimums tell employers: "Don't give a beginner a chance."

But the media don't see that. It's easy to see, and interview, workers who get an increase after a minimum wage law goes into effect. It's harder to see the worker who loses a job, or more commonly, never is offered a job because the minimum would force an employer to pay him more than the employer thinks the job is worth. Such losses are invisible, but widespread. One company closes because it can't afford to pay higher wages. Another decides to automate, to produce its product with fewer workers, and another never expands. Most important, some businesses never open. The people who were never hired don't complain—they don't even know that they were harmed. They are the unseen victims.

At least the people of Santa Monica woke up and overturned the "living wage." That's the good news. The bad news is that more than a hundred other "living wage" ordinances passed elsewhere. In Washington, D.C., companies with government contracts must pay employees at least $12.50 per hour. In Manchester, Connecticut, it's $15.54. In Richmond, California, $16.69.

But if living-wage advocates really believe government minimums help workers, why stop at $16.69? Why not $100 per hour?

At $100, even a diehard interventionist understands that workers would be hurt. But the principle is the same at every level. Every little bit hurts when government forces employers to deviate from market-set prices. Wages are a function of productivity, not whim, so when the minimum is set, some workers won't be hired.

For some minimum wage advocates, such bad consequences are not exactly unintended. Consider the support the minimum wage gets from companies like Wal-Mart. Why do they want a higher minimum? Economist Alex Tabarrok of George Mason University answers, "Because it raises the costs of their rivals. This is why unions have typically been in favor of the minimum wage even when their own workers [already] make much more than the minimum." Where there is "humanitarian" government intervention, there is often a special interest.

What workers need is not meddling politicians—but free labor markets.

Lately, some central planners got upset because a few workers get paid nothing at all. I'm talking about internships. Do you know of businesses that invite college students to work in return for on-the-job training? Might they be giving your son or daughter valuable job experience right now?

President Obama's Labor Department decided that such businesses "exploit" your children. The department didn't declare an absolute ban, but decreed internship permissible only if the employer gets "no immediate advantage" from the intern's activities. In fact, the department advised that it's better if the employer's work "may be impeded."

What? Impeded? I've had interns like that, and wanted to scream at them. Fortunately, those interns were exceptions. Most of my interns provided lots of "immediate advantage." They made my work possible.

It began in 1974 when I asked my TV bosses to pay for research help. They laughed: "You think we're made of money?"

So I asked colleges if students wanted internships. Many did, and from then on I got some of my best help from unpaid college students. Did I exploit them? Most told me that they loved the experience. One said, "I learned more than at college, and I didn't have to pay tuition!"

For many, their internship led to careers in journalism. They were happy; I was happy. What's the problem? The problem is that unions don't like it. Obama's Labor Department hired 250 investigators to catch exploiters like me. I asked the department to provide someone to appear on my show, but they declined.

Instead, *Village Voice* writer Anya Kamenetz, who wrote a column titled "Take This Internship and Shove It," came on to defend the Obama rule. "If you start working for free, where's it going to end? . . . Employers could say . . . why should we be forced to pay the guy who cleans the floors?"

Because if they didn't pay, they wouldn't get people to clean floors! But we shouldn't expect a *Village Voice* writer to understand markets.

Shortly before the Obama Labor Department announced its no-free-interns policy, my old employer ABC, always in sync with the latest in Democratic Party thinking, started paying interns $10 an hour. That was a good deal for well-connected students who got internships—but lousy for the majority who didn't. Because of the new cost, ABC cut the number of interns by half.

What's happened to the rights of contract and free association? If student and employer come to an agreement, both expect to benefit or the agreement won't happen. The student is no indentured servant. If the employer "exploits," the student can quit. The contract ought to be nobody's business but theirs.

WHAT INTUITION TEMPTS US TO BELIEVE:

Markets are cruel. Government is kind.

WHAT REALITY TAUGHT ME:

Governments' attempts at "kindness" are cruel.

When I talk about getting rid of regulations, it's not because I want rich employers to get fat off the labor of workers. It's because I've learned that markets are fluid—and the best way for more workers to find jobs they like is to leave everyone free to make any contract they want to make.

When we outlaw the low-wage job that would have taught a teenager skills and the internship that would have given a kid a foot in the door, we don't insulate people from the hardships of the market. We insulate them from knowledge about how to function in an ever-changing economy.

That's not compassion. That's a denial of reality.

The best way to help workers achieve a better future is to get the government to butt out and let the market work.

It's also the only way to solve the health-care "crisis."

5

FIXING HEALTH CARE

WHAT INTUITION TEMPTS US TO BELIEVE:
American health care is a costly mess, and someone,
probably government, must do something about it.

WHAT REALITY TAUGHT ME:
Government already dominates health
care—and that's the problem.

Right before President Obama took office, the media suddenly got
hysterical about American health care. You heard their claims:
America spends more than any other country—$6,000 per person—
yet we get less. Americans die younger than people in Japan and

Western Europe. Americans worry about paying for care. Millions lack health insurance.

So what should be done?

I know! said the president. Bigger government will give us more choices and make health care cheaper and better. He proceeded to give us that. Bigger government, that is. The cheaper/better/more choices part—not so much.

Costs have risen. "Better" is too early to judge. As for "more choices"? No. We have fewer. Some people have lost coverage.

Because ObamaCare required insurance companies to cover every child regardless of preexisting condition, WellPoint, Humana, and Cigna got out of the child-only business. Principal Financial stopped offering health insurance altogether—one million customers no longer have the "choice" to keep their insurance (something that Obama promised about a zillion times we would be able to do).

Ironically, in the year after ObamaCare passed, some of its biggest proponents asked to be exempted from it. More than a hundred organizations got waivers. The largest group that got an exemption? A big teachers union.

Advocates for government-run health care stick to their talking points, despite reality smacking them in the face. In my waning days at ABC, Michael Moore released the movie *Sicko*. It claims that Cubans get better health care than Americans: "They believe in preventive medicine. . . . [I]t seems like there's a doctor on every block . . . a clinic in every neighborhood." Moore told me, "This isn't just me saying this, you know. All the world health organizations have confirmed that if there's one thing they do right in Cuba, it's health care. There's very little debate about that."

Oh, there's plenty of debate.

It's true that a United Nations report claimed that Cubans live longer than Americans. But the UN just reports what the Cuban government tells them. Governments (especially socialist ones) lie. Twenty years ago, Soviet officials insisted there were no poor people in Russia. Why would anyone believe Cuban health statistics?

Cuba claims low infant mortality, but doctors there tell us that if a baby dies soon after birth, they don't count the baby as ever having lived.

When I pressed Moore, he backed away from his movie's claims about Cuba. "Let's stick to Canada and Britain," he said.

Okay.

WHAT INTUITION TEMPTS US TO BELIEVE:

Under government health care, people get equal treatment.

WHAT REALITY TAUGHT ME:

They get equally second-rate treatment.

In England and Canada, health care is "free." Of course, "free" just means it's paid for through taxes. That's a good thing if the goal is to reduce individuals' anxiety about paying medical bills. It's theoretically a good thing if your goal is equality of treatment. But that's about it.

If you want a checkup and you don't mind waiting—or if you have a heart attack that is life-or-death *right now*—you might think government health care is fine. But that's where it ends. Say you have endless headaches (could be a brain tumor) or need a knee replacement (extremely painful) or are going blind and need cataract surgery. To get treatment, you will wait . . . and wait . . . and wait . . .

because making people wait is one way government keeps its costs down.

In the U.S., Medicare hasn't really done that yet—they just shovel money out the door. But that will soon end.

Where governments control health care but want to limit the cost, everyone has to get in line. (Okay, not everyone—the rich and politically connected jump the line. Economist June O'Neill, director of the Congressional Budget Office from 1995 to 1999, studied the U.S. and Canadian health-care systems and found that the relationship between income and health is greater in Canada than the United States.) Since medical services seem free, demand increases. Governments deal with that by rationing—limiting what's available. Advocates of government health care hate the word "rationing" because it forces them to face an ugly truth: Once you accept the idea that taxpayers should pay, then individual choice dies. Someone else decides what treatment you get, and when.

Now, in a sense, there's nothing wrong with rationing. Resources aren't unlimited, so choices must be made. But who gets to make those choices—you . . . or a bureaucrat? Either the decisions will be determined by force, by government, or they will be made voluntarily, by individuals spending their own money. The latter is better. Some want to spend for every ounce of health care that might keep them alive. Others would rather leave that money to their children.

At least in America, you still have *some* choice. You can pay to get what you want. Under government health care, bureaucrats like the ones who had trouble simply counting votes in Florida will decide how long you wait for your knee operation or cataract surgery.

The British National Health Service recently made the pathetic promise to reduce the waiting time for hospital care to four months. Have a toothache? The wait to see dentists is so long that some Brits pull their own teeth. One man made headlines in England for using novel dental tools on himself: pliers and vodka.

In America, socialists scare the elderly by saying that conservatives want to cut Medicare. Conservatives scare the elderly by talking about "death panels." Sarah Palin popularized the term, saying, "My baby with Down syndrome will have to stand in front of Obama's 'death panel' so his bureaucrats can decide, based on a subjective judgment of their 'level of productivity in society,' whether they are worthy of health care."

But that problem isn't unique to ObamaCare. When someone else pays for your health care, that someone else gets to decide when to pull the plug. The reason can be found in Econ 101. Medical care doesn't grow on trees. It must be produced by human and physical capital, and those resources are limited. Politicians can't repeal the law of supply and demand.

Call it "death panels" or not, a government that needs to cut costs will limit what it spends on health care, especially to people nearing the end of life. Medical "ethicists" have long lamented that too much money is spent in the last several months of life. Given the premise that it's government's job to pay, it's only natural that some bureaucrat will decide that eighty-year-olds shouldn't get hip replacements.

When he pushed for ObamaCare, the president insisted that he was not "trying to bring about government-run health care." What a relief! He said that if we were starting from scratch, a single-payer system is what he'd back. But he didn't think that was politically achievable. So Obama said he would just improve our system with a little "government management."

"But government management does the same thing," says Sally Pipes of the Pacific Research Institute. Pipes is from Canada, so she knows something about "equality" medicine. "Either we let a free market distribute those resources according to who is most willing to pay for them, or we let government give them out 'equally.' "

Despite the rationing, polls show most Canadians *like* their free health care. That gave me pause. But Dr. David Gratzer reminded me that most people, when they get the survey phone call, aren't sick. Gratzer is a Canadian who also liked Canada's government health care. But then he started treating patients. "The more time I spent in the Canadian system, the more I came across people waiting for radiation therapy, waiting for the knee replacement so they could finally walk up to the second floor of their house. . . . You want to see your neurologist because of your stress headache? No problem! Just wait six months. You want an MRI? No problem! Free as the air! Just wait six months."

More than a million and a half Canadians say they can't find a family doctor. Some towns hold lotteries to determine who gets to see one. In Norwood, Ontario, a producer for my show watched as the town clerk pulled four names out of a big box and then telephoned the lucky winners. "Congratulations! You get to see a doctor this month."

Think the wait in an American emergency room is bad? In Canada, the average wait is twenty-three hours. "We can't send these patients to other hospitals," Dr. Eric Letovsky told us. "Every other emergency department in the country is just as packed." Canadian doctors told us that sometimes they couldn't even get heart attack victims into the ICU.

Fortunately for Canadians with money, there is a safety valve: the large, wasteful, selfish country just south of the border.

Shirley Healy's doctor told her she had only a few weeks to live because a blocked artery kept her from digesting food. Yet Canadian officials, eager to be responsible and save the country money, declared her surgery "elective." Under the Canadian system, if your surgery is "elective," you wait. So Shirley came to America for treatment. "The only thing elective about this surgery was I elected to live," she said.

WHAT INTUITION TEMPTS US TO BELIEVE:

Profit and medicine don't mix.

WHAT REALITY TAUGHT ME:

Pursuit of profit is what brings innovation.

It's true that America's partly profit-driven health-care system is expensive. We spend much more than other countries. But by spending more, we get more. As Canada's Dr. Gratzer points out, the United States "is the country of medical innovation. This is where people come when they need treatment. . . . [We're] surrounded by medical miracles. Death by cardiovascular disease has dropped by two thirds in the last fifty years. You've got to pay a price for that type of advancement."

Canada and England don't pay that price, because they freeload off American innovation. We invent it—the world then uses it. Were America to adopt their government-managed system, we could worry less about paying—yippee—but we'd get current-level care, forever. That's not good enough for me.

What's more important than health? I define "health" as freedom from pain and the ability to do things I like for as many years as possible. This definition has no necessary connection to health "insurance" that politicians obsess about. It's much more about innovation. Before free markets created prosperity, humans lived just a few decades. It was entrepreneurial advances in housing and sanitation that first extended our lives. Then progress in science led to vaccines and antibiotics that extended life further.

That set us up to suffer from degenerative diseases of old age—strokes, bad knees, dementia. These are good problems to have. It's great that most of us now at least reach a period we call old age. Now we need innovation to make those years productive and less painful. We've got some: robotic prosthetic limbs, MRI machines, artificial hearts, microscopic cameras that peer inside the body during surgery, hip and knee replacements. But I want more. Without the greed of drug companies and medical researchers like my brother Tom, there would be far fewer of those innovations. We'd live with more pain and die sooner. Most of those advances have happened in America because America is the one country that has allowed the profit motive to work—at least partially.

If government ran health care, those advances would slow to a crawl, because governments don't innovate. They just keep doing what they did last year. It's only the hope of fat profit that gets people to break free from their comfortable habits and gets investors to risk the big money required to invent the new drugs and cutting-edge medicine that we really want.

Michael Moore is correct when he says that Canadians and Europeans live longer, but one reason they live long is that they have access to those American inventions.

The other reasons have little to do with health care. Americans die younger because more Americans are fat like Moore (I give him credit—he laughed when I told him that), we shoot each other more often, and we crash our cars more often.

Moore told me that my trust in free markets is so retrograde that I sound like I'm from the "thirteenth century." Ha ha. Yet I noticed later that when he decided to get treatment for his weight problem, he didn't go to Cuba or Canada. He went to a private spa in Florida.

WHAT INTUITION TEMPTS US TO BELIEVE:

Health care is too important to be left to the
vagaries of market competition.

WHAT REALITY TAUGHT ME:

Health care is too important *not* to be
disciplined by market competition.

In Canada, we did find one area of medicine that offered easy access to cutting-edge technology. In these clinics, you can get a CT scan, endoscopy, thoracoscopy, laparoscopy, etc. quickly. Unfortunately, these clinics are open only to patients with four legs. Veterinary medicine is still private in Canada. Dogs can get a CT scan in one day. For people, the waiting list is a month.

Canadian vet care is cutting-edge because market competition demands that. Market competition so routinely brings us better cars, phones, shoes, medicine—that we don't even think about the mechanism that created those wonderful things. We just assume the supermarket will have thirty thousand products, will be open 24/7, and that the food will be cheap. Government could never produce that—look at what's happened when government tried. Heck, in the agriculturally rich Soviet Union, there was so little food that mothers sent their kids into the fields to kill mice and rats. Yet now, somehow, under President Obama's management, government will give us better health care? Give me a break.

Yet doctors are often hostile to markets. Dr. Atul Gawande, in an otherwise interesting *New Yorker* article on health-care costs, described talking to surgeon Lester Dyke about the idea of a true market in health care. This is how their intuition worked:

> We tried to imagine the scenario. A cardiologist tells an elderly woman that she needs bypass surgery and has Dr. Dyke see her . . . they're supposed to haggle over the price as if he were selling a rug in a souk? "I'll do three vessels for $30,000, but if you take four, I'll throw in an extra night in the ICU"—that sort of thing? Dyke shook his head. "Who comes up with this stuff?" he asked.

Adam Smith, for one. The market does manage to sort that stuff out. It's not surprising that Drs. Dyke and Gawande cannot imagine it. As Friedrich Hayek wrote in 1944, "It may indeed prove to be far the most difficult and not the least important task for human reason rationally to comprehend its own limitations." Dyke's elderly patients wouldn't have to haggle over price before surgery because those decisions would in effect have been made by thousands of previous patients, by the minority who pay closest attention. If there were a market, word about where to go to get the best care or lowest prices would quickly get around. Hospitals would advertise prices. Rating agencies would evaluate them for quality. Even in nursing homes, word would get around that hospital X is a rip-off while hospital Y and Z give better treatment for less. In situations where Dyke's patients don't have the opportunity to make a choice, health insurance companies would have already done the haggling on the patient's behalf.

Drs. Dyke and Gawande have mastered the anti-free-market sneer: "markets are good for crass consumer goods, like washing machines and computers, but not for health care. It is too complicated for people to understand."

Health care is certainly complicated. But think about how complicated a car is. Yet car buyers don't need to be experts on automotive engineering. It just takes a few car buffs to guide the market—and the rest of us free-ride on their effort by listening to them, maybe reading car magazines, and most important: noticing the reputations of automakers. The good companies grow and bad ones atrophy. When government butts out, competition and cost-conscious buyers assure all of us that all cars, computers, cell phones, etc. are pretty good.

The worst car I can buy in America is much better than the best cars that governments' central planners could invent. The best the entire Soviet bloc produced were the Trabant and the Yugo. Remember those cars? They are the automotive equivalent of ObamaCare: consumer goods from government "experts." The world was fortunate that in other countries, markets were around to offer something better. When the Soviet empire collapsed, Yugos and Trabants disappeared along with the Berlin Wall. Government products and services cannot compete.

But think about this: if all automakers were government-managed, today we'd just assume that Yugos and Trabants were as good as cars could get. When governments stifle innovation, we cannot know what we might have had. We cannot imagine a Lexus (or an iPhone or Lipitor) until some greedy entrepreneur produces it.

In 2009, the Detroit Medical Center bragged that it was one of the first hospitals in America to track patients' medication with bar codes. Congratulations! But supermarkets did that forty years before. Tracking hospital medications is more important than tracking candy and Coke, but candy and Coke got there decades before simply because they aren't funded by third parties and a sclerotic government bureaucracy. This third-party payment system even discourages doctors from adopting today's most efficient form of communication—email. Does your doctor give out his email address? Bet he doesn't. Insurance companies don't pay for that.

More modernization would happen in medicine if only more of us spent our own money for care. That's because it's consumers spending our own money—consumers dealing directly with producers—that make the market work.

WHAT INTUITION TEMPTS US TO BELIEVE:

More Americans need health insurance.

WHAT REALITY TAUGHT ME:

Insurance is part of the *problem*.

Insurance companies were delighted when Obama and the "reformers" talked about how millions of American don't have health insurance, and promised that ObamaCare would get more people insured. But that was a move in the wrong direction. One of America's biggest health-care problems is not that 48 million people lack insurance—it's that 250 million Americans have too much of it.

The average American doctor now spends 14 percent of his income on insurance paperwork. A North Carolina doctor we interviewed hired four people just to fill out forms. He wishes he could spend that money on caring for patients.

I don't blame the insurance companies. Paperwork is their

pathetic attempt to protect themselves against fraud. People *do* cheat. They demand money for care that never happened. Doctors cheat, too, and we patients rarely check, because we rarely pay the bills ourselves.

This brings me to the bigger problem with health insurance: by insuring so much of our health care, we ensure that we are blind to its cost. Do you *know* how much your doctor charges for a checkup? How about for blood tests? Do you even ask?

Did you even shop for your health insurance? Compare prices? Probably not, because your employer probably provides your insurance. Why do they do that? They don't pay for your food and clothing.

Employers buy your health insurance because during World War II, government forbade companies to give workers raises. To attract better workers, employers then offered benefits like health insurance. The tax code helped this along by treating employer-based health insurance more favorably than coverage you buy yourself.

A fun footnote: My father, a poor German immigrant, made enough money to buy a house thanks to those price controls. During World War II, Sears Roebuck wasn't allowed to raise prices. However, if companies "added value" to a product, they could. So they told their suppliers to add something. My father made towels. He came up with the idea of "name towels"—a towel with your name on it. Sears could sell that for more. So America got name towels—and I got a home in the suburbs—from World War II price controls.

Unfortunately, America also got stuck with employer-based health insurance. Getting health insurance at work is especially dumb today, when Americans change jobs, on average, every four years.

Because employers pay most of the bills, the patient doesn't shop for insurance. Because the patient has insurance, he doesn't care what services cost. Because he doesn't care and doesn't shop around, the cost of care goes up and up.

Suppose you had grocery insurance. You wouldn't care what food cost. You wouldn't even know what it cost.

Why compare prices? If someone else pays 85 percent of your bill, you buy the most expensive cuts of meat. Prices would sky-rocket. That's what health insurance does to the cost of health care. Patients rarely even ask what anything costs. Doctors often don't know. Patients don't ask, "Is that MRI really necessary? Is there a cheaper place?" We consume without thinking, because someone else pays.

Third-party payment destroys the shopping process that is the essence of a market. College economics departments like to run a test where two groups of people go to a restaurant. One group orders dinner and gets separate checks. The other group splits the check. That group orders more. Another appetizer? An extra glass of wine? Why not? You'll pay only a fraction of the cost. The end result? Everybody is stuck with a higher bill.

The Guttmacher Institute says women paid an average $372 for abortions when the women or charities paid the fee. By contrast, the bill for abortions in hospitals was $5,407.

What holds costs down is patients acting like consumers, looking out for ourselves in a competitive market. Then providers, even insurance companies, fight to win business by keeping costs down.

Today we don't even see ads from health insurance companies—bragging that their prices are lower. They don't need to advertise prices. There's no consumer market. We watch funny Geico commercials. But Geico sells car insurance. Health insurance companies are silent about what they charge.

It's a big reason that the price of health care has risen at about twice the rate of inflation. When someone else pays, *costs go up.*

There are a few tiny pockets of health care, like cosmetic and Lasik eye surgery, where prices haven't risen. It's not because of any price controls. Cosmetic and Lasik surgery are specialties where patients pay with their own money. No insurance company or government bureaucrat is involved. So patients shop around, and competition holds prices down.

If you've ever had Lasik or plastic surgery you'll notice something else unusual: Patients are treated like valued customers. Waiting rooms are nice. Waiting time is brief. Doctors constantly make improvements because they must please their customers. They even give patients their email address and cell phone numbers.

Quality increased, and prices dropped. That's what markets accomplish.

WHAT INTUITION TEMPTS US TO BELIEVE:

We need comprehensive medical insurance.

WHAT REALITY TAUGHT ME:

Insure only against catastrophes.

Flood insurance, homeowners' insurance, life insurance, car insurance . . . all protect us from financial ruin if disaster strikes. But what is *health* insurance? People file claims every year—maybe every month—for routine expenses. That's not the way insurance is supposed to work! If your car insurance covered oil changes and gasoline, we'd behave . . . well . . . the way health-care consumers behave. We wouldn't even know what gasoline cost.

Most Americans would be better off if we paid all but the biggest medical bills out of pocket and saved insurance for catastrophic events. Truly needy people would rely on charity. There were lots more medical charities before the all-too-visible hand of government pushed them aside.

We do need insurance for unexpected bills that might bankrupt us. If people paid for insurance themselves, they would likely buy high-deductible policies (roughly $1,000 deductibles for individuals, $2,100 for families) because premiums are lower. That's the kind of insurance that Whole Foods offers its employees. If a worker has a sore throat or sprained ankle, he pays. But if he gets cancer or heart disease, insurance covers it.

Whole Foods puts about $1,500 a year into a Health Savings Account (HSA) for each worker. It's not charity—it's money Whole Foods would have otherwise spent on more expensive cover-most-everything insurance. If an employee doesn't spend the $1,500 on medical care this year, he keeps it in his HSA, and the company adds more next year.

CEO John Mackey told me that when he went to the new system, "[o]ur costs per employee went way down." And today, many workers have more than $10,000 in their accounts. "That's their money," Mackey said. "It builds up over time because the money is compounding for them."

It will cover all sorts of future expenses. Most important, since employees control the money, their behavior changed. Whole Foods workers started asking "how much things cost," Mackey said. "They may not want to go to the emergency room if they wake up with a stomachache in the middle of the night . . . unless it really is an emergency. They schedule an appointment now."

Before, there was no need to ask about costs, because an insurance company picked up most of the tab. Now saving money makes sense to employees because the money belongs to them.

Some say that HSA accounts will lead people to scrimp on health care. That's why our wise government must step in to protect them.

Mackey has the right response. "The premise in those kinds of questions is that people are stupid. They're not smart enough to make these decisions for themselves. It's an elitist attitude. The individual is the best judge of what's right for the individual."

WHAT INTUITION TEMPTS US TO BELIEVE:

Insurance companies should treat everyone equally.

WHAT REALITY TAUGHT ME:

With insurance, equality is not good.

Obama—and the Clintons before him—expressed outrage over insurance companies charging people different rates based on their risk profiles. Politicians want insurers to cover everyone for the same "fair" price. It's not "fair" to charge sick people more. As I write this, even Bill O'Reilly and others who oppose most ObamaCare mandates support the one that forbids discrimination against people with a preexisting condition. "Discrimination" does sound bad.

A system where everyone pays the same amount is called "community rating." That sounds fair. No more cruel discrimination against the obese or people with cancer. But community rating is as destructive as ordering flood insurance companies to charge me nothing extra to insure my very vulnerable beach house, or ordering car insurance companies to charge Lindsay Lohan no more than they charge you. Such one-size-fits-all rules take away insurance companies' best tool: risk-based pricing. Risk-based pricing encourages us to take better care of ourselves.

But when politicians complained about discrimination, the health insurance industry was happy to play along. They even offered to give up on gender differences. Women go to the doctor more often than men and spend more on medicines. Their lifetime medical costs are much higher, and so it makes all the sense in the world to charge women higher premiums. But Senator John Kerry pandered, saying, "The disparity between women and men in the individual insurance market is just plain wrong, and it has to change!" The industry caved. The president of its trade group, Karen M. Ignagni, said that disparities "should be eliminated."

Caving was safer than fighting the president and Congress, and caving seemed to provide the industry with benefits. Insurance companies wouldn't have to work as hard. They wouldn't have to carefully analyze risk. They'd be partners with government—fat and lazy, another sleepy bureaucracy feeding off the welfare state. Alcoholics, drug addicts, and the obese wouldn't have to pay any more than the rest of us.

Sadly, this just kills off a useful part of insurance: encouraging healthy behavior. Charging heavy drinkers more for insurance gives them one more incentive to quit. "No-discrimination" pricing makes health-care costs rise even faster. Is it too much to expect our rulers to understand this?

Of course, the average citizen doesn't understand, either. When

I argued that medical insurance makes people indifferent to costs, I got online comments like "I guess the 47 million people who don't have healthcare should just die, right, John?"

The truth is, almost all people do get health *care*, even if they don't have health *insurance*. Hospitals rarely turn people away; charities pay for care; some individuals pay cash; some doctors forgive bills. I wish people would stop conflating the terms "health care," "health insurance," and "ObamaCare." Reporters ask guests things like "Should Congress repeal health care?" I sure don't want anyone's health care repealed.

Reporters also routinely called ObamaCare health "reform." But the definition of reform is *making something better*. I doubt that ObamaCare will do that. We should call it the mandatory health insurance law, or health insurance *change*, or big intrusive complex government micromanagement. Or maybe just: ObamaCare.

WHAT INTUITION TEMPTS US TO BELIEVE:

Prevention saves lives and money.

WHAT REALITY TAUGHT ME:

Preventative care extends some lives but doesn't save money.

After ObamaCare passed, medical costs rose and some companies dropped health insurance altogether. I confronted an ObamaCare lobbyist about that. He said those unintended consequences are "not a problem." He changed the subject by saying that under Obama-Care, "people can get preventative care."

"Prevention" is a favorite of the policy elite. They claim that if insurance companies are forced to pay for "wellness" education and regular checkups, that will save America money by keeping us healthier. But their assumption is false.

John C. Goodman of the National Center for Policy Analysis says, "[L]iterally hundreds of studies from over the past 40 years show preventive medical services usually increase medical spending."

That's true for several reasons. First, some preventative care is "wellness" nonsense that's a waste of money. Second, some checkups lead to "false positives"—extra biopsies and surgeries that shorten lives. Third, even care that extends lives doesn't necessarily save money. Consider this: I take Lipitor. The pills may prevent heart disease—but a lifetime of pill-taking increases spending. And I might never have gotten heart disease.

Spending more isn't always a bad thing—think of the vastly increased amounts that Americans spend on recreation and consumer electronics. We spend more because we like the new options. It's not a problem—because we spend our own money.

WHAT INTUITION TEMPTS US TO BELIEVE:

America still has a free market in health care.

WHAT REALITY TAUGHT ME:

We don't. Government and business have
colluded to corrupt much of the market.

Many of our health-care decisions are already made by government, or government colluding with industry.

We think of big business and big government as opponents. But they're often not. In ObamaCare, businesses saw a chance to make money from taxpayers. Big Pharma and Big Insurance saw Big Profit—ObamaCare would guarantee them customers. What could be better than that?

It illustrates economist Steven Horwitz's First Law of Political Economy: "No one hates capitalism more than capitalists." In this case, big business wanted to shape—and profit from—interventionist health-care reform. Can you think of the last time a major business supported a truly free market? Big Medicine's lobbyists didn't favor everything in the original Obama plan, of course—pharmaceutical companies opposed allowing Medicare to impose price controls on drugs—but in general, insurance companies and Big Pharma were on board.

So why do the mainstream media assume that opponents of socialized medicine are mouthpieces for big business when big business supported government control? Because it fits the narrative: Business is bad, greedy, Republican, and selfish. Government is for the people, equality, and care for the poor.

Democrats and the mainstream media were further confused when masses of citizens objected. Many dismissed the protests as "AstroTurf" campaigns—not real grass roots. "When handfuls of Code Pink ladies disrupted congressional hearings or speeches by Bush administration officials," Glenn Reynolds writes, "it was taken as evidence that the administration's policies were unpopular, and that the thinking parts of the populace were rising up in true democratic fashion. . . . But when it happens to Democrats, it's something different: a threat to democracy."

STEPS ON THE LONG ROAD TO GOVERNMENT-RUN HEALTH CARE

- **Prior to the twentieth century:** health care sold by individual doctors; patients pay for specific services
- **Early twentieth century:** government, mostly local, begins to subsidize small-scale clinics for the poor
- **Circa 1940:** government begins pulling people into job-based health insurance
- **Circa 1960:** hospitals become heavily government-subsidized and regulated (inflation price spiral begins)
- **1965 on:** Medicaid becomes the primary means of paying for the health care of the poor
- **1965 on:** Medicare becomes the primary means of paying for the health care of the old. (Congress said Medicare would cost $12 billion by 1990. In 1990, it cost $107 billion. Today it costs $468 billion.)
- **1993:** Under the supervision of Hillary Clinton, Congress nearly imposes total government-run health care. It is beaten back with great publicity, but under the radar, half of American health care is already government-paid.
- **2006:** government pays for drugs under Medicare Part D
- **2010:** ObamaCare.

This is *not* a good trend.

WHAT INTUITION TEMPTS US TO BELIEVE:

A "public option" will increase competition.

WHAT REALITY TAUGHT ME:

Watch out! That's a trick.

Progressives say government health care is superior. They challenge libertarians, saying, "Why do you oppose a government insurance policy, a 'public option'? If the free market is as superior as you say, then consumers will choose private insurance. Why won't you let government compete?"

Because politicians cheat.

Government-run health insurance could do something no private firm can do: milk captive taxpayers. The politicians promise that the public option would compete fairly. It wouldn't offer below-market premiums and then raise taxes when it lost money. It would break even or make a profit, just like private companies. But they said that about Fannie Mae, Freddie Mac, and federal flood insurance, too. All are now are deep in debt, taxpayers are on the hook for billions, and the private market for mortgages and flood insurance is crippled.

A government insurer would have lower borrowing costs (because lenders assume it would never default). In the short term, the public option would use those advantages to price private insurance out of the market, until government care was all that was left. Then, as the money runs out, the rationing would begin in earnest.

Perhaps that was what was intended all along; the progressives would have achieved total government health care by stealth.

WHAT INTUITION TEMPTS US TO BELIEVE:

Government must do more for the elderly.

WHAT REALITY TAUGHT ME:

It is time for government to do less for the elderly.

Americans love Medicare. Older Americans say it should cover *more*. A McClatchy-Marist poll even found that 73 percent of Republicans and 92 percent of Democrats opposed cutting it.

They need a wake-up call.

It is high time the American government did less for the elderly. I know it is forbidden to say things like that, but Medicare is unsustainable. It has an astounding $34 trillion unfunded liability—that means politicians promise us $34 trillion more in Medicare benefits than they can pay. Social Security is "just" $5.3 trillion in the hole.

For a TV special called *You Can't Even Talk About It*, I spoke with residents of La Posada, a development in Florida that made *Forbes*'s list of top ten "ritzy" retirement communities. These folks are well-off. Because Medicare pays for their health care, I called them "greedy geezers." They replied angrily, "We've paid our dues! I worked for years, and every week FICA payments were deducted from my check. I'm just getting back what I paid in."

That was true when we older people were considerate enough to die at a reasonable age. But rudely, we keep living longer. When FDR started Social Security, most Americans didn't even reach age 65. Today the average life span is 78 years, and increasing. Also, we want all the cool new medical innovations that make our lives better. As a result—and the rich seniors in the Florida retirement community didn't know this—today's elderly collect much more from Medicare than they paid in. Two to three times more. No wonder people love Medicare. Everyone likes getting "free" stuff.

Medicare is a Ponzi scheme. America locked up Bernie Madoff for one of those, but Medicare is a bigger one. In fact, calling it a Ponzi scheme may be too nice: a Ponzi scheme may involve some investment, but there's no investing going on here. People think the

Medicare and Social Security money deducted from their paychecks was stored in a trust fund. But there is no trust fund. As usual, politicians spent the money immediately, as soon as it came in. The "trust fund" is an accounting gimmick. Future Medicare payments will have to come directly out of young people's paychecks.

Like Social Security, Medicare is a pyramid scheme: the growing number of newcomers in the system pay the people who entered the system earlier—until, inevitably, the supply of newcomers dries up and it's no longer possible to pay off all the earlier participants. Entitlements structured this way aren't sustainable, especially when the elderly keep living longer. There just aren't enough new workers to pay into the system.

I give the La Posada seniors credit. Once we talked about this for two hours, and they saw the statistics, most changed their minds. They said it might be fair to increase the retirement age, or raise copayments, or cut richer seniors off—once they got back what they paid in, or something like that.

But most seniors don't have two-hour discussions. They don't know the truth. Liberal groups like AARP sure don't tell them. And seniors *vote*. Young people don't.

The coming entitlements bankruptcy is the biggest threat to America's future. Few politicians want to face this truth.

I'm not optimistic about this one.

6

THE ASSAULT ON FOOD

WHAT INTUITION TEMPTS US TO BELIEVE:
Greedy food companies would happily make us
sick and fat, so government must protect us.

WHAT REALITY TAUGHT ME:
Capitalism has improved our health more
than government ever can.

Instinct tells us to fear poison. If our ancestors were not cautious about what they put in their mouths, they would not have survived long enough to produce us.

Unfortunately, a side effect of that cautious impulse is that almost any time someone claims some chemical in food is a menace, we are primed to believe it, even without good evidence. That makes it easy for government to leap in and play the role of protector.

Take New York City's ban on trans fats in restaurants. It's now been imitated in all of California. Cities like Seattle, Baltimore, Philadelphia, and Boston have banned it, and others plan bans. Yet "trans" fat is no more fattening than other fats. The only unique thing about it is that it slightly decreases your "good cholesterol" level. The effect is minuscule, and evidence now suggests that dietary cholesterol has little impact anyway.

Nonetheless, when New York City banned trans fats, one city health official implied that without the ban children would otherwise have died of heart disease. Children dying of heart disease? There's no stopping the hyperbole about food once it starts—and that quickly leads to restrictions on *your* freedom to eat what you want.

The trans-fat ban meant that french fries stopped tasting as good and margarine vanished from restaurants. Restaurants switched to butter, as if butter were suddenly heart-friendly. (Ironically, margarine made with partially hydrogenated vegetable oil—otherwise known as trans fat—was once hailed as the key to heart health and superior to butter.)

Trans fat was even banned from soup kitchens, as if subtle cholesterol effects are the poor's biggest problem. Remember the days when *hunger* was their biggest problem?

WHAT INTUITION TEMPTS US TO BELIEVE:

Since too much salt hurts some people, we should eat less salt.

WHAT REALITY TAUGHT ME:

Most of us can eat salt without worrying.

About 10 percent of the population ought to be on a low-sodium diet. If you have hypertension, too much salt may increase your blood pressure. For the rest of us, salt doesn't much matter. But once a demonized substance is identified, the food police ratchet up a war against it. After banning trans fats, New York City mayor—and prominent food nag—Michael Bloomberg announced a "voluntary" effort to reduce salt content in restaurants and processed foods by 25 percent. It didn't end there. "Voluntary" is never enough for the food police.

New York state senator Felix Ortiz proposed a ban on the use of *any* salt in restaurant kitchens—with a thousand-dollar fine for each instance of salt-adding. His proposed bill said, "No owner or operator of a restaurant in this state shall use salt in any form in the preparation of any food." Fortunately, salt, as opposed to other victims of the nanny state, has influential lobbyists. Chefs condemned the ban as absurd, and the bill hasn't passed. So far.

Next, the Food and Drug Administration announced its first plan to introduce legal limits on the amount of salt allowed in food products. The *Washington Post* described the FDA's anti-salt push this way: "The FDA would analyze the salt in spaghetti sauces, breads, and thousands of other products ... government would set limits for salt in these categories, designed to gradually ratchet down sodium consumption. The changes would be calibrated so that consumers barely notice."

The hubris here is staggering. The agency knows enough about not just my taste buds, but *all* consumers' taste buds, that they can finely "calibrate" sodium levels so that Americans "barely notice"?

Who is the government to decide how much salt is good for me— or you, or even someone with hypertension? It happens that I have low blood pressure. I don't need to cut back. There is no "right" amount of salt consumption that applies to all 300 million Americans. In fact, a study in *Current Opinion in Cardiology* found that people who ate low-salt diets were *more* likely to die of cardiovascular disease.

Dr. Michael Alderman, head of the American Society of Hypertension, says that "no single universal prescription for sodium intake can be scientifically justified."

They seem to know this in other countries. The United States is virtually unique in waging a war on salt, and our anti-salt bureaucracy produces virtually all of the world's alarming anti-sodium studies. The rest of the planet worries about more important things.

WHAT INTUITION TEMPTS US TO BELIEVE:

Some foods are just bad.

WHAT REALITY TAUGHT ME:

There are few "good" and "bad" foods.

Soda became the next battlefield. In 2009, the governor of New York, which is basically a laboratory for crazy new food restrictions, proposed a $465 million excise tax on the syrup that sweetens soft drinks. Officials launched a "public awareness" campaign that included putting up repulsive posters all over New York City subways depicting soda as a vile glop that clogs arteries. But "natural" orange and apple juices contain just as much sugar per glass (about ten spoonfuls) as Coke. No *one* food is uniquely fattening. The government later admitted that an important reason for the tax was simple "revenue enhancement."

For "the sake of the children" is a favorite line of the food police. Many states have removed soda from school cafeterias (this is in addition to the thirty-three states that now have "sin" taxes on soda). California, New Jersey, and New York City even banned school bake sales. Under a law signed by Governor Mike Huckabee—now my popular Fox colleague—public schools in Arkansas measure every kid's body mass index (BMI) and report it to parents like a grade on their report card. BMI, a height-to-weight ratio, is a crude standard that makes short people and densely muscular people appear to be fat. BMI measurements declare George Clooney overweight and Tom Cruise obese.

When I gave Huckabee a hard time about his law, he said, "We made no decisions for a parent. We simply gave parents empowering information." I suppose that's true, but public schools can barely teach reading and writing. Now Arkansas schools spend time on BMI silliness.

The food nannies' attempts to nudge everyone toward healthier choices have comic consequences. Politicians in Illinois passed a 6 percent tax on candy. This required a government bureaucracy to rule on what is candy and what is tax-free "food." They ruled that Kit Kat bars, because they contain flour, are "food," while Hershey bars are "candy." Sales clerks often have no clue, so they make random tax decisions at the cash register. But politicians achieved their objective: money that might have been put to productive use now goes to the bureaucracy.

Oh, that wasn't their objective?

WHAT INTUITION TEMPTS US TO BELIEVE:

We can't trust big corporations like
McDonald's and Burger King.

WHAT REALITY TAUGHT ME:

Yes, we can!

I don't claim that corporations operate out of love and goodwill. But the marketplace offers us *choice*—and each company knows that. Therefore, some will offer healthy options—increasingly so—as more Americans demand them. It seems contradictory to say that Americans' interest in healthy eating has increased as we got fatter, but it's a big country full of contradictory trends. As we grew wealthier, some of us seized the opportunity to overindulge, but others used that newfound wealth to explore food choices that would have been exotic and largely unknown a few decades ago.

Burger King even tried offering its customers tofu burgers, though they weren't popular. They'll keep experimenting, though—the most successful franchises continually do—and some healthier items will probably catch on. No one bought a salad at McDonald's years ago.

Yet the media tell us that the "obesity crisis" shows that we consumers can't help ourselves, so it's just obvious that government should impose new taxes and limits on your choices. Lawsuits are filed against fast-food restaurants for "making" people fat. Cities mandate calorie counts on menus (although one study showed that people in those restaurants consumed *more* calories).

Los Angeles outlawed new fast-food restaurants in a poorer part of town. Councilwoman Jan Perry pushed the law. When I gave her a hard time about it, she said people there don't eat well because they're tempted by bad choices.

It's not just the bad science and bad economics here that worry me. What happens to notions of individual responsibility? Why think carefully about food choices—or anything, really—if the government promises to make your decisions for you?

WHAT INTUITION TEMPTS US TO BELIEVE:

The Food Police want to help us make better choices.

WHAT REALITY TAUGHT ME:

Government has guns. Police take away choices.

I started using the term "Food Police" as a joke to refer to uptight nutritionists and groups like the (misnamed) Center for Science in the Public Interest that condemn just about every food besides wheat germ. But sometimes real food police show up, eager to use all their police powers. Don't believe me? Try selling raw milk.

Now, I think food faddists who buy raw food and unpasteurized milk are silly. Pasteurization may destroy some nutrients, but there's no credible science that suggests unpasteurized milk is healthier. Pasteurization kills germs that cause nasty diseases.

Still, the risk of illness is fairly small, and in a free country, you should have the right to make foolish choices.

If buyers of unpasteurized milk get sick, word will get out, and those sellers will be punished by the market. Whole Foods voluntarily stopped selling raw milk because it would have raised their liability costs. The free market would keep food safe.

But that's not good enough for our intrusive government. As the *Los Angeles Times* reported in 2010:

With no warning one weekday morning, investigators entered an organic grocery with a search warrant and ordered the hemp-clad workers to put down their buckets of mashed coconut cream and to step away from the nuts.

Then, *guns drawn* [emphasis mine], four officers fanned out across Rawesome Foods in Venice. Skirting past the arugula and peering under crates of zucchini, they found the raid's target inside a walk-in refrigerator: unmarked jugs of raw milk. "I still can't believe they took our yogurt," said Rawesome volunteer Sea J. Jones.

Later, police arrested three people who work at the grocery. "How can we not have the freedom to choose what we eat?" one raw-food aficionado asked the L.A. *Times*. The *Times* writers highlighted the food nannies' reasons for the raid: "Regulators say the rules exist for safety and fairness."

Fairness? The *Times* added that the raid was "to provide a level playing field for producers." But providing a level playing field has nothing to do with protecting consumers. If government arrests people to "level a playing field," that's crony capitalism. Producers who pasteurize use government to shut down competitors who don't.

WHAT INTUITION TEMPTS US TO BELIEVE:

Chemicals added to our food cause cancer.

WHAT REALITY TAUGHT ME:

Nature, at the wrong dose, causes cancer.

People are paranoid about "man-made chemicals." They worry that many are in our food—and of course, they are. As scientists get better at detecting tiny amounts of things, they find traces of chemicals everywhere. This gives activists at the Environmental Defense Fund the opportunity to sucker reporters into writing headlines like "Obscure Chemicals in Consumer Products." It's true, but that doesn't mean anything.

Dose matters, and trace amounts of deadly chemicals are normally far too small to have *any* discernible biological effect, let alone do harm. The importance of dose is a basic principle of toxicology—one stressed by responsible groups, like the American Council on Science and Health, that strive to combat unscientific scares.

The source of such scares is often the regulations themselves. If a chemical is found to be a carcinogen, it is banned from food. That sounds reasonable. But how is "carcinogen" defined? Our wise government defines it as any chemical that can induce tumors in lab rodents *no matter how high the dose*. When the regulations were written in the mid-twentieth century, it didn't occur to regulators that chemicals could cause tumors in massive doses but be harmless in the tiny amounts we normally encounter.

In fact, scientists didn't expect to find many "carcinogenic" chemicals at all. Then they ran their rodent tests and were surprised to discover that by the broad standard, about *half* of man-made chemicals are "carcinogens." That meant that the government should ban half the chemicals upon which industry—and thus civilization—rely. The bureaucracy has slowly begun to do that. Chemicals that were in use decades ago were mostly grandfathered in under chemical regulations, but since the 1970s, all new chemicals must pass EPA tests—and about half of new chemicals fail to get EPA approval. Manufacturers race to keep up with the regulations—constantly reformulating products with new chemicals that haven't yet run afoul of rodent tests. This raises the price of everything you buy.

This might sound like a steep but necessary price for safety, but such regulations don't make us safer. The chemicals used as substitutes may be worse—they just haven't run afoul of the tests yet. Even sticking to "all-natural" chemicals is not a solution, since tests showed that—oops—both natural and man-made chemicals induce rodent tumors at about the same rate. But why don't we ban half of nature—half the universe, if you will—to be "safe"?

Because our intuition suggests that "natural" is better. It never occurred to the bureaucrats who wrote the first regulations that nature might be as dangerous as the "unnatural" products of human industry. So nature gets a pass. But nature's chemicals are no safer.

The fuss over the chemical bisphenol A (BPA)—used in plastic bottles—shows how strange antichemical paranoia can get. Canada, several U.S. cities and states, and several European legislatures announced they will ban BPA because of claims it might disrupt hormones in children, causing obesity or neurological problems. But the evidence didn't actually show that BPA did those things. Europe's equivalent of the FDA concluded: "[T]he data currently available do not provide convincing evidence of neurobehavioral toxicity." Richard Sharpe of the University of Edinburgh explained: "Some early animal studies produced results suggesting the possibility of adverse effects relevant to human health, but much larger, carefully designed studies in several laboratories have failed to confirm these initial studies."

Yet many "environmental" groups tell people that BPA causes breast and prostate cancer, obesity, diabetes, attention deficit hyperactivity, autism, liver disease, ovarian disease, disease of the uterus, low sperm count, and heart disease. When a chemical is blamed for so many disorders, that's hysteria, not science. But once hysteria starts, it's hard for politicians and bureaucrats to pass up the chance to cater to people's fears.

The World Health Organization knows as well as the rest of the European scientific community that BPA is no threat—but if the WHO, or the U.S. government, proclaims BPA safe, that would enrage the activists who are out to save the world from BPA. Then the scientists would have to answer letters from frightened anti-BPA zealots. Two FDA scientists, Ronald J. Lorentzen and David G. Hattan, noted the bias, writing: "The disquieting public invocations made by some . . . about the perils of exposure [to BPA] . . . galvanize the public debate." When even notoriously risk-averse FDA scientists speak out, the scaremongers must have gone absurdly far.

The FDA can't declare BPA perfectly safe because nothing is perfectly safe. So instead the FDA announced an extensive new campaign to study BPA, making it sound like they are worried—despite knowing full well there's no evidence of a real problem.

A documentary called *Tapped* helped spread the paranoia. (Film schools and "independent" film festivals are populated by silly lefties who parrot nonsense that capitalism-hating environmental groups preach. The films win awards from the "socially conscious.") In *Tapped*, toxicologist Dr. Stephen King—no relation to the prolific author—says that we should be "horrified" at the chemicals in our drinking water. The film implied that BPA from plastic bottles is especially dangerous, but when my staff contacted Dr. King, he sent us a study that said that the chemicals found in bottled water were at levels no different from those routinely found in tap water. Again, there's nothing special going on—chemicals are everywhere. *Tapped* claims cancer rates are up because of BPA and other chemicals in water, but that too is not true. Deaths from cancer are down and cancer incidence rates are flat or declining (despite new screening methods that detect cancers sooner).

Not only is there no good evidence that BPA in plastic hurts people; there *is* evidence that it saves lives. The American Council of Science and Health points out that "[s]ince BPA became commonplace in the lining of canned goods, food-borne illness from canned foods—including botulism—has virtually disappeared."

So BPA saves lives, but its producers are vilified. This is nuts. Media malpractice. But fearmongering gets ratings, and few things are scarier than an invisible substance that may seep into your body, give you cancer, and poison your children.

What's remarkable is that a small handful of activists, knowing what sorts of scare stories the media like, generate almost all the scares. A blog called "Truth or Scare," written by someone who calls herself "Junk Science Mom," identified one of the biggest culprits:

> If you believe what you see and hear in the media, those fighting an unnecessary battle against bisphenol-A (BPA) are altruistic individuals concerned about health. . . . But there is an ugly truth behind the scenes that you will never hear about in the media. Greed, propaganda, political agendas, profits, lies and scams. And it all can be tied to one person and one powerful PR firm. David Fenton and Fenton Communications.

I can't prove "lies and scams," but David Fenton helped bring us the groundless scare about the chemical Alar on apples years ago. Fenton went from directing public relations for *Rolling Stone* magazine to peddling progressive causes and environmental scares. Now he has a PR business with seventy employees. Fenton gets paid to spread fear. As the blogger writes, "He is the puppet master, and we moms are his puppets. He orchestrates the scare, and we, being fearful for our children, unknowingly carry out his plan for him. He comes out a winner, and we are duped into wasting our time, money and energy fighting a battle that never needed to be fought."

We hear so much talk in the media about dangerous chemicals, it would be easy to get the impression that most scientists worry about them. But they don't. Ask some.

WHAT INTUITION TEMPTS US TO BELIEVE:

Radiation kills people.

WHAT REALITY TAUGHT ME:

It's a way to make food safer.

There is something unsafe in our food, but it's not chemicals—it's bacteria. The Centers for Disease Control and Prevention says that more than 1 million Americans are poisoned every week by something they ate, and food poisoning kills about 5,000 people each year.

Groups like Safe Tables Our Priority (STOP) lobby Congress for cleaner-food mandates. One parent, Rainer Mueller, who joined the group after his son died of food poisoning, was surprised to learn that bacteria is everywhere.

"It's impossible to get food completely clean, especially if the bacteria are inside the food," he said. "You can scrub the outside all you want, and you'll get it clean, but you won't get it safe."

But there *is* one proven way to make food safer: irradiate it.

Irradiation is the process of moving food through a stream of ionized energy. It's a little like an X-ray machine, except the point is to kill bacteria.

Studies show that irradiation works. Irradiated meat stays fresh longer; irradiated strawberries stay fresh for up to three weeks. Astronauts eat irradiated food because NASA wants to prevent food poisoning.

Omaha Steaks, the gourmet mail-order meat company, irradiates all its hamburger meat. The company's president, Bruce Simon, says ground meat that's not irradiated should come with a "danger" label, because no matter how carefully anyone disinfects a production plant, they can never kill all the harmful bacteria.

"Our plants are cleaner than any emergency room I've ever been in. But it only takes four cells to make a person sick. With irradiation, I know I can kill those cells."

With so much food-borne illness, why doesn't America irradiate more food? Because scientifically illiterate activists organize protests, shouting things like "Don't nuke our food!" A group called Food & Water Watch tells people that irradiated food causes "cancer, premature death, and lower body weight." Americans believe it because we're already frightened of radiation. People think, the horrors! Three Mile Island! Jane Fonda! Nuclear bombs!

Irradiation opponents also claim that irradiation destroys the quality of the food. Food & Water Watch's president, Wenonah Hauter, told me that irradiated fruit "smells like singed hair and tastes like wet dog." That was a repulsive thought, so we offered samples of irradiated and nonirradiated papaya to random people on the street. Many preferred the irradiated version. They said it tasted fresher and sweeter.

Irradiated food tastes good and might save hundreds of lives, but groups like Food & Water Watch have lobbied so effectively that today less than 1 percent of all beef and poultry is irradiated in the United States.

Major health organizations like the WHO, the FDA, and the CDC all say that irradiation is safe, effective, and would save lives. If we irradiated 50 percent of all meat, the CDC says, nearly a million bacterial infections could be avoided.

But we don't do it. The scaremongers won the public relations war.

WHAT INTUITION TEMPTS US TO BELIEVE:

Natural is better.

WHAT REALITY TAUGHT ME:

"Natural" means dying young.

Just as our intuitions prime us to worry about radiation and poison, they incline us to think that pristine natural environments are health-enhancing. But such "green" health beliefs are driven more by ignorance and aesthetics than by science.

Take the idea that grass-fed "free-range" beef cattle are better for the environment—and you—than factory-farmed cattle. It *feels* right. Steer raised in a more "natural" environment must be better.

Michael Pollan, the prolific food author and activist, knows how to capture those nature-loving aesthetic impressions and combine them with just enough science to produce bestselling books. Because factory-farmed cattle are fattened on corn, Pollan wrote in the *New York Times*, "what was once a solar-powered ruminant [grass-fed steer] has been turned into the very last thing we need: another fossil-fuel machine." I guess steer are "fossil-fuel machines" because fossil fuels are burned to ship corn to them instead of letting them eat what's naturally under their feet.

Pollan and others portray organic and "free-range" food as better for the environment. The American Grassfed Association adds that "harmony is created between the land and the animals." People believe this stuff. Nobody likes the idea of cattle jammed into feedlots. For one of my shows, I asked my audience which cows would produce healthier meat, and most chose "free-range." One said: "Free-roaming grass-fed cows lived a happy life out in sunshine!"

But Dr. Jude Capper of Washington State University studied the data. She told them, "Based on the carbon footprints, grass-fed is far worse than corn-fed."

Worse? How can that be? "Because the animals take 23 months to grow. [Corn-fed cattle need fifteen.] That's eight extra months of feed, water, land use, and also an awful lot of waste . . . they give off methane nitrous oxide—very potent greenhouse gases . . . that's like adding almost one car to the road for every single animal."

Once again, so-called environmentalists get it wrong. Modern technology saves money *and* is better for the earth. Because feedlot animals mature faster, they do less environmental damage than "natural" cows do.

People also think that naturally raised animals are healthier to eat. "There is absolutely no scientific evidence for that," Capper said. "There is some very slight difference in fatty acids, but they are so minor that they don't make any significant human health impact."

What about hormones that the cattle are given? Surely they cannot be good for us. Capper says, "Every food we eat—tofu, beef, apples—they all contain hormones. There's nothing, apart from salts, that doesn't have some kind of hormone in them."

This false intuition that "natural" is always better is dangerous and foolish. Natural aflatoxin, sometimes found in peanuts, causes liver damage. Natural microbes kill people.

We are less likely to be harmed by such things in the modern, industrialized world than in the "all-natural" days of our ancestors. For most of the human race's existence, life expectancy at birth was about twenty. From the Renaissance through the industrial revolution, it was about forty. Thanks to "unnatural" things like antibiotics, that span has doubled. We should be grateful for the science, industry, and capitalism that made it possible.

The idea that avoiding industrial agriculture enhances the environment and human health is just another myth, rooted in our idyllic desire for a world of happy beasts roaming free in a world without smokestacks. It's intuitive. But it's wrong.

WHAT INTUITION TEMPTS US TO BELIEVE:

The government is a neutral arbiter of truth.

WHAT REALITY TAUGHT ME:

Be skeptical of everyone.

For every study that says X is bad for you, another study disagrees. Citing conflicting studies begins to look like an unending snowball fight. How is a layman to decide? I once assumed that consumer activists and environmentalists were more reliable than industry. Heck, they want to help the world, but industry just wants to get rich. Now I know better. The activists want money, too, and fame.

But then who will be the arbiter? "Natural" food folks may

be scientifically illiterate, but their opponents in industry can't be trusted. To pursue the truth, it's intuitive to turn to government—government scientists just want what's best for us.

Except . . . government scientists have conflicts, too.

Who becomes a government regulator except people who want to regulate? Some come from activist groups that hate industrial agriculture. Some come from industry and later hope to convert their government job into a higher-paying industry job. Some just want attention. They know that saying "X will kill you" gets more attention than saying that X is probably safe.

Also, their opinions keep changing. Think how many times the famous "food pyramid" has been revised. Now it's not even a pyramid, it's more like a pie wedge from Trivial Pursuit.

I don't suggest that we ignore the experts and eat like pigs. Today's majority opinion—eat more whole grains, fruits and vegetables, a small amount of dairy, and less fat, salt, sugar—is probably good advice. Beyond that, the nutrition scientists and doctors will thrash it out, anyone who is interested in his health will pay attention, and in time more truths will emerge.

But the scientific question should not overshadow the more fundamental issue at stake—something more important than health: freedom. *Who* should decide what you can eat: you? Or the state? Should the government decide what we may eat, any more than it decides where we live, or how long our hair will be? The Food Police claim that they just want to help us make informed choices. But that's not all they want to do. They want government to *force* us to make healthy choices.

The moral issue of force versus persuasion applies even if all the progressives' ideas about nutrition are correct. Even if I would be better off eating no fat, sugar, and salt, that would not justify forcing restaurants to stop serving me those things. Either we live in a free society or we don't.

It is no coincidence that the biggest push for more food regulation came at a time when Congress obsessed about the rising cost of medical care. When government pays for your health care, it will inevitably be drawn into regulating your personal life. First politicians promise to pay. Then when their deficit becomes unsustainable, they propose to control *you* because you eat too much.

Where does it stop? If we must control diet to balance the government's budget, will the health squad next ban skydiving and extramarital sex? How about another try at Prohibition?

Government attracts do-gooders and meddlers who believe that, as Mark Twain put it, "Nothing so needs reforming as other people's habits." Or as Twain's spiritual descendant, H. L. Mencken, said about puritanism, government health officials seem to have "the haunting fear that someone, somewhere, may be happy."

Sometimes the Food Police like to strike an innocent pose, claiming that they just want to give people information. Information is good. But it's not free. Mandated calorie signs in restaurants cost money. Those costs are passed on to consumers, and the endless parade of calorie counts and warning labels make us numb to more important warnings—like "This Coffee Is Scalding Hot."

It's not as if dietary information isn't already available. Health and diet websites abound. Talk shows routinely discuss the latest books on diet and nutrition. TV shows like *The Biggest Loser* focus on obesity. Diet gurus are celebrities. That's enough. We have information. We don't need government force.

Let the marketplace of diet ideas flourish. Let claim meet counterclaim, but let's not let government put its very heavy thumb on one side of the scale.

WHAT INTUITION TEMPTS US TO BELIEVE:

Food rules are a minor nuisance.

WHAT REALITY TAUGHT ME:

Every government rule is backed by force.

For most of us, the food police are merely annoying, but if you have the audacity to want to enter the food business you will be reminded: government is force. If you run afoul of its many rules, it doesn't just give you a lecture.

The National Marine Fisheries Service (NMFS) decided that a seafood shipment from Honduras to Alabama was improperly packed in clear plastic bags, rather than the cardboard boxes allegedly required by Honduran law. Even though America has no such law, when the $4 million shipment arrived, NMFS agents seized it and put two American businessmen in jail. They served six years in American federal prisons for breaking the obscure Honduran regulations, even though the Honduran government later informed American authorities that the regulation requiring cardboard boxes had been repealed.

Something's happened to America, and it isn't good. When legislatures and regulators keep passing new rules, and even enforce dubious rules from other countries, it becomes easy for *everyone* to get into trouble.

When the justification is "protecting our health and food supply," it's hard to object. But it's nasty to live in a nation of a million rules.

And these are not the bottom-up rules that people generate through voluntary associations. These are imposed, top-down rules.

Congress creates, on average, one new crime every week. Federal agencies create thousands more—so many, in fact, that the Congressional Research Service itself said that merely counting them would be impossible. State and local bureaucrats create their own sets of crimes on top of that. This is a bad trend. As Lao Tzu said, "The more laws and order are made prominent, the more thieves and robbers there will be." But I've given up expecting anything other than a continual increase in laws and regulations. After all, the powerful assumption behind so much of government's policy regarding food (and everything else) is that *everything good should be encouraged by law* and *everything bad should be discouraged.* Stated that way, it sounds like common sense.

But since everything is arguably to some degree helpful or harmful, this is a formula for totalitarianism. What is totalitarianism if not the view that *everything* falls within the purview of the state? Everything within the state, nothing outside, as Mussolini put it. That doesn't mean our government is brutal like a fascist regime—but it's becoming just as *invasive,* reaching into every nook and cranny of our lives.

The seventeenth-century philosopher Thomas Hobbes started the practice of using the term "leviathan" to refer to a powerful central government to which we give up some or all of our rights. He thought this leviathan was a good and necessary thing. But even Hobbes assumed that the central government's most important function was protecting us from violence.

He never imagined Leviathan would plan our dinners.

7

CREATING A RISK-FREE WORLD

WHAT INTUITION TEMPTS US TO BELIEVE:

Government should outlaw life's bigger risks.

WHAT REALITY TAUGHT ME:

Government has no rational way of deciding
which risks are worth taking.

A child leaving home alone for the first time takes a risk. So does the entrepreneur who opens a new business. I no more want government to prevent us from doing these things than I want it to keep us in padded cells.

When government gets in the business of deciding which risks are acceptable and which aren't, nasty things happen.

WHAT INTUITION TEMPTS US TO BELIEVE:

Millions of Americans cannot be trusted with handguns.

WHAT REALITY TAUGHT ME:

Yes, we can.

Many governments ban possession of handguns. Liberals consider that a noble stand against violence.

Most of the media did not notice when the Centers for Disease Control and Prevention found no good evidence that gun control decreases crime. Believe me, the CDC looked for it. They wanted to find it. That they didn't should be no real surprise, since a gun law isn't likely to be obeyed by criminals—it merely disarms potential victims. Gun control may *increase* crime. But such facts rarely get through to my liberal colleagues:

- Chris Matthews of MSNBC: "I wonder if in a free society, violence is always going to be a part of it if guns are available."
- Keith Olbermann: "Organizations like the NRA . . . are trying to increase deaths by gun."

Trying to increase deaths? Well, Olbermann usually can't be topped for absurdity. But I admit that I believed similar nonsense. Living in Manhattan, working at CBS and ABC, everyone agreed that guns are *evil*. Barbara Walters, my cohost on *20/20*, probably didn't even think she was being political when she ended one story about gun violence by asking how many more people had to die before Congress would act—as if unregulated guns are just bad, like untreated cancer. On *The View*, she told Rosie O'Donnell that it made her sad when Rosie said, "We're never going to get a gun control law." I wonder if Rosie's armed bodyguards also make Barbara sad.

It took my reading of research published by—horrors—conservatives to discover that she and I were mostly wrong. Now I know that gun control is not crime control.

We hear about murders and armed robberies, but we rarely hear about crimes *stopped* because would-be victims showed a gun and scared criminals away. Those thwarted crimes and, sometimes, lives saved often aren't reported to police (sometimes for fear the gun will be confiscated). When they are reported, the media usually ignore that. No bang, no news. Back in 1999, the media became so obsessed with a day trader's shooting rampage in Atlanta that they barely noticed when, the very next day in a suburb of Atlanta, a man stormed into a truck parts business with a shotgun but was disarmed by an alert worker with a pistol. He'd bought the pistol only hours earlier, after hearing about the day-trader incident. The media were too busy debating whether we should outlaw guns, or day-trading—or both—to cover that.

Because guns sometimes save lives, gun *laws* can cost lives.

Suzanna Hupp and her parents were having lunch at Luby's cafeteria in Killeen, Texas, when a man pulled out a gun and began shooting diners. He killed people methodically, even stopping to reload. If someone had a gun, they could have easily stopped the shooter. Suzanna's parents were two of the twenty-three people killed. Suzanna owned a handgun, but because Texas law did not permit her to bring it into the restaurant, she'd left it in her car. She came on my show to say that she could have stopped the shooting spree, and saved her parents, if she had had her gun. (Texas has since changed its law.)

Today, forty states allow adults to carry concealed handguns (my New York City colleagues are shocked when I tell them this). Vermont, Alaska, Arizona, and Wyoming have the most libertarian approach: they don't even require a permit.

Every time another state proposes liberalizing gun laws, the mainstream media predict outbreaks of gun violence. "Angry people will shoot each other after car accidents, card games, and domestic quarrels!"

But it rarely happens.

What does happen? John Lott, in *More Guns, Less Crime*, revealed that crime fell by an average 10 percent in places where laws were passed that made it easier to own a gun (disclosure: Lott's son works for me). One probable reason for the drop: criminals suddenly worry that their next victim might be armed.

In countries with tough gun control laws, like Canada and Britain, almost half of all burglaries occur when residents are home. But in the United States, only 13 percent of burglaries occur when someone's at home. The difference is that in the United States, where households contain guns, burglars fear entering our homes.

For years, Washington, D.C., had the toughest gun laws in America. But it's not like that stopped people from shooting each other. D.C. still earned the nickname "murder capital of the U.S." Bob Levy, chairman of the Cato Institute, believed that the District of Columbia's gun law was unconstitutional, so he decided that he would sue to get the law changed. He'd never owned a handgun himself, so he recruited plaintiffs who *wanted* to own one.

Dick Heller volunteered. He's a security guard who lives in a dangerous neighborhood. He was licensed by the police to carry a gun on the job, but he was not allowed to have a gun at home. D.C. law effectively permitted him to protect others, but not to defend himself in his own home. It left all D.C. residents defenseless against a home invasion.

In 2008, the U.S. Supreme Court ruled that D.C.'s ban was unconstitutional and that Heller could keep a gun at home. D.C. mayor Adrian Fenty predicted that "[m]ore handguns in the District of Columbia will only lead to more handgun violence!" But violent crime went down.

The *Heller* victory applied only to Washington, D.C. Two years later, the Supreme Court made it clear that just about all Americans have the right to bear arms. It ruled in favor of Otis McDonald, an elderly man who lives in a dangerous part of Chicago. He wanted to buy a handgun, but Chicago forbade it. He told ABC News, "If they come in here, break the door open, I can't do nothing." The Supreme Court said that such laws are unconstitutional.

Lawyer Alan Gura, who argued for the gun owners in both the *Heller* and *McDonald* cases, came on my show to point out that gun bans don't stop criminals: "No criminal is going to say, I was gonna hold up that liquor store, I was gonna hold up that couple in the park, but I couldn't get the permit to get the gun, so I'll give up." *McDonald v. Chicago* will gradually lead to restrictive gun laws falling throughout America. But liberal bureaucrats will resist at every step.

It is still nearly impossible to carry a handgun for self-defense in my hometown. To keep a gun at home, you must pay $340 and fill out a fifteen-page application about why you want the handgun. It can be rejected for any reason. Want a realistic toy handgun? Banned. Want to carry a handgun on your person? Forget it.

WHAT INTUITION TEMPTS US TO BELIEVE:

Around kids, we should have zero tolerance for weapons.

WHAT REALITY TAUGHT ME:

Zero tolerance leads to zero common sense.

In the name of "safety," governments keep passing paranoid rules. Brian Walsh and Paul Rosenzweig's book *One Nation Under Arrest* describes some of the absurd things that happen when schools impose "zero tolerance" policies.

Fort Myers, Florida, honor student Lindsay Brown parked her car at her high school. A county police officer looked inside her car and saw a butter knife with a rounded tip. Because Lindsay's school had a zero tolerance policy for knives, Lindsay was arrested, handcuffed, and hauled off to county jail, where she spent nine hours on a felony weapons possession charge. School principal Fred Bode told a local paper, "A weapon is a weapon."

At New Jersey's Wilson Elementary School, four kindergartners, five-year-olds, played cops and robbers. One yelled: "I have a bazooka." The four boys were suspended for three days for "making threats." I always think school administrators will cringe with embarrassment when these cases are publicized, but I'm often wrong. School principal Georgia Baumann said, "We cannot take any of these statements in a light manner."

Zero tolerance for things resembling violence quickly bleeds over into zero tolerance for . . . well, much of anything. Twelve-year-old Ansche Hedgepeth committed this heinous crime: she left school, entered a Washington, D.C., subway station to head home, and—ate a french fry. An undercover officer arrested her, confiscated her backpack and shoelaces, handcuffed her, and took her to a Juvenile Processing Center. Only after three hours in custody was the twelve-year-old released. The chief of Metro Transit Police said: "We really do believe in zero tolerance. . . . Anyone taken into custody has to be handcuffed for officer safety." Hedgepeth now carries an arrest record. At least publicity over this stupidity got Washington's Metro to rescind its zero tolerance policy.

In countless schools, though, children learn about obedience to a very authoritarian and arbitrary government—a lesson that is more easily ingrained than algebra equations. Unlike rational individuals rapidly adjusting to nuances of specific situations, government's one-size-fits-all solutions make life sadder without making it safer.

RISK-TAKERS OF HISTORY WHO WOULD LIKELY BE PUNISHED TODAY

- In 1519, Ferdinand Magellan left Spain to circumnavigate the globe. He started with 240 men and five ships. Three years later, only one ship returned, with eighteen men alive—Magellan not among them. A worthwhile trade-off? Would you trust the Department of Transportation to decide that question?
- Madame Curie won a Nobel Prize for pioneering work in the study of radiation. She died from aplastic anemia that she got from exposure to radioactive isotopes.
- Popular TV personality and *Twilight Zone* creator Rod Serling worked for years in a high-risk job: parachute tester.

- Since Sir Edmund Hillary ascended Mount Everest in 1953, more than 1,900 other people have climbed Everest—and 180 have died. In 1990, prior to improvements in climbing equipment and techniques, the fatality rate was an alarming 37 percent. Today the fatality rate is about 4 percent. Could you imagine any activity in the United States with a 37 percent—or even a 4 percent—death rate being legal?

WHAT INTUITION TEMPTS US TO BELIEVE:

Gambling is addictive and leads to broken marriages and bankruptcies, so we cannot trust adults to gamble responsibly.

WHAT REALITY TAUGHT ME:

"We" shouldn't get to decide.

Everyone has a different tolerance for risk. One person takes out a second mortgage to start a business. Another thinks that sounds nerve-racking, if not insane. Neither person is wrong. Government cannot know each person's preferences, or odds of success. Even if it did, what right does it have to tell them what to do?

This obvious line of reasoning goes out the window once the topic turns to activities that make autocrats nervous, like gambling. But why? Some of us like to gamble. State governments make money running lotteries. Where casinos are legal, Americans legally bet a hundred million dollars *every day*. Much more money is bet illegally.

So authorities crack down. State bureaucrats never punish

themselves for running lotteries, but Texas police once raided a branch of Veterans of Foreign Wars that ran a poker game for charity.

Chad Hills of Focus on the Family came on my show to say that cracking down on gambling is the right thing for authorities to do. Hills worries that gambling "addiction" will lead to bankruptcy, crime, and suicide.

Well, I worry about that, too, but the bans don't stop those things from happening. Hills claimed that the law "makes it extremely difficult. You have to be fairly desperate to do it."

But you don't. To find a place to gamble illegally, all you have to be is fairly interested. Prohibition doesn't rid society of an activity. It drives it underground or overseas. Overseas, others profit from America's ban. Underground, it's less subject to respectable social conventions. Both are bad for America.

On that same show, professional poker player Andy Bloch pointed out that allowing gambling doesn't necessarily increase *problem* gambling. After online gaming was legalized in the United Kingdom, "there was no significant increase in the number of problem gamblers."

Even if there were an increase, people ought to be responsible for the consequences of their bad habits. Conservatives, like Focus on the Family, usually advocate for personal responsibility. They should apply it to gambling, too.

WHAT INTUITION TEMPTS US TO BELIEVE:

Charging victims for a rescue adds insult to injury.

WHAT REALITY TAUGHT ME:

People do more dumb things when we protect them from the costs of their stupidity (see banks and bailouts in chapters 1–3).

Here's a thought experiment to push the envelope: government should stop paying for the rescue of reckless people.

Right now, the same government that fears the consequences of you eating fatty foods or playing blackjack will rush to help you out if you, say, get drunk and go rock climbing. Almost every day, rescuers save someone, somewhere. Rescuers spend lots of taxpayer money and put their own lives on the line.

Many of those rescued took foolish risks. You see it on YouTube. A drunk says, "I fell down the hill. I really don't know what happened." Ha ha. It's a joke. Except taxpayers pay.

People go ice fishing on Lake Erie. The ice cracks. They call 911, and twenty-one government agencies respond. Sheriff Bob Bratton of Ottawa County, Ohio, complained: "The helicopter from the Coast Guard? Four thousand dollars an hour." Sheriff Bratton says—and I agree—that the fishermen should pay for their own rescue.

"No," said Rick Ferguson, who owns a nearby bait shop. "We already pay that in tax dollars that we pay." One rescued fisherman, Randy Hayes, told me, "If you start charging people, people won't call when they truly do need help." But they will; New Hampshire charges reckless people who need help. People still call 911.

Sparsely populated Grand County, Utah, launches a hundred rescues a year because tourists come there to try extreme sports. "When people go out and do ridiculous things, they ought to be held accountable," says Sheriff Jim Nyland. The county started charging for rescues.

John Rushenberg was rescued after hiking—in flip-flops. It was the second time he'd needed rescuing. On TV, he laughed about it. Nyland billed Rushenberg two thousand dollars. Rushenberg told us that he hoped people watching my television program would chip in to pay his fine. I don't think they did.

Nineteenth-century libertarian writer Herbert Spencer wisely said, "The ultimate result of shielding men from the effects of folly is to fill the world with fools."

Government also warps people's estimation of risks when it does things like subsidize flood insurance. I built a beachfront house. I asked my father for help with the mortgage and he said, "What? Are you nuts? It's on the edge of an ocean!" He was right, but I explained that I couldn't lose: for a premium of just a few hundred dollars a year, federal flood insurance would reimburse me in the unlikely event that the ocean rose up and took the house. Government offers this deal because congressmen claimed it would save taxpayers money. Instead of just writing checks after flood emergencies, Congress would get money up front in insurance premiums. Yippee—more bargains from my government!

Congressmen claimed that people didn't buy private flood insurance because private companies charged too much. They argued: We can sell it cheaper. And we won't lose money because floods don't happen all over America at the same time. We'll price our insurance so that the program is not a drain on the Treasury.

As usual, they were wrong. Private flood insurance is expensive for a reason. Don't bureaucrats ever think to themselves: "If this is a viable risk, why hasn't some private business already done it"? They don't think that—and we pay. The federal program is now $19 billion in the hole. Not only have taxpayers lost money, but subsidized insurance encourages more of us to build on the edge of oceans and rivers.

Speaking of that, I should thank *you*. I never invited you to my beach house, but when the ocean washed it away, you paid. One winter storm knocked it down. Government flood insurance covered my loss. Thanks! I feel bad about it. And I promise, I won't rip you off again.

But we're *all* on the hook and probably *will* be ripped off again because federal flood insurance now insures 5.5 million homes.

An irony in all this is that damage to coastal homes is often cited as a reason we must "do something" about global warming. But if sea levels rise, American taxpayers could escape much of that cost simply by ending the government subsidy that encourages people like me to build on the beach. Instead, Congress debates ruinously expensive Al Gore–style carbon regulations, and local governments pass building codes that outlaw construction in potential flood zones. Why not allow people to take their *own* chances with their *own* money?

Government never seems to pick a "reform" that involves it spending or regulating less.

WHAT INTUITION TEMPTS US TO BELIEVE:
Government must protect us from unproven
medicines and medical devices.

WHAT REALITY TAUGHT ME:
Protection kills people.

In what sense are we free if we can't decide for ourselves what medicines we take?

Dr. Alan Chow invented a retinal implant that allows some blind people to see. Demonstrating that to the FDA took seven years and cost $50 million. Then the FDA decided it wanted *more* tests.

Those would cost $100 million. Chow doesn't have $100 million. Investors won't loan him the money because they say there aren't enough blind people to justify their $100 million risk.

So Steven Lonegan, who has a degenerative eye disease that will gradually blind him, can't have the implant. On my show, I told him that the bureaucrats said their restrictions are for his own safety. He practically screamed at me, "There's nothing safe about going blind! I don't want to be made safe by the FDA. I want it to be up to me to go to Dr. Chow to make the decision myself."

But it's not up to Lonegan or Chow. It's up to the autocrats of the nanny state. I confronted the FDA's Terry Toigo about that. She calmly and quietly explained that such restrictions are necessary to protect the integrity of the government's safety review process. Frustrated, I said: "Why are you even involved? Let people try things!"

She replied, "We don't think that's the best system for patients, to enable people to just take whatever they want."

But letting people take whatever they want *is* the best system for most everyone.

For another of my shows, I talked to Bruce Tower, a prostate cancer patient. He wanted to try a drug that showed promise against his cancer, but the FDA would not allow it. One bureaucrat told him that government had protected him from dangerous side effects. Tower's angry response: "Side effects? Who cares? Every treatment I've had I've suffered from side effects. If I'm terminal, it should be my option to endure any side effects!"

People suffer because the government "protects" us. We may or may not be safer because of its rules, but we are always less free. That trade-off is rarely debated when bureaucrats talk about limiting risk.

Regulators want an orderly world where drugs are tested under their highly controlled and often sleepy supervision. That may indeed be a more reliable way to determine which medicines are safe and effective. It allows regulators to reduce the number of variables that might distort the results of a test. But the policy is cruel to people who suffer and die *waiting* for a drug to be approved.

Don't we own our own bodies? Why, in a supposedly free country, do Americans, even when we are dying, meekly stand aside and let the state limit our choices?

The FDA's intrusion on our freedom is supplemented by another agent of the nanny state: the Drug Enforcement Administration. The DEA jails pain management doctors who prescribe quantities of painkillers that the DEA considers "inappropriate." It's true that some people use drugs like Vicodin and OxyContin to get high. Some harm themselves. Some doctors don't ask questions. But it's hard to separate "recreational" drug users from the people who are really in pain. Some cancer patients need large amounts of Oxy-Contin. What's a doctor to do? If he prescribes what those patients need, the DEA will notice.

After the DEA jailed some doctors, pain specialists got scared. Some are scared enough that they underprescribe. If you are in pain, this is a terrible thing. Sick people suffer needlessly.

Think I exaggerate? Check out the website of the Association of American Physicians and Surgeons. It warns doctors: *don't* go into pain management. "Drug agents now set medical standards . . . could be years of harassment and legal fees." Today, even old people in nursing homes, hardly candidates for drug gangs, sometimes don't get pain relief they need.

The DEA told me that "good" doctors have nothing to worry about. But Siobhan Reynolds, who started the group Pain Relief Network after her late husband was unable to get sufficient pain medicine, says we should not believe them. She says the DEA's cherry-picked medical experts often persuade juries to jail any doctor who administers higher doses of pain relief than government zealots think appropriate. News of those jail terms spreads. Doctors learn to be stingy with pain meds. (Isn't the drug war grand? More on its perverse effects in chapter 10.) Reynolds has now shut down the Pain Relief Network because "pressure from the U.S. Department of Justice has made it impossible for us to function."

WHAT INTUITION TEMPTS US TO BELIEVE:

Seat belt laws save lives.

WHAT REALITY TAUGHT ME:

Seat belt laws also *cost* some lives . . . and
nobody ever talks about that.

Even the most reasonable safety regulations have costs as well as benefits. Consider the regulators' favorite example: seat belts. They save fifteen thousand lives a year, according to the National Highway Traffic Safety Administration. People say: "How dare you libertarians doubt the need for government in the face of those fifteen thousand lives?!"

Okay! I get it! I acknowledge that seat belts save lives. I could just say, yes, this is one area where a government mandate helped more people than it hurt. I could say that, but instead I'll stick my neck out and argue that even seat belt laws may kill more people than they save.

I know this is hard to get your head around, but consider this: University of Chicago economist Sam Peltzman argues that increased safety features on cars have the ironic effect of encouraging people to drive more recklessly because they worry less about accidents. It's called the Peltzman Effect—a variation on what insurance experts call "moral hazard." Studies do show that people drive faster when they are snugly enclosed in seat belts. Give people padding and they tend to play rougher. Perhaps the best safety device would be a sharp spike mounted to the dashboard—pointed right at your chest.

Peltzman crunched the numbers and concluded that seat belt laws had "not decreased highway deaths." Passengers were less likely to die in accidents because of the laws, but there were also more accidents. More pedestrians were hit, too.

Even if Peltzman is wrong, there's another reason to think seat belt laws have been counterproductive: Before government made seat belts mandatory, some automakers already offered them as options. Imagine that! Letting customers decide how much safety they want. Volvo ran ads touting seat belts, laminated glass, padded dashboards, etc., as the sort of things that responsible parents should want. Those safety measures contributed to Volvos' higher cost, but some people still chose them. People care about their safety. As word spread that seat belts save lives, more people would have ordered them. I concede that government action expanded seat belt use faster than would have otherwise happened in a free market. If that were the only issue, then—absent the Peltzman Effect—government force saved lives.

But it's not the only issue. Government action also stifled seat belt innovation, and that will kill people.

Let me explain: The first seat belt law required a certain kind of belt. That set the standard and relieved auto companies of the need to compete on seat belt safety and comfort. No longer did Volvo need to try to invent a better seat belt than GM's; it would have been foolish if it tried. The new seat belt would have to clear onerous and expensive regulatory hurdles. Even if it were safer, the first time someone was injured wearing one, personal injury lawyers would swarm, knowing that they could convince some juries that deviation from the government standard was "reckless." For carmakers, it is safer to stick with the government standard. Drivers and passengers, of course, are also stuck with the government standard, and that makes us less safe because we'll never see the improvements carmakers *might* have made.

But if every auto company were constantly trying to invent a better belt, today, instead of one seat belt, I'd bet there'd be six types, and all would be better and more comfortable than today's standard. Because they would be more comfortable, more passengers would wear them. Over time, the free-market safety achievements would save more lives.

Of course, there's no double-blind experiment to be done. I can't prove a counterfactual. Once again, we don't know what good things we might have had if the heavy foot of government didn't step in to limit our options.

In a free country, it should be up to individuals, once we're adults, to make our own choices about risk. We should be able to make our own decisions in all areas of life, so long as we do not harm the bodies or property of others. Patrick Henry didn't say, "Give me safety, or give me death." *Liberty* is what America is supposed to be about.

Let's start treating people as though their bodies belong to them, not to a coddling and protective government.

8

MAKING SURE NO ONE
GETS OFFENDED

The very *first* amendment that the Founders chose to add to the Constitution was the one that said speech should be protected. They couldn't be more clear: "Congress shall make no law abridging the freedom of speech . . ."

But words wound. Cruel comments can make people miserable. Crude speech in schools makes it tough for kids to learn. Sexist comments in the workplace can make it tough to work. Many people support rules against speech that offends religious groups or minorities. Even media organizations like the *New York Times* endorse restrictions on political speech when that speech is funded by rich people or corporations.

Many people are willing to undermine the right to free speech because it just seems intuitive that some speech is *so* hurtful that society is better off without it. People on both the right and the left support free speech right up until it counts—which is to say, when something finally offends them. Or scares them.

WHAT INTUITION TEMPTS US TO BELIEVE:

It's nice for people to have their say, but some speech
is so hateful and offensive that we must limit it.

WHAT REALITY TAUGHT ME:

No one can be trusted to silence others.

I once held a racist bake sale. I stood in midtown Manhattan shouting, "Cupcakes for sale." In front of me were identical cupcakes and a sign that read:

CUPCAKES

Asians	$1.50
Whites	$1.00
Blacks/Latinos	50 cents

This wasn't my idea. I copied a stunt that students tried at Bucknell University. They wanted to make people think about the wisdom of affirmative action policies. The Bucknell students never got to finish their experiment because a school official shut it down.

Fortunately, college administrators don't get to boss me around, so I stood in a shopping mall with my racist sign, yelling "Cupcakes!"

People stared. One white man yelled at me. A black woman said, angrily, "It's very offensive, very demeaning!" One black man sneered that I'd "probably poisoned the cupcakes."

I understand why people got angry. Highlighting racial difference makes us uncomfortable. Neither the Bucknell students nor I wanted to anger minorities. We just wanted to start a discussion about the oddly condescending nature of affirmative action.

A university is supposed to be a place for open discussion, but some kinds of speech are off-limits on campuses like Bucknell's. Bucknell officials eventually said they would authorize a *debate* on affirmative action, but not the bake sale.

Fortunately, the Foundation for Individual Rights in Education (FIRE) is around to defend speech on campus. FIRE threatened to take Bucknell to court unless it rescinded its debate-only rule. "Using this absurd logic, Bucknell would have to require its College Democrats to say nothing political on campus unless they give equal time to Republican candidates, or [require] its Catholic Campus Ministry to remain silent about abortion unless it invites prochoice activists to speak," said FIRE's Adam Kissel.

That's exactly right. Even biased speech deserves protection. My affirmative action cupcake "event" led to some useful discussions. Anger turned into insight. People said my racist price list made them think harder about affirmative action. Those are discussions students should have.

WHAT INTUITION TEMPTS US TO BELIEVE:
People who raise controversial issues are
natural allies of free speech.

WHAT REALITY TAUGHT ME:
People "raising issues" often don't want *other* voices heard.

Sometimes when a camera crew and I are outside in the city, demonstrators get in my face and loudly scream something like "Fox lies!" They keep screaming to try to prevent me from interviewing people. If no crowd gathers to support them, they usually go away.

I assume they learned this technique on college campuses, where activists often scream to drown out speakers who have "wrong" opinions. Speakers with wrong opinions tend to be conservative. Ward Connerly, a black man who opposes affirmative action, is sometimes forced to stop speaking because of all the screaming.

I got my first taste of this intolerance at Brown University years ago. I was there to report on protests against date rape. At Brown, the definition of rape had come to include having sex with someone who was drunk. I realize that drunk "consent" is not really consent, but Brown's rule was so broad that it would have criminalized most of the sex that happened when I was in college.

So I did a politically incorrect thing. To spark debate, I told the crowd of protesters, "I'm not sure I understand the new definition. When I was a student, rape meant physical force. But now—"

I never got to finish. The activists screamed, "Get off this campus! Rape is not TV hype! Come on, everyone, louder: rape is not TV hype!"

One student wanted to be interviewed, but the protesters drowned him out. Then they disconnected my microphone cord.

These students were brainwashed into believing that some ideas are beyond the pale and must not be heard. But the beauty of free speech is that no one in authority gets to decide that. No president, no priest, no imam, no group of people has that authority. There is no single authority. Everyone can speak.

Colleges, companies, and governments now have all sorts of rules banning sexist, racist, and other forms of offensive speech. These rules are well intended, but they effectively give the power of censorship to whoever is most easily offended. That gives everyone a perverse incentive to become more sensitive. When getting offended gives people power, people get offended more easily.

At Indiana University–Purdue University Indianapolis, Keith John Sampson read the book *Notre Dame vs. the Klan*. He read it outside, in public. The book is in no way pro-Klan, but because the cover of the book depicts Klan members, one minority student complained that simply seeing Sampson read the book "offended" her. The university then charged Sampson with racial harassment! Fortunately, a letter from FIRE got his punishment revoked.

I once interviewed law students at Seton Hall University and asked them what speech should be forbidden for the "common good." Their list was long. Many wanted to ban sexist speech and hate speech. "No value comes out of hate speech," said one future lawyer. Another wanted to ban blasphemy. "The gravity or harm outweighs the intrinsic value," he said. One even wanted to ban hunting videos, saying they are "unnecessary cruelty to sentient beings." Only when I embarrassed the students by pulling out a copy of the Bill of Rights and started writing in the many restrictions they had put on the First Amendment did one student say, "We may have gone too far."

I wish future lawyers understood that America is a special country *because* we have free speech. In Ecuador, it's illegal to criticize the tax system. In many Islamic countries, enforcers wander the streets on the lookout for blasphemous conversations. China's Communist Party not only limits criticism of the government, but recently they even banned stories about time travel. A party official explained that such stories "have monstrous and weird plots, use absurd tactics, and promote feudalism, superstition, fatalism, and reincarnation."

In many "free" countries—like India—reporters must register with the government. In the hands of more authoritarian regimes, such rules surely silence people: better stick to the party line than risk having your license revoked.

Even Canada, so close to the United States both geographically and culturally, bans speech that exposes people to "contempt." Such laws allowed the Canadian Human Rights Commission to threaten sanctions against magazine editor Ezra Levant for republishing the Danish cartoons of Muhammad that led to riots in the Middle East. Another Human Rights Commission debated hate speech charges against humorist Mark Steyn, who wrote a column titled "The Future Belongs to Islam." After supporters of Levant and Steyn blasted the commission as "kangaroo courts" that had launched "an assault on one of the most basic principles of justice," no punishment was meted out, but the writers still had to pay hundreds of thousands of dollars in legal fees to fend off Canada's speech police.

In America, legal attacks on political speech are rare—but there are lots of assaults on commercial speech. A Washington state bagel store owner was fined for hiring someone to wear a sandwich board that advertised "Fresh Bagels." The city said the sign was aesthetically unappealing. But then, so are a lot of things in this country. Washington authorities prosecuted using zoning regulations rather than claiming a right to censor, but it's still an attack on speech.

Conservatives try to ban flag burning. They say that a ban wouldn't violate the Constitution because burning a flag is an "act," not speech. Nonsense. I was relieved when the Supreme Court struck down state laws forbidding it. Since then, conservatives have mounted attempts to pass an amendment to the Constitution just to reinstate those laws. Why so eager to cleanse the nation of this rare political protest? It is just speech.

WHAT INTUITION TEMPTS US TO BELIEVE:

Everyone knows certain things are just offensive.

WHAT REALITY TAUGHT ME:

People's standards vary wildly.

Conservatives feel comfortable legislating protection of a beloved national symbol and progressives are comfortable banning what they call hate speech because it's intuitive to believe that all right-thinking citizens *agree about what is offensive*. If "everyone knows" that, say, flag burning is unacceptable, then it's just common sense to censor that speech.

In the homogeneous environment of left-leaning college campuses, "everyone knows" that blacks, poor people, and homosexuals are in need of special protection (but there's no need to worry about whether Baptists are offended by someone who mocks Christ).

It seems intuitive that in workplaces, there should be rules against sexual harassment. No one wants workers harassed. But what speech qualifies as "harassment"? Sex talk that some call appealing flirtation threatens others. It's fine when the employer arbitrates that question—it's his company, after all. But laws are different. We have many employers, but just one government. When a court decides what constitutes a "hostile environment" or an "inappropriate remark," it decides for everyone. But everyone isn't the same. What shocks one person—perhaps rightly so—may seem funny and appropriate to another.

When pornographer John Stagliano (a libertarian, of course) first appeared on my show, he was under threat of prison time and $7 million in fines because he distributed films like *Milk Nymphos*, which feature people engaging in unusual sex acts. Other porn producers sold similar stuff, but the Justice Department went after Stagliano, probably because his business was big. They had no trouble finding some jurors who said his films violated community standards. But in an era of the Internet and national video distribution, allowing the community standards of one town to rule would give the most prudish town in America the power to decide the viewing habits of all of America. A judge finally dismissed the government's case. Good. People living in the prudish town are always free to choose not to purchase the stuff.

Regional differences—not to mention individual differences in taste—are far too subtle and nuanced to be turned into law and enforced by jail threats or fines. The codes of conduct at Fox News and at the Playboy Mansion are not going to be the same, and there is no sane reason to expect that they will be.

And tastes change over time. Years ago, many towns banned the novel *The Catcher in the Rye*, calling it "obscene" and "explicitly pornographic." Now people call it a classic, and adolescents read it in school.

WHAT INTUITION TEMPTS US TO BELIEVE:

A little censorship makes for a more polite society.

WHAT REALITY TAUGHT ME:

Censorship makes everyone angrier.

People who censor claim they want a more civil and tolerant society, even though few things are more intolerant than telling people to "shut up."

Speech can be hurtful, but it's better to meet speech with speech—even nasty speech—than to use the power of government to silence people.

I've learned to put up with my share of criticism.

"Oust John Stossel," said the organization ColorofChange.org. In a newspaper, they explained that because of my "backwards and hateful ideas . . . it's time that Fox drop Stossel . . . we'll go directly after the network with a public campaign unlike anything we've pursued to date." Media Matters added: "By airing Stossel's repugnant comments, Fox legitimizes his indefensible position." What "indefensible" position? Once more, race was the topic: I told Fox's Megyn Kelly, "Private businesses ought to get to discriminate."

This came up after Republican U.S. Senate candidate Rand Paul told Rachel Maddow that he didn't support some civil rights laws. Paul was immediately attacked by Democrats *and* Republicans. He went silent on the topic, so I stepped up to say that he was right. Articles 1–7 of the Civil Rights Act, the parts that ban discrimination by government, are good laws, but the articles that ban *private* discrimination were an overreach by big government.

"I won't go to a place that's racist," I told Kelly, who has a knack for finding the most inflammatory libertarian issue and confronting me about it. I said I would criticize that business, "but it should be their right to be racist."

Please read that carefully: I condemned racism. I said I'd boycott a racist's business. But my heresy was to say that I thought the two articles of the Civil Rights Act that outlaw private discrimination violate freedom of association. As a libertarian, I say: Individuals should be allowed a sphere of privacy where government does not intrude. A White Person's Club ought to be allowed. So should a Black Pride Association and the Black Students Association. Heck, they *are* allowed. That's why I told Kelly, "It's time now to repeal that part of the law."

To the left, I committed heresy because I failed to accept the entire catechism. I didn't say that we need *government* to fight racism and prohibit racist policies in private establishments. For this, they demand that I be fired. And that, too, is their right—but it's a reminder how ugly these disputes would get if government had the power to censor. Or fire people.

I say, if you disagree with me, argue with me. Shun me. And, yes, even boycott me. Just don't bring in government to settle the issue.

WHAT INTUITION TEMPTS US TO BELIEVE:
We need to get big money out of political campaigns.

WHAT REALITY TAUGHT ME:
In politics, money is speech.

Asking government to decide which political opinions are too disruptive or influential is a dangerous precedent. Politicians naturally think that people who challenge their power need to be restrained. Senator John McCain thinks that. He championed the "campaign finance reform" laws that, among other things, forbade anonymous donors to run ads in the crucial weeks just prior to national elections (when most voters finally pay attention).

McCain-Feingold was one of the nastier assaults on free speech. After all, obscenity and racist speech are marginal things—but political speech (and religion) is *exactly* what the Founders were eager to protect when they wrote the First Amendment. They wanted to make sure the republic was open to competing political factions. (Not that they were perfect—some voted for the Alien and Sedition Acts to punish critics of the government.)

McCain's arrogant eagerness to give government power to censor ("No one thinks we need so much money in elections!") was enough to turn me off to him, and it was nice to watch the Supreme Court overrule McCain-Feingold piece by piece. I also enjoyed what happened after President Obama, upset by a court ruling against the law's ban on corporate speech, gave an unprecedented upbraiding of the justices during one of his State of the Union addresses: They just sat there stoically while he bad-mouthed them, but some of the justices stopped attending Obama's State of the Union speeches.

My ABC colleagues loved McCain-Feingold. Some conservatives think journalists liked the law because it exempted media corporations. ("Ha. We can speak about politics, but you can't." That suits the *Washington Post* and *New York Times* just fine.)

But I don't think it was just media self-interest. It goes back to our intuitive, gut instinct: big money is bad, corporations are bad, and rich people spending money to influence politics is very bad. When the Supreme Court agreed that even corporations must be free to fund political ads prior to elections, the mainstream media were so upset, they sounded like there had been a coup d'état.

The *New York Times* said the decision "strikes at the heart of democracy." The *Washington Post* quoted someone saying it "threatens to undermine the integrity of elected institutions."

The case grew out of a documentary critical of Hillary Clinton that a group called Citizens United wanted to run on cable TV. McCain-Feingold made that illegal because it banned anonymously funded campaign ads within three months of an election.

The swing justice, Anthony Kennedy, couldn't have been more clear: "When Government seeks to use its full power, including the criminal law, to command where a person may get his or her information or what distrusted source he or she may not hear, it uses censorship to control thought. This is unlawful."

Yes!

He also said, "Because speech is an essential mechanism of democracy—it is the means to hold officials accountable to the people—political speech must prevail against laws that would suppress it."

Yes!

Progressives condemned the Supremes for "judicial activism" because the ruling overturned two precedents. Progressives usually *like* judicial activism and dumping bad precedents. I also thought they favored free speech. I was wrong. To its credit, at least the American Civil Liberties Union took Citizens United's side.

People's stance on free speech often depends on whose ox is gored (as the great defender of free speech Nat Hentoff put it in the title of his book *Free Speech for Me—But Not for Thee*). In condemning the decision, the offended progressives engaged in amazing mental contortions. It "was wrong because nothing in the First Amendment dictates that corporations must be treated identically to people," said the editorial in the *Washington Post*. Don't progressives realize that corporations (and unions, which also had their speech rights protected) are associations of individuals—individuals who have rights? Presidential candidate Mitt Romney was mocked when he said, "Corporations are people, they're made up of people." But Romney was right.

One need not be a fan of corporations to see that restricting anyone's speech is dangerous. One government lawyer said that even corporate-funded *books* favoring candidates could be illegal. That should scare progressives—the Federal Election Commission put an anti-Bush book written by George Soros under scrutiny. Laws limiting speech are used more often against radicals than against the corporate establishment.

It is shameful that leftists let their hatred of corporations lead them to throw free speech under the bus. There is a smarter way to get corporate money out of politics: shrink the state. If government has fewer favors to sell, citizens will spend less money trying to win them.

WHAT INTUITION TEMPTS US TO BELIEVE:

Conservatives at Fox will censor liberal ideas.

WHAT REALITY TAUGHT ME:

No, they don't.

When it became clear to me that ABC News would not let me report on markets in ways that I thought best, I knew that it was time for me to leave. But much as I resent the narrow-mindedness of my former bosses, I won't complain that I was "censored."

The term "censorship" should not be thrown around lightly. Censorship implies government coercion. When private organizations limit what employees may say, that's not censorship—that's editing, or setting rules of conduct. If I wanted to say things that ABC did not like, I had the freedom to go elsewhere—and eventually I used it. No complaints.

Well, not *too* many.

When I was at ABC, conservatives and libertarians sometimes told me, "You should move to Fox! You'd be more comfortable there."

They were right. But I wanted to stay at ABC to share with liberals what I'd learned about free markets. ABC viewers rarely got to hear anything good about business or markets or *de*regulation. I thought it my duty to at least introduce them to economics. And anyway, on *20/20*, I reached 10 million people! Fox's audience was much smaller.

But that was then. Now *20/20* mostly seems to do stories about pretty people who disappear under suspicious circumstances, and the show's audience has dropped. Fox's has grown. Tuesday nights, when I'm on Bill O'Reilly's show, we reach as many people as ABC reaches. And I get to discuss what I care about: politics and policy.

When I announced my departure on my ABC blog, plenty of viewers said they were happy to have me leave: "Goodbye. You suck. You have found a much better home for your garbage."

Oh well. I can't please everyone.

My libertarian beliefs don't please everyone at Fox, either. Some Fox viewers don't like my questioning defense spending, or the existence of God, or saying that I think that homosexuality is just fine. They bristle when I say that immigration and pornography and drugs and prostitution and gambling ought to be legal. These beliefs are abhorrent to many Fox viewers.

And yet Fox lets me say those things. When liberal friends heard I was moving to Fox, they assumed that I wouldn't be allowed to do shows on subjects like gay marriage or military waste. But they were wrong. No boss has even sent me a skeptical email about it. The only time I was ever "censored" (edited, really) was when I wanted to show some of those Danish anti-Muhammad cartoons. (It's "easy for us to be brave in New York," said my boss, but airing the cartoons might endanger our colleagues in the Middle East. His argument made sense.)

My liberal friends might be surprised by Fox's open-mindedness, but I'm not. I've found that it's the liberals, who preach tolerance, who are most intolerant. Conservative groups invite me to speak at their events. Occasionally a person who booked the speech says something like "This is a pro-life group. Don't mention abortion." Or "it's a very conservative audience. I hope you won't discuss legal drugs and prostitution." But I *do* discuss those things, and after I tell conservatives that I think homosexuality is fine, or why I believe that drugs and prostitution should be legal, or that some abortion should be legal, they politely *applaud*. They still thank me for coming and say that they enjoyed the speech.

Liberals think conservatives are dogmatists who silence liberated people. But it's liberals whose minds are often closed. I wasn't surprised that NPR eventually fired commentator Juan Williams.

Conservatives who disagree with me send me reasoned arguments. "Here's why illegal immigrants are a big threat . . . here's why I think drug legalization is dangerous . . . here's why I know that God exists and next time you do a show on that you should book this guest . . ." Leftists send me emails like this one: "You are intelectually [sic] dishonest and a hack . . . a corporate shill."

Many leftists complain that I'm not "objective." An interesting buried premise behind that complaint is the assumption that the work of other reporters is not shaped by their opinions. It is true that my colleagues at ABC, CBS, and NBC rarely revealed their political beliefs. I was one of the few who did. I told viewers that I value individual liberty and favor the free market over government coercion. I thought that this candor might earn me credit from those who disagree. By putting my views out there, everyone could judge my reports accordingly.

But it did not win me credit with those who disagreed. It was as if I was the *only* reporter with an ideology. That, of course, is absurd. Every reporter has political beliefs. The difference is that I am up-front about mine. Sometimes I think we'd be better off—and our use of free speech more productive—if more media imitated one aspect of European culture: openly partisan newspapers and TV stations that come right out and tell you what political factions they favor. That way we'd at least know where everyone stands, and you'd know I'm far from alone in having a political philosophy.

Sure, some reporters would voice extreme opinions—but so what? Readers and viewers come to learn whom they can trust. A rough-and-tumble contest of opposing views is preferable to government-mandated "objectivity" required by old laws like the

Fairness Doctrine, which gave government the power to decide which opinions must be "balanced."

We should never let government decide which ideas are worthy of protection and which are not.

If that means unleashing partisanship and even an occasional crackpot, I say, bring it on!

9

EDUCATING CHILDREN

WHAT INTUITION TEMPTS US TO BELIEVE:

Public schools are one of the best parts of America.

WHAT REALITY TAUGHT ME:

Government schools are one of the worst parts of America.

President Obama's "stimulus" included $100 billion for K–12 education and public school workers. Obama said the money was needed desperately to "save teachers from layoffs." His secretary of education, Arne Duncan, said school districts "have literally been cutting for five, six, seven years in a row. And, many of them are through, you know, fat, through flesh and into bone."

That's what we've heard for years. Public schools are *starving*.

Americans don't care enough about education! Teachers are underpaid. The graph below, from Andrew Coulson of the Cato Institute, shows the absurdity of such claims. Spending has gone through the roof but test scores are flat.

While most every other service in life has gotten better, faster, and cheaper, education has remained stagnant, unchanged since we started measuring it in 1970.

Inflation-Adjusted Cost of a Complete K–12 Public Education, and Percent Change in Achievement of 17-Year-Olds, Since 1970

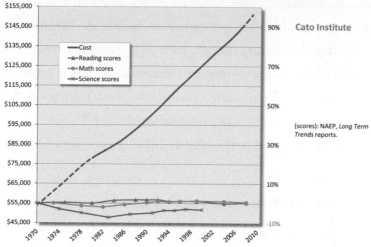

Cato Institute

(scores): NAEP, *Long Term Trends* reports.

Why no improvement? Because K–12 education is a government monopoly. Monopolies don't improve.

In every other sector of the economy, market competition forces providers to improve constantly. It's why most things get better. Often cheaper, too (except when government interferes, as in health care).

But the government school monopoly claims education is different. It is "too important to leave to market competition." At a teachers union rally, even actor Matt Damon, whose mother is a teacher, showed up to deride competition as "MBA-style thinking."

Competition may be okay for selling movies and cell phones, they say, but learning is too complex. Parents aren't real "customers" because they don't have the expertise to know which school is best. They don't know enough about curricula, teachers' credentials, etc. That's why education must be centrally planned by government "experts."

Those experts have been in charge for years. They are what school reformers call the "BLOB." Jeanne Allen from the Center for Education Reform says that attempts to improve the government monopoly have run "smack into federations, alliances, departments, councils, boards, commissions, panels, herds, flocks, and convoys that make up the education industrial complex, or the BLOB. Taken individually, they were frustrating enough, each with its own bureaucracy, but taken as a whole they were (and are) maddening in their resistance to change. Not really a wall—they always talk about change—but more like quicksand, or a tar pit where ideas slowly sink."

The most powerful part of the BLOB is the teachers unions.

WHAT INTUITION TEMPTS US TO BELIEVE:

Teachers unions want what's best for teachers and kids.

WHAT REALITY TAUGHT ME:

Teachers unions want what's best for unions.

When the *Washington Post* asked George Parker, head of the Washington, D.C., teachers union, why he fought a voucher program that let some kids escape failing government schools, he was unusually candid: "As kids continue leaving the system, we will lose teachers. Our very survival depends on having kids in D.C. schools so we'll have teachers to represent."

Albert Shanker, the late teachers union president who first turned teachers unions into a national political force, was even more honest. Shanker callously said, "When school children start paying union dues, that's when I'll start representing the interests of school children."

Union leaders first. Teachers second. Kids third. Maybe fourth or fifth, after the school board, the principals union, or some other part of the BLOB.

WHAT INTUITION TEMPTS US TO BELIEVE:

Education would improve with more money.

WHAT REALITY TAUGHT ME:

Throwing money at the BLOB is part of the problem.

The BLOB claims teachers are underpaid. At that union rally Matt Damon also said teachers "take a shitty salary and [work] really long hours."

That is what most people believe. But today American teachers average more than $50,000 a year. That's not "shitty." Compute teachers' hourly wage and it turns out to be more than what most architects, accountants, and nurses make.

Government vomits money on schools. Today taxpayers spend a stunning $13,000 a year per student—about a quarter of a million dollars per classroom. For that much, you could hire four good teachers!

Yet the secretary of education claimed districts had "cut into bone." What nonsense. As Coulson puts it, "Back in the real world, a K–12 public education costs three times as much as it did in 1970." Secretary Duncan was pandering, unless he was actually fooled by how school districts (and other government agencies) describe budget cuts. Normal people assume a "cut" means less money is spent. But that's not what bureaucrats mean. If a district spent much more, but less than it asked for, administrators consider it a cut. "They compare the current year budget to the budget that they initially *dreamed* about having," says Coulson.

School staffing increased too. "Over the past forty years," says Coulson, "public school employment has risen *ten times faster than enrollment*." Check out his chart:

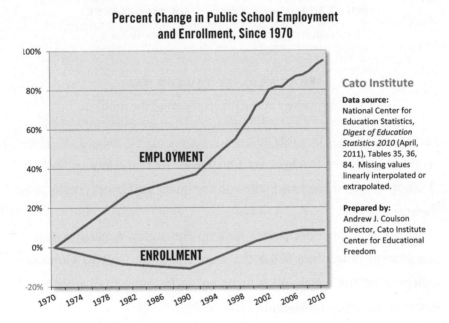

Percent Change in Public School Employment and Enrollment, Since 1970

Cato Institute

Data source: National Center for Education Statistics, *Digest of Education Statistics 2010* (April, 2011), Tables 35, 36, 84. Missing values linearly interpolated or extrapolated.

Prepared by: Andrew J. Coulson Director, Cato Institute Center for Educational Freedom

More money and staff brought no improvement. Kevin Chavous discovered that when he was the Education Committee chairman of the Washington, D.C., City Council. He arranged for the school system to get an additional $300 million. "I gave them more than what they asked for. I gave the teachers the highest increase they had ever had. And during that period, ten thousand students left the system.

Teachers got more money than ever to educate ten thousand fewer kids, and the test scores went down."

I asked him where all the money went. "They grew central office. They had more deputies to the assistant to the deputy to the assistant. They had all these people who were regional superintendents. They grew the bureaucracy. . . . It's not about the money, it's about what you do with the money."

It definitely is, because some charter schools do better with *less* money. Charter schools are a new kind of public school that are allowed to ignore some of the BLOB's endless rules. The American Indian Charter School in Oakland, California, was once a failing school, but now its students get among the highest test scores in the state. The school's "chief," Ben Chavis, turned the school around, even though he got less money per student than nearby government-run schools.

Chavis accomplished this without the "certified" teachers so revered by the BLOB. Only a quarter of his teachers are certified. He scoffs at the establishment's rituals, like formal teacher evaluations. "I don't do no teacher evaluations. All I do is go into a class, and if the kids ain't working, your ass is fired."

Most of his students are considered "economically disadvantaged" (75 percent qualify for a free lunch), but his students go on to colleges like the University of California, Berkeley; Cornell University; and the Massachusetts Institute of Technology.

"When economists look at the effects of a school upon a kid's educational performance," says Coulson, "they use words like 'small,' 'medium,' and 'large.' But the effect of attending American Indian is 'five times better than large. I like to call it 'ginormous.' "

In my part of the country, a chain of charters called Success Charter Network educates New York City kids whom the BLOB labels "at risk." In BLOB schools, these kids got low grades and dropped out. At Success schools, their test scores are among the best in the city. I write this after spending time at one of their Harlem schools. I'm *very* impressed. I spent a fortune to send my kids to one of New York's best private schools, where most of the kids were alert, cheerful, verbal, and eager to learn.

But at Harlem Success, nearly *all* the kids were alert, cheerful, verbal, and eager to learn. I challenged fourth graders. "School is boring," I said, "especially writing, and math." They practically yelled at me: "No! School is exciting. I *like* to learn."

I don't presume to understand what they do at the charters that makes the kids so eager. They do employ some clever tricks: at Success Network, teachers sometimes wear an earpiece so a "master teacher," sitting at the back of the classroom, can give them advice while they teach. "We view teachers as athletes in the Olympics and they need constant support and coaching to be at the top of their game," says Success founder Eva Moskowitz.

The school day at many charters is longer. That means longer hours for the teachers, too. Don't they get annoyed? Burnt out? "When you see the results that we're getting, it's hard to be ticked off by it," one teacher told me.

Maybe that's the trick, or maybe it's something else. The beauty of breaking out of the government monopoly and permitting choice and competition is that we don't need to know. Word gets out about which schools are better. It doesn't take long before every parent knows that, say, Harlem Success schools make for happy kids who learn. Even parents who barely give a damn soon find out. That's how markets work. Consumers don't need to be experts on food or electronics to know that Kroger supermarkets and iPhones are pretty good. Word gets out. Good providers succeed and bad ones gradually disappear.

But when the BLOB is in control, schools rarely improve, and bad ones don't disappear. Bad teaching and waste and indifference live on and on.

WHAT INTUITION TEMPTS US TO BELIEVE:
Public schools are part of the American melting pot.

WHAT REALITY TAUGHT ME:
Government schools pull us apart.

Advocates for government schools argue that public education is "the great equalizer." Rich and poor and different races mix and learn together. It's a beautiful concept. But it is a lie. Rich parents buy homes in neighborhoods with better schools.

As a result, public—I mean, government—schools are now more racially segregated than private schools. University of Arkansas education professor Jay Greene examined a national sample of school classrooms and found that public schools were significantly more likely to be almost entirely white or entirely minority. In another study, he looked at who sat with whom in school lunchrooms. At private schools, students of different races were more likely to sit together.

Government-run schools sometimes pull whole communities apart. When government controls the curriculum, parents and teachers fight about prayer, teaching evolution, what food should be served, dress codes, which textbooks are used, etc. In 2010, Texas's Board of Education voted to remove the secular views of Thomas Jefferson from its textbooks and add conservative heroes like Phyllis Schlafly. The left went berserk. If the left-leaning parents had it their way, they'd add left-wing values. Both sides want to control what every student learns. School choice allows more parents to have what they want.

In 1844, rioters in Philadelphia burned down a Catholic church. "It is telling that the Bible Riots were not over what was preached in St. Augustine's church, but rather over what was taught *in Philly's public schools*," writes Andrew Coulson. "America has seen comparatively little religious conflict surrounding our places of worship, but an endless series of battles over the religious (and other) content of our public schools. The reason is simple: no American has to pay to build another man's temple, shrine, church, mosque, synagogue, or coffee-shop; but we all have to pay for the public schools."

Greene and Coulson shouldn't call them "public" schools. If these schools truly belong to the public, members of the public would get to decide which schools their kids attend. Public just means "free," but in this case free just means that government runs it, and you pay for it at tax time.

Calling them *government-run* instead of *public* schools makes the picture clearer: government schools are inefficient, centralized bureaucracies just like everything else government does. Instead of treating them as sacred because of the important task they have, we should be horrified that this job has been left to government.

WHAT INTUITION TEMPTS US TO BELIEVE:
Teachers need tenure to protect them from arbitrary dismissal.

WHAT REALITY TAUGHT ME:
Being able to fire people is the only way
to keep schools accountable.

Former D.C. schools chancellor Michelle Rhee told me a story about visiting a high school with terrible attendance. She asked a teacher,

"Where are all the kids?" She was told that low attendance was expected on a Friday, especially when it was raining. She then noticed a crowded classroom. "There were thirty kids . . . not enough desks for the kids that were there. I'm watching the teacher. This is a pretty engaging lesson. So I go up to one of the kids, a young man. And I said, 'What do you think about the teacher?' He said, 'This is my best teacher, bar none.' "

Later that morning Rhee left the school and saw that same student and two of his friends leaving. "I said, 'Excuse me, young man. Where do you think you're going?' And they said to me, 'Well, our first-period teacher, the one that you saw, he's great. So we came to school. But our second-period teacher is not so good, so we're going to roll.' This is not the picture that the American public has of truants! These children were making a very conscious decision to wake up early and to come to school for first period, 'cause they knew they were going to get something out of it, and then to leave after that because they weren't going to get any value."

And this great teacher gets paid no more than the others. The BLOB frowns on giving extra pay for excellence. They *snarl* at the idea of ever firing a teacher. Public school teachers typically get tenure once they've taught for about three years. Tenure means that it's just about impossible to fire them. They basically have a job for life.

In Paterson, New Jersey, it's former police detective Jim Smith's job to investigate claims against bad teachers and to go through the BLOB's insane process of trying to fire *really* bad ones. He told me that he can't even fire a six-hundred-pound teacher who urinated into a container in his classroom and then had his seven-year-old students carry his urine to the bathroom.

Smith was more successful dismissing a teacher who hit kids. But the cost? "It took me four years and $283,000; $127,000 in legal fees plus what it cost to have a substitute fill in, all the while he's sitting home having popcorn."

This is not how it works in real life, the private sector. Before General Electric got so political and became a "partner" with big government, it was a phenomenal growth company. Its CEO at the time, Jack Welch, said what was crucial to its success was "identifying the bottom 10 percent of employees, giving them a year to improve, and then firing them if they didn't get better." He said "there is no sugarcoating this—they have to go." This pruning of deadwood is good for any institution—it's "creative destruction." It makes most everyone more efficient. It's often even good for the fired employees, many of whom find new wealth and happiness in jobs for which they are better suited.

But government institutions almost never make such cuts. Even when forced to shrink their workforce, they usually do it though "attrition." They don't make actual decisions about which workers are more or less productive. They just wait until some workers—often the better ones—leave for other jobs. The deadwood gets to stay.

Welch's idea about firing people influenced charter school leader Deborah Kenny. Because her schools are nonunion, she can fire. "We fired as many as we must and as little as we can," she told me. It's made a big difference. Her students outscore the union school students on all the standardized tests. She says that good teachers want the bad teachers out. "Somebody who doesn't carry their weight . . . brings down the morale of the whole team of teachers."

I asked some charter teachers if it bothered them that they could get fired at any minute. "If I'm not doing my job and I was fired for that, so be it," said one. Another told me, "If I was a doctor and I wasn't good, I mean I wouldn't have a job. No one would come to me, right?"

But unions say that failing teachers must be given chances to improve. Lots of chances. "We need to lift up the low performers and help them do better," Nathan Saunders, head of the D.C. teachers union, told me. "There's a cost of firing teachers . . . the quality of life of that person is deeply affected by that termination."

Boo-hoo. Notice that he didn't mention the cost to the kids who are stuck in a class with the teacher being given a second, third, or fourth chance.

WHAT INTUITION TEMPTS US TO BELIEVE:

Reformers who improve government schools will be rewarded.

WHAT REALITY TAUGHT ME:

People don't like change.

When D.C. mayor Adrian Fenty appointed Michelle Rhee to be schools chancellor, Rhee was a schoolteacher who'd never run a school, much less a school *system*. "People said, he's lost his mind," she told me. "I was a thirty-seven-year-old girl from Toledo, Ohio."

Some people said she was out of *her* mind to take on the dysfunctional D.C. system. There were "no books in the library. Kids didn't have supplies and pencils. And then the following week, I visited the warehouse of the school district, where there were boxes and boxes of books and scissors and computers."

She asked why the supplies didn't get to the schools. "People at the warehouse said, 'They're just going to get lost.' "

Surrounded by such staggering incompetence, Rhee did what she says any CEO would do: "I started to fire people. And that did not go over particularly well."

Her general counsel ran into her office and told her she couldn't fire people unless they did something "egregious." What qualified as "egregious"?

According to Rhee, "You have to have hit a kid, and we have to have the videotape to show it, because five teachers and the principal seeing it is not enough. Or you have to have stolen money from the district, and we have to have the bank receipt to prove that you did. Short of that, really nothing counts as egregious."

Eventually Rhee found a loophole in the union contract that allowed her to fire 200 of 4,000 teachers. She also fired her own daughter's principal. "That was a chilly night at home," she said.

People called her the "hatchet lady" and the "big bad witch." *Time* magazine put her on its cover with a broom.

Ultimately, firing people cost Rhee her job. Mayor Fenty was voted out of office (a loss that was largely attributed to Rhee's unpopularity). Rhee quit before the new mayor fired her. "I just had this maybe naïve assumption that because we were delivering results, because people could see that the schools were better places, they're going to want to see the school reform continue. And I was wrong. I could not have been more wrong."

Rhee rocked the wrong boat. She made the BLOB mad.

WHAT INTUITION TEMPTS US TO BELIEVE:
If education reforms clearly improve student success,
then they will be welcomed by the BLOB.

WHAT REALITY TAUGHT ME:
The BLOB rejects almost any change.

When a reporter asked President Obama if he thought that his daughters could get a high-quality rigorous education in the D.C. public schools, he said, "If I wanted to find a great public school for Malia and Sasha to be in, we could probably maneuver to do it. But . . . I will be blunt with you, the answer is no right now. The D.C. public schools are struggling."

So the president sent his kids to private school—the same one Chelsea Clinton attended and that Vice President Biden's grandkids attend. Tuition is about $32,000 a year (that's not so much more than the $28,000 per year spent in D.C. public schools per pupil on K–12 education, but the results are more impressive).

About the same time as his kids enrolled in private school, the president cut off a small D.C. school voucher program that allowed some poor kids to have options like his kids have. Fortunately, when Republicans won the House in 2010 and elected John Boehner as Speaker, Boehner insisted that Obama restore the vouchers. Obama did.

The president is just one of many voucher opponents who prefer private schools for his own family. Heck, when I interviewed two teachers union leaders for my most recent *Stupid in America* TV special, I was surprised to learn that both attended private schools and were grateful for the good education.

But they sure don't make it easy for other kids to have what they got. When charter schools were proposed for Newark, New Jersey, union boss Joe Del Grosso said: "Over my dead body they're going to come. . . . I'm going to physically try and stop them. . . . Why should they be in *our* schools?" (Notice he says "our" schools—as if schools belong to his union rather than the kids.) He continued: "Fox and CNN, are *they* in the same building? I don't think so."

But Fox and CNN cannot banish competition. Competition is *why* we have Fox, CNN, and a hundred other channels. Competition is what's finally given us some charter schools that actually make some kids excited to learn.

WHAT INTUITION TEMPTS US TO BELIEVE:
Charter schools don't get better results, and if they do
it's because they pick kids who are easier to educate.

WHAT REALITY TAUGHT ME:
Charters often get better results with the
same randomly selected kids.

The BLOB is desperate to perpetuate stories of charters failing to outperform "their" schools. In 2006, the U.S. Department of Education announced the results of a big study: "Children in public schools generally performed as well or better in reading and mathematics than comparable children in private schools." The media ate it up. The *New York Times* put the study on its front page, along with a quote from teachers union (National Education Association) president Reg Weaver, who claimed it showed "public schools were doing an outstanding job." The BLOB still trots out this study every time charter schools are proposed.

Please.

The actual data suggested that private and charter school kids scored higher. It was only after the researchers adjusted the data for the students' "race, ethnicity, income, and parents' educational background" that the BLOB schools appeared to do better.

Such regression analysis is a valid statistical tool. But it's also prone to researcher bias, and there's plenty of that at BLOB Central, the Department of Education. Harvard University researchers tried to reproduce the government-commissioned study using several data adjustments, but they couldn't do it. The Harvard researchers concluded that the government-funded study was biased. Surprise!

Even the BLOB's researchers acknowledged that "[i]deally, to ascertain the difference between the two types of schools, an experiment would be conducted in which students are assigned [by an appropriate random mechanism] to either public or private schools." The *New York Times* didn't find it "fit to print" *that*.

In 2010, the Department of Education came out with the results of one of those experiments—a "gold standard" study that compared students who were accepted via lottery at twenty-eight different charter schools to students who applied to the same schools but who were randomly rejected in the lottery.

They found no significant difference in test scores, but parents were almost twice as likely to be happy with the charter school— 70 percent of lottery winners said their school was "excellent," compared to 38 percent of lottery losers. Kids liked the charter schools more, too, 75 percent to 62 percent.

The study found that some schools drastically increased kids' scores but that others did worse than traditional public schools. But that's okay. When a charter school fails, it goes out of business. When the BLOB schools fail, they just keep failing. No matter how bad they get, they almost never close.

The beauty of charters—or, far better, allowing diverse market competitors—is that, over time, good schools will expand while the bad ones die. There are no such prospects for change in the BLOB-controlled system.

Michelle Rhee says the charter school success phenomenon is not a result of charters choosing students. "I'd have a school where 10 percent of the kids were on grade level. And right down the street I would have a KIPP [charter] school where the kids are picked by lottery, and 90 percent of the kids were proficient. . . . They are getting kids who are scoring very low in proficiency, and by the time they leave they are achieving like suburban kids are."

Successful charters we visited were filled with the "at risk" kids whom the BLOB claims charters exclude.

Almost all parents do care about their kids and want them to learn and succeed—yes, even poor parents, despite the assumption made by a surprising number of liberals that many poor parents just don't care. Visit Harlem in the spring and you can see how much they care. During lottery week, thousands wait in long lines hoping to get their kids into one of the few charters allowed by the BLOB: Thousands of kids enter the lottery, hoping to be allowed to attend a school like Harlem Success. Only a few hundred kids are lucky enough to be picked. Kids and parents cry when they lose.

WHAT INTUITION TEMPTS US TO BELIEVE:

We need government schools to educate the poorest of the poor.

WHAT REALITY TAUGHT ME:

Government schools are so bad that even the
poorest of the poor pay to escape them.

Some of the money I make giving speeches goes to a charity that helps kids escape New York City's lousy public schools. It pays most of their tuition at Catholic school. When I visit those parochial schools, I'm always amazed how many parents work two or three jobs just to get their kids a decent education. It's not a religious thing; half the students aren't Catholic. Parents want their kids to succeed.

James Tooley spends most of his time in the poorest parts of Africa, India, and China. Those countries copied America's "free public education," and Tooley wanted to see how that's worked out. What he learned is that in India and China, where kids outperform American kids on tests, it's not because they attend the government's free schools. Government schools are horrible. So even in the worst slums, parents try to send their kids to private, for-profit schools.

"What private schools?" I asked. How can the world's poorest people afford tuition? And why would they pay for what their governments offer for free?

Tooley says parents with meager resources still sacrifice to send their kids to private schools because the private owner does something that's virtually impossible in government schools: replace teachers who do not teach. Government teachers in India and Africa have jobs for life, just like American teachers. Many sleep on the job. Some don't even show up for work.

As a result, says Tooley, "The majority of [poor] schoolchildren are in private school." Even small villages have as many as six private schools, "and these schools outperform government schools at a fraction of the teacher cost."

As in America, government officials in those countries scoff at private schools and parents who choose them. A woman who runs government schools in Nigeria calls such parents "ignoramuses." They aren't—and thanks to competition, their children won't be, either.

WHAT INTUITION TEMPTS US TO BELIEVE:

Head Start is a success because it helps kids
when they're just learning to learn.

WHAT REALITY TAUGHT ME:

Even Head Start is an expensive failure.

Even with today's new passion about federal budget cuts, one program is sacred: Head Start.

It's intuitive that spending $166 billion to give the neediest of kids a head start before kindergarten would help them do better in school. But guess what: The U.S. Department of Health and Human Services found that while Head Start helps kids in kindergarten, the improvement doesn't last. By first grade there was no difference in test results. Head Start made no difference!

Head Start is now forty-five years old, so it's had time to prove itself. Cato's Andrew Coulson points out, "If Head Start [worked], we would expect now, after forty-five years of this program, for graduation rates to have gone up, expect the gap between needy and privileged kids to have shrunk, expect students to be learning more. But none of that is true."

Doesn't matter. The money keeps coming.

Now the BLOB wants more. They (and President Obama) want every child in America to start school *before* kindergarten. Taxpayers would pay for it. It's another intuitively popular idea. When polled, most Americans said they favor government-funded pre-K.

But I doubt that most people have thought it through.

Mia Levi has thought about it a great deal because she runs six preschools. She told me, "This whole thing is a scam." You'd think that she'd favor the program, since it would give her free government money, but she's the rare person who understands that government money comes with limits on freedom. "I don't want to have to answer to the government. Our programs are far superior."

Levi has to work hard to improve her schools because she knows that, unlike K–12 education, parents have options. "If we didn't do our job, families go down the street to the next school. Public schools aren't doing their job, and they just keep opening their doors. That *they* are the ones to define quality is laughable."

The "free" pre-K movement has the whiff of scam about it. Most American kids already attend preschool. Parents pay for it, and those who can't afford it can get subsidies or use free programs like Head Start.

"It's a flagrant waste of money," Levi said. "It's as if I went shopping for myself because I needed a dress for a party and I bought a dress for everybody else whether they needed it or not."

Libby Doggett, who leads one of the biggest pre-K advocacy groups, says that "high-quality" government programs benefit children, and Oklahoma and Georgia have them already. So I checked test results in those states. I didn't find progress. Despite the spending of billions of tax dollars on preschools for ten years, Oklahoma's students lost ground.

Doggett replied: "We don't want to just focus on IQ scores. We want to look at how children are doing in their social and emotional, their noncognitive development." Give me a break. If the huge government program can't perform the basic (and measurable) educational task of raising math and reading scores, why should we give the central planners money because they promise to improve the kids' "emotional development"?

WHAT INTUITION TEMPTS US TO BELIEVE:

Education is too important to be left to the
uncertainty of market competition.

WHAT REALITY TAUGHT ME:

Education is too important to leave to a government monopoly.

American parents, and especially those in wealthy suburbs, think their kids' public schools are pretty good. But most are not. Jay Greene created something called the Global Report Card (Global reportcard.org), which allows parents to compare academic performance of nearly every U.S. school district. While suburban public school districts look good compared to their neighbors, they are mediocre compared to schools in the rest of the world. Only 6 percent of 14,000 public school districts in the United States have math scores that place them in the upper third of global performance.

Without real competition, parents don't know what their kids *might* have had.

Few of us can imagine the wonderful possibilities until we see the options. When phone service was a government-blessed monopoly (you younger readers may not know that it was), all phones were black and all calls were expensive. Only when the monopoly was broken up did we get cheap calls and the variety of phone choices we have now. The postal service couldn't "get it there overnight." None of the brilliant managers at that government monopoly could make it happen. But once FedEx appeared, suddenly even the postal service could get it there overnight (sometimes).

It's not that the government is staffed (entirely) by dumb and lazy people. It's just that it's hard to think of better ways to do things until competition makes them apparent.

If there were a free market in education, parents would demand that their school spend more on good teachers. Top teachers might make two hundred thousand dollars a year (many cities already spend more than that per classroom). Students would learn more. Competition brings out the best in everyone.

I don't presume to know what the successful formula will be. As Hayek put it, competition is a "discovery process," constantly ferreting out places where improvement can be made. They may not be where we anticipated. For years, the BLOB rhapsodized about smaller classrooms. But, oops, smaller class sizes did not increase performance. Bill Gates spent billions building smaller high schools. That didn't help, either. Neither did special training for principals that billionaire philanthropist Eli Broad funded. I give Broad and Gates credit—they spent their own money, took measurements, and when they found no improvement, looked for other solutions. The BLOB spends *your* money and continues failed experiments forever.

Once there's competition, the better schools will emerge. I bet most will use some form of Internet instruction. Think about this: Two hundred years ago, most towns had a best singer. If you lived in that town, that singer's songs were as good as it got. But today, thanks to radio, then records, then CDs, and now the Internet, the best singers reach the whole world. We've seen no such improvement in education, because the BLOB prevents change.

But the Internet allows great educators to evade the BLOB.

Who is the world's best teacher? Maybe it's Sal Khan. Could your kids have Khan as a teacher? Well, today, yes, you can.

Khan is a nerdy investment adviser whose cousin asked him to tutor her. "I had to do the same lecture over and over again. So I had a friend who said, 'Sal, why don't you put some of your lectures on YouTube?' "

Khan did. Soon he noticed that thousands of people had watched his lectures. "I started getting comments on YouTube . . . like, 'I hated mathematics and I was about to drop out of college. Now I'm staying, and I want to be an engineer.' "

His YouTube numbers kept rising. Now Khan is funded by Bill Gates. His videos are viewed millions of times. We videotaped a California school district that uses Khan's videos in fifth-grade classrooms. The teachers were skeptical at first but now say they are impressed at Khan's ability to get kids to like learning. "They're happy to walk in the door every morning," one teacher told us. "They're excited about doing math. It isn't like, ugh, we're doing math. It's like, 'Oh! We're doing math! Great!' "

We saw fifth graders doing high school math. Khan says, "It's funny—they have this innocence about it. They don't know that it's supposed to be difficult. They just view it as a game."

The Khan videos are just one of several new Internet learning systems. In Florida, some students now take most classes online. Perhaps we're close to an era in which, thanks to online classes— or new charter schools, or other experiments that I can't even imagine—education will be fun and easy for all kids.

Competition can make that happen. But first we must make the educators compete to serve our kids.

10

THE WAR ON DRUGS: BECAUSE ALCOHOL PROHIBITION WORKED SO WELL . . .

WHAT INTUITION TEMPTS US TO BELIEVE:

Drugs hurt people, so we do everyone a service by banning them.

WHAT REALITY TAUGHT ME:

The *war* on drugs harms more people than the drugs.

Look at this graph:

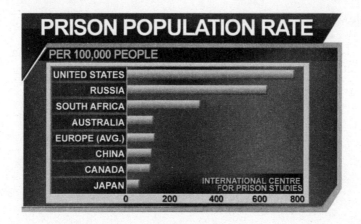

In 1971, the United States locked up fewer than 200 of every 100,000 Americans. Our incarceration rate was similar to that of other Western democracies. Then, President Nixon declared war on drugs. After that, the incarceration rate nearly tripled. Now we lock up a much higher percentage of our people than any other country—more even than the authoritarian regimes in Russia and China.

Jailing so many Americans allows even China to criticize America's human rights record.

Narcotics officers keep announcing "successes." They knock down doors and hold press conferences to show off big drug busts. Yet the busts don't affect most of the drug trade.

The media (including Fox News) run frightening stories about Mexican cocaine cartels and marijuana gangs moving into America. Few of my colleagues stop to think that decriminalization might end the violence. But it would. There are no French wine "cartels" or Corona beer "gangs." No one "smuggles" liquor anymore. Liquor dealers are now called "businesses" instead of gangs and they "ship" their products instead of smuggling them. They settle disputes with lawyers rather than guns.

Drug laws create violent crime by handing the trade over to people who operate outside the law.

WHAT INTUITION TEMPTS US TO BELIEVE:

Drugs cause crime.

WHAT REALITY TAUGHT ME:

The drug *war* causes the crime.

On some levels, the government and even the cops are aware of the ridiculousness of the drug war. In busy midtown Manhattan, I sometimes smell marijuana. People smoke in public. Police usually leave them alone.

But other times the police act like a military force engaged in urban combat. SWAT raids were once an extreme measure, rarely used, conducted only when there was fear that a grave crime would be committed, something requiring "Special Weapons and Tactics." Now SWAT teams conduct a hundred raids a day. Every day, at least a hundred people wake up to the terror of their home being broken into and armed men yelling at them. Most of those people violated some law, but not all did—informants lie, and police make mistakes.

In the town of Berwyn Heights, Maryland, marijuana was randomly shipped to Cheye Calvo's home as part of a smuggling operation. Calvo didn't even know about it. When police raided his home, "I assumed it was just a terrible, terrible mistake," Calvo told my Fox audience. "But the more I looked into it, the more I realized business as usual brought the police through our front door. This is just what they do. We just don't hear about it. The only reason people heard about my story is that I happened to be a clean-cut white mayor."

That's right, Calvo is the *mayor* of Berwyn Heights. The county police didn't know they had raided the mayor's home. They later acknowledged their mistake, but would they have admitted making a mistake if Calvo were poor or black?

When police departments have machine guns and tanks at their disposal, criminal offenses that were once part of a metaphorical "war" are treated like targets in a real war—and more innocent Americans are caught in the cross fire.

I don't understand why the private use of recreational drugs justifies the militarization of the police, violent disregard for our civil liberties, and the jailing of millions of nonviolent people. I understand that some people who are high on drugs wreck their lives. Some hurt others. But just as we hold drunk people accountable when they do stupid things while intoxicated or drink and drive, we should punish drug users for harm they do, not for what they ingest or sell.

Everything can be abused, but that doesn't mean government can stop it. Government goes astray when it tries to protect us from ourselves.

Few drug users hurt or rob people because they are high. Drug crime occurs *because* the drugs are illegal and available only through a black market. Sellers arm themselves because they cannot ask the police to protect their persons and property.

In turn, some buyers steal to pay the high black-market prices. It's not that some drugs are so powerfully addictive that drug users are driven to steal. The U.S. government says heroin and nicotine are similarly addictive, but people don't rob convenience stores to get Marlboros. People rob to get drugs because drug prohibition creates a black market.

WHAT INTUITION TEMPTS US TO BELIEVE:
The war on drugs must be waged to reduce drug
use and drug crime in black neighborhoods.

WHAT REALITY TAUGHT ME:
The drug war *causes* crime in black neighborhoods.

John McWhorter, a former Berkeley linguistics professor who is now a senior fellow at the Manhattan Institute, indicts the war on drugs for "destroying black America." McWhorter, by the way, is black.

McWhorter sees prohibition as *the* saboteur of black families. "It has become a norm for black children to grow up in single-parent homes, their fathers away in prison for long spells and barely knowing them. In poor and working-class black America, a man and a woman raising their children together is, of all things, an unusual sight. The war on drugs plays a large part in this."

Going to prison is now a "badge of honor" in the black community. McWhorter says, "Enduring prison time is seen as a badge of strength. It's regarded [with some justification] as an unjust punishment for selling people something they want. The ex-con is a hero rather than someone who went the wrong way." This attitude did not exist before drug prohibition.

He enumerates the positive results from ending prohibition. "No more gang wars over turf, no more kids shooting each other . . . Men get jobs, as they did in the old days, even in the worst ghettos, because they have to."

Would cheaper and freely available drugs bring their own catastrophe? "Our discomfort with the idea of heroin available at drugstores is similar to that of a Prohibitionist shuddering at the thought of bourbon at the corner store. We'll get over it."

WHAT INTUITION TEMPTS US TO BELIEVE:

At least the feds allow states to experiment
with medical marijuana.

WHAT REALITY TAUGHT ME:

No, they don't.

Early one morning, DEA agents raided Charlie Lynch's California home. They shouted, "Open the door, or we're gonna tear it down!" Lynch says, "I opened the door, and about ten to fifteen agents with shields, bulletproof vests, guns, masks . . . threw me on the ground and . . . held a gun to the back of my head."

DEA officers then seized thirty pounds of marijuana.

How did the DEA discover that Lynch possessed marijuana? Maybe they were tipped off by the public ribbon-cutting ceremony Lynch held for his marijuana *business*—the one that the mayor of his town attended, along with city councilmen and the president of the Chamber of Commerce. The local police were invited, too. Lynch sold medical marijuana, which has been declared legal by California and fifteen other states.

But the federal government is not bound by state laws, and President Obama, who admits that he smoked marijuana ("I inhaled," he said when asked during his campaign; "frequently; that was the *point*"), now directs his Justice Department to arrest others who do what he did.

WHAT INTUITION TEMPTS US TO BELIEVE:

"Medical marijuana" is just a clever excuse to get high.

WHAT REALITY TAUGHT ME:

Sometimes it is. So what?

There's no proof that marijuana works better than conventional anti-nausea drugs, but many cancer patients say that it does. Singer Melissa Etheridge told me smoking marijuana helped her endure chemotherapy when she had breast cancer. Pills her doctors gave her to treat the side effects created new side effects. "Take one drug for pain. It makes you constipated. So then you have to take the drug that helps you not be constipated. But that drug [gives you] diarrhea, and so you take another drug to combat the side effects of that."

Then Etheridge's doctor recommended marijuana. She found it worked much better than the pills.

It worked for Owen Beck, too. He was in high school when I interviewed him. "I was playing soccer, and [my leg] was really hurting," he said. Tests showed it was cancer. Doctors amputated Owen's leg and started him on a course of chemotherapy. Chemo tortured him the way it tortured Etheridge. "It destroys your appetite," he said. "And whatever you can eat, you throw up."

When prescribed medicine didn't relieve the side effects, his doctors suggested marijuana. "With the marijuana, I could do what I needed to do during the day and just not be in pain. I could be comfortable."

Of course, marijuana doesn't grow itself. Okay, it often does, but cultivating those plants is illegal. And so people like Melissa Etheridge and Owen Beck have to buy their medical marijuana from someone. Owen bought his from Charlie Lynch's dispensary.

The local sheriff, Pat Hedges, wasn't happy that California legalized medical marijuana. So he had his officers stake out Lynch's dispensary to see if Lynch broke any part of California's law. Lynch didn't. After a year of spending taxpayer money to diligently document that marijuana was indeed being sold by a marijuana dispensary, the sheriff came up with a new idea: he handed the case over to the feds.

The DEA, which puts marijuana in the same category as drugs like heroin, arrested Lynch for violating federal law. Authorities took Lynch to federal court, where his lawyers were not even allowed to tell the jury that medical marijuana is legal in California. Not surprisingly, the jury found Lynch guilty of selling marijuana.

Then came the election of President Obama. Right before Lynch was to be sentenced, Obama's Department of Justice seemed to call for a halt to such ridiculous prosecutions. Deputy Attorney General David Ogden directed U.S. attorneys not to focus federal resources on "individuals whose actions are in clear and unambiguous compliance with existing state laws." Since Lynch's actions were in "clear and unambiguous compliance with existing state laws," the judge postponed sentencing. But a week later, he went ahead and sentenced Lynch to a year and one day in prison.

After that, the Justice Department issued a *new* memo, making it clear that they will raid and prosecute medical marijuana dispensaries after all.

Charlie Lynch is out of jail while appealing his sentence, but his girlfriend left him, his friends are afraid to talk to him, and he's filed for bankruptcy. He says his life has been destroyed.

WHAT INTUITION TEMPTS US TO BELIEVE:
America should send a consistent message
about which drugs are acceptable.

WHAT REALITY TAUGHT ME:
States should be allowed to experiment.

Whatever happened to America's federal system, which recognizes states as "laboratories of democracy"? Alaska, Arizona, California,

Colorado, Delaware, Hawaii, New Jersey, Maine, Michigan, Montana, Nevada, Oregon, New Mexico, Rhode Island, Vermont, Washington, and Washington, D.C., all voted to eliminate penalties for physician-approved possession of marijuana. But the feds say federal laws trump state laws, and the Supreme Court agreed.

This is not the way it was supposed to work. The plan in the Federalist Papers delegated a few powers to the federal government, and reserved the rest to states. The system was hailed for its genius. Instead of having decisions made in the center—where errors harm the entire country—a mistake in California would hurt only Californians. People could move to another state if they really hated a rule. Everyone would learn from the experiments.

It's another good idea destroyed by a Big Federal Government.

Something doesn't go away just because the government decrees it illegal. It simply goes underground. Then the black market creates worse problems. Since sellers cannot rely on police to protect their property, they arm themselves, form gangs, and kill competitors.

Alcohol prohibition gave America Al Capone. Drug prohibition gives us Mexican criminal gangs and funds Middle Eastern terrorists.

Such prohibition-caused crime leads to calls for even bigger government. In Colombia, I watched as my government spent my tax money on planes that dropped herbicides on fields. The farmers told me this made them hate America.

But the State Department called their spraying a big success! After all, it did cut back on the Colombian drug trade. But that just squeezed the balloon. The trade moved across the border to Mexico. Then the president of Mexico squeezed the balloon—and now the trade spills over into Peru, Guatemala, and the United States. This is not progress.

WHAT INTUITION TEMPTS US TO BELIEVE:

Maybe marijuana is okay, but more
serious drugs should be banned.

WHAT REALITY TAUGHT ME:

Adults should get to decide for themselves, period.

I once attended a party given by the Marijuana Policy Project, a group that pushes for more reasonable marijuana laws. The party celebrated a tiny victory: a medical marijuana bill had been approved by one of New York's two legislative bodies. Celebrities took turns at a microphone, saying how great it was that the legislature had finally acted. I then took the mic and said that it was pathetic that they were so excited about the mere partial passage of a medical marijuana bill, when *every* substance should be legal.

The *New York Post*'s popular Page Six gossip page reported on that: "The crowd went silent at his call to legalize hard drugs."

"How could you say such a ridiculous thing?" demanded one ABC employee when that article appeared. "If you do crack just once, you are hooked. Legal hard drugs would create more addicts. And that leads to more violence, homelessness, out-of-wedlock births . . ." and so on. Her diatribe is a good summary of the drug warriors' arguments. Most Americans agree with her.

But what most Americans believe is wrong.

WHAT INTUITION TEMPTS US TO BELIEVE:

Do crack or heroin once, and you're hooked.

WHAT REALITY TAUGHT ME:

Most people who try drugs give them up. Really.

The media have told us that some drugs are so powerful that one "hit" or "snort" will hook the user forever. Worse, users of crack become homicidal, or at least indifferent to life and death. Harvard economist Jeffrey Miron calls these claims a "grotesque exaggeration. . . . Crack has been out there for 25 years. It's available in every city. If it were going to cause that kind of violence, everyone living in cities would be dead by now. . . . [L]ots of people try [crack] and they realize it's either not that much fun, not that interesting, or they have concerns about negative side effects and they stop. . . . [P]eople who use all sorts of risky things in their teens and early 20s stop doing them for lots of reasons as they get older."

This isn't just Miron's opinion; this is what the government's own statistics show. The National Institutes of Health found that 36 million Americans have tried crack. But only 12 percent used it in the last year, and fewer than 6 percent used it in the last month. If crack is so addictive, how did 88 percent of the users quit?

Nearly 4 million Americans have tried heroin. But the government says only 195,000 used it in the past month. That is just 5 percent of the people who have tried heroin. The government's own data show that *alcohol* creates more heavy users than heroin or crack.

People have free will. Most who use drugs eventually wise up and stop, or moderate their use. The one-hit-and-you're-hooked reputation from these drugs is a myth. The vast majority of users give it up without a treatment program.

Even people who continue to use drugs usually live responsibly, as Jacob Sullum points out in the book *Saying Yes*. Some drug users wreck their lives, but most hold jobs and carry on productive lives.

WHAT INTUITION TEMPTS US TO BELIEVE:

Drug legalization would lead to more drug use.

WHAT REALITY TAUGHT ME:

Maybe not.

That *New York Post* reporter at the party also wrote, "Stossel admitted his own 22-year-old daughter doesn't think [legalization] is a good idea." What my daughter actually said was that she feared that legal cocaine would lead to more cocaine use. And therefore, probably, more abuse. That alone might be a reason to keep drugs like cocaine illegal.

It's possible that legalization might increase the amount of use, or abuse. But evidence from European countries suggests otherwise.

In the Netherlands, marijuana has been tolerated for years. Yet the Dutch are less likely to use than Americans. Thirty-eight percent of American adolescents have smoked weed, while only 20 percent of Dutch teens have. One Dutch official told me that "we've succeeded in making pot boring." Of course, heroin and cocaine are different, but Portugal decriminalized those as well in 2001. What happened? Teenagers immediately ran out in the streets and shot up!

Actually, no. That didn't happen. Drug use among Portuguese

teens declined. So did the rate of new HIV infections caused by dirty needles. General drug use stayed about the same.

Why didn't teen drug use increase? Because prohibition doesn't deter many people, and it certainly doesn't stop people from getting drugs. Teenagers tell researchers that weed is easier to obtain than alcohol. Heck, we can't even keep drugs out of prisons, so how do we expect to keep them out of the rest of America? Prohibition doesn't even accomplish its first goal.

But let's assume my daughter was right, that legalization would lead to more experimentation and more addiction. I *still* say legal is better. While drugs harm many, the black market harms more.

And regardless of the harm, what about *freedom*? Once we become adults, we should own our own bodies. No one should be allowed to tell adults what we may or may not ingest. Once I accepted that principle, it wasn't intellectually honest to argue that "only marijuana" should be legal—and only for certain sick people. *Every* drug should be legal, and it should be up to adults to decide whether to consume them, medically or recreationally.

WHAT INTUITION TEMPTS US TO BELIEVE:

Drugs erode people's morals.

WHAT REALITY TAUGHT ME:

The drug war corrupts cops and politicians.

Another devastating side effect of the drug war is damage to the legal system. Drug prohibition gives governments an incentive (an addiction, if you will) to continue the war in order to fund its own bureaucracy.

In America, liberty and property supposedly can't be taken from you unless you're convicted of a crime. But check out a government surplus auction. The police sell bikes for $10, cars for $500. Much of the merchandise was seized in drug raids. It's a fast-growing business. In 1986, the Justice Department made $94 million on forfeitures. Now their pool of loot totals a billion dollars.

"It's led to horrible abuses," says Scott Bullock of the Institute for Justice, the libertarian law firm. "Under this bizarre legal fiction called civil forfeiture, the government can take your property, including your home, your car, your cash . . . keep all or most of the property that they seize . . . use it to improve their offices, buy better equipment." Obviously, that creates a big temptation to take stuff.

The police can seize your property if they *think* it was used in a crime. If you want it back, *you* must prove it was not used criminally. This reverses a centuries-old safeguard in Anglo-American law against arbitrary government power.

"A district attorney's office in Texas used forfeiture money to buy an office margarita machine. Another used forfeiture money to take a junket to Hawaii for a conference," *Reason*'s Radley Balko told me. When the lawyer was confronted about it, his response was "A judge signed off on it, so it's okay." But it turned out the judge also went on the same junket.

In another case, people found cash in a man's car and confiscated it even though they had no evidence that the money had been illegally obtained. Balko says, "The state's argument was that maybe he didn't get it from selling drugs, but he might use that money to buy drugs at some point in the future. Therefore, we're allowed to take it." Sounds like that Tom Cruise movie *Minority Report*, where the police predict future crimes and arrest the "perpetrator."

"Give people the wrong incentives, and it's not surprising that they stretch the definition of law enforcement," Balko said. "You should not have people enforcing the laws benefiting directly from them." Right.

WHAT INTUITION TEMPTS US TO BELIEVE:

Legalization sends the wrong moral message.

WHAT REALITY TAUGHT ME:

Ridiculous laws erode respect for all law.

Even people who concede that the war on drugs has failed are reluctant to end it. Some fear legalization would make young people think that drugs are okay. But that seems specious. We tell young people that mountain climbing and cigarette smoking are dangerous, but we don't make them illegal.

Still, the message-to-kids idea may be why even liberal California rejected Proposition 19, a full marijuana decriminalization bill, as Fox's Bill O'Reilly predicted it would.

O'Reilly bet me ten thousand dollars (to go to charity) that Prop 19 wouldn't pass, and won. He argued that full decriminalization would lead to more drugs being sold to kids. "That's what's happening, man, and you don't care. *Stossel doesn't care.*"

I do care. But caring does not require supporting government action.

When O'Reilly yells at me about drugs, he always cites the same statistic: "Seventy-five percent of child abuse is caused by adults on drugs!" He then says that I "don't care about the kids!" But his statistic just demonstrates that the current law doesn't stop drug use.

The statistic is bogus anyway. It comes from Joseph Califano and his militant antidrug group, the National Center on Addiction and Substance Abuse, or CASA. The 75 percent is based on a survey that is more than ten years old, and "drugs" includes *alcohol*—which causes *most* of the abuse.

Califano represents the worst tendencies of the central planning autocrat. He's a longtime government bureaucrat and cabinet secretary, who in his autobiography brags about being an architect of President Lyndon Johnson's "Great Society": "I was exhilarated by the prospect of putting the thumb of the federal government on the scale," he writes. "Of course I enjoyed exercising the power. . . . The role of the federal government was forever changed; its expanded responsibility has been accepted by every successive president."

Unfortunately, he's right about that. I'm annoyed that O'Reilly cites him.

Califano is even blind to the fact his own research reveals the futility of the drug war. He surveys teens and finds that despite its illegality, marijuana "continues to be easier to buy than beer."

If drugs were legal, I suppose that at first, more people would try drugs. But most would give them up. Eventually, once the "forbidden fruit" excitement is gone, drug use would diminish, as it has in Portugal and the Netherlands. Crime would decrease, more young men would find real jobs, and the police could focus on real crime. Governments would collect drug taxes instead of spending a fortune on a futile war. Win-win.

When the public is this divided about an issue, there's a strong argument to be made that it's something that should be left to voluntary social pressure instead of legal enforcement. That's how most Americans decide whether to drink alcohol or go to church every week. Private, voluntary social networks have their own ways of punishing bad behavior and send more nuanced messages about what's unacceptable. Government's one-size-fits-all rules don't improve on that.

WHAT INTUITION TEMPTS US TO BELIEVE:

Steroids are a big new threat.

WHAT REALITY TAUGHT ME:

Relax.

The same applies to government's extension of the drug war to performance-enhancing drugs, like steroids. Some of this campaign is about politicians' lust for attention. Targeting steroid use by athletes gives congressmen an excuse to launch a showboating intrusion into sports. Congress, supposedly busy dealing with a ruinous deficit, still somehow finds time to subpoena famous athletes and hold hearings on steroid use. I didn't think baseball was an urgent national problem, but Congress felt it necessary to hold *a dozen* hearings on baseball-related controversies. Of course, berating Roger Clemens gets politicians more media attention than addressing, say, civil forfeiture laws. "This is part of our duty," Representative Elijah Cummings, Democrat of Maryland, told me, "to protect the American people." Steroids are "a serious public health problem." Both statements are wrong. It's not his duty. Steroids are not a serious public health problem.

Steroids briefly enjoyed a spin as the media's scare du jour. Scary claims were on TV every day: steroids cause brain tumors, heart attacks, and an anger problem nicknamed "roid rage." (Years ago, when a pro wrestler beat me up, people said that steroids made him do it.) Alarmists like Dr. Gary Wadler go on TV and say, "The threat is dying! The threat is suicide!"

But Dr. Norman Fost, a bioethicist at the University of Wisconsin, told me that the scare is bunk. The anti-steroid movement is mostly hysteria, much like the hype directed against other drugs: "The horror stories . . . some of them are just frankly made up." Fost insists there's no correlation between steroids and brain tumors.

When I confronted Wadler about that, Wadler, to my surprise, admitted that there's no correlation. And he wasn't so certain about other claims. When I asked him if steroids cause strokes, he said, "It's on a possible list." Heart attack? "The likelihood of anabolic steroid abuse being associated with heart disease is real." Note the waffle words "possible" and "associated." He uses them because, unlike smoking and cancer, there are no good epidemiological studies that show steroids *cause* those problems. *Every* drug is "associated" with side effects. Advil is associated with ulcers and shock. Why single out steroids? Because sports are sexy, "roid rage" is scary, the athletes are huge, and bringing them to Washington gets congressmen face time on TV.

Yes, steroids may cause problems. But "[p]eople everywhere take enormous risks way greater than even the hyped-up risks of steroids," says Fost. He says steroid use should be legal. "Athletes are going to use these things, so it would be better to have them on the table where informed doctors can help them get the right drug with the right dose."

What about sportsmanship? Legal steroids would tempt "natural" athletes to try steroids just to keep up. But America can deal with that without Congress making it a national crisis. Colleges and sports leagues can set their own rules and do their own tests on athletes. Some sports might allow steroid use. Fost told me, "I don't know why you would think this is cheating any more than the hundreds of other things athletes do to enhance their performance."

To doctors like Wadler, any use of a drug that's not medically necessary is "abuse." But that's just another piece of our hypocritical attitude about drugs. Entire fields of medicine thrive doing "unnecessary" procedures—like breast enhancement and hair replacement.

Wadler says a crackdown on steroids is necessary because steroid use "enhances a criminal element." But there's a "criminal" element only because zealots like him make steroid use a criminal activity. Wadler gave me a dirty look when I said that to him on TV.

That wrestler who hit me later said: his boss told him to hit me. He didn't mention steroids.

WHAT INTUITION TEMPTS US TO BELIEVE:

Mind-altering substances are always dangerous.

WHAT REALITY TAUGHT ME:

Mind-altering substances alter minds.

If we adults own our own bodies, we ought to get to control what we put in them. It's a legitimate function of government to protect me from reckless drivers and drunken airline pilots—but not to protect me from myself.

Economist Ludwig von Mises wrote: "[O]nce the principle is admitted that it is the duty of the government to protect the individual against his own foolishness [w]hy not prevent him from reading bad books and bad plays...? The mischief done by bad ideologies is more pernicious... than that done by narcotic drugs."

That connection between drugs and "bad books" and "bad

ideologies" is closer in the minds of some advocates of the drug war than Mises realized. The anarchist writer Robert Anton Wilson says that power-craving regimes have tended throughout history to forbid the use of mind-altering substances: Islamic regimes forbid alcohol, central-government-loving progressives were the great advocates of alcohol prohibition, and religious conservatives are ardent supporters of the current drug war.

Altering our minds is perhaps our most basic right. We alter our minds—often for the better—every time we read a book, have an argument, fall in love, or reconsider bad public policies.

If you've been in favor of the drug war, I hope reading this chapter quite literally "altered your mind."

11

WARS TO END WAR

I'm uncomfortable writing this chapter. After years of consumer reporting, I do understand markets. I've watched government attempt to improve on markets—and make things worse. I've watched free enterprise accomplish things governments could never do, and accomplish them so quietly and peacefully that most people didn't even notice. I understand and appreciate free enterprise, and that's what most of this book is about.

But defense? That's different. I've never studied war or covered international conflicts. I've learned that government tries to do too much, but *defense* is something government is *supposed* to do. It's in the Constitution.

Our military has an extraordinary record. Again and again, it has fought to achieve peace, and then . . . gone home. "Every other country in the history of the world, when it's defeated an adversary, it demands reparations," says Fox News national security analyst K. T. McFarland. "Pay us back for what it cost us to defeat you. What did the United States do at the end of World War II? The Marshall Plan. We sent money."

I cheered when our military retaliated against Al Qaeda. That seemed like a necessary war—a response to the attacks of 9/11. But I became skeptical when we stuck around to try nation building.

I was also skeptical when President Bush took us to war in Iraq. Saddam Hussein hadn't attacked America. I did believe that he had "weapons of mass destruction"—even Democrats believed that at the time. I read the Natan Sharansky book that Bush kept next to his bed. Sharansky wrote that there are "free societies and fear societies" and "if freedom comes to the Middle East, there can be peace." My lefty friends said Bush invaded Iraq to "get the oil," but that's silly. Bush sincerely believed Sharansky's claim that a democratic Iraq would be the beginning of real peace. He wanted to protect America and help the world. But Presidents Johnson and Nixon sincerely believed that the Vietnam War was necessary to protect America. They were wrong. Now we *trade* with Vietnam.

Successful interventions are the exception. For every World War II, there's a Bay of Pigs. When we helped the Afghani mujahedeen fight the Russians, we armed rebels like the ones led by Osama bin Laden. Intervention frequently goes wrong.

Ron Paul and many libertarians say we should immediately bring our soldiers home—pull our troops out of not just Iraq and Afghanistan, but also Germany, Japan, South Korea, etc. Libertarians have been right about most everything, and I suspect they are right about this, too.

But what if China attacks Taiwan? The United States made a "commitment" to peace and stability in the region. Can we do that without troops nearby? Weren't our interventions in Kosovo, Bosnia, Serbia, Grenada, and Kuwait a good thing? These places may not be beacons of freedom today, but they seem better off thanks to American intervention. And our intervention in Korea saved millions of South Koreans from the tyranny of communism.

WHAT INTUITION TEMPTS US TO BELIEVE:

Lunatics want to murder us, so we must kill them
over there before they kill us over here.

WHAT REALITY TAUGHT ME:

Such thinking leads to an overextended military.

The *Wall Street Journal* editorializes with such certainty that we must stay "engaged" in the Middle East "to prove bin Laden's central contention—that Americans have no stomach for a long-term fight—wrong. . . . Taking care to avoid a perception of weakness ought to be a chief consideration of U.S. policy makers."

Avoiding "a perception of weakness" is worth risking soldiers' lives and trillions of dollars?

Testing a microphone during his presidential campaign, John McCain once sang "Bomb bomb Iran" to the tune of "Barbara Ann." Smart defense hawks like Bill Kristol say we should consider a military strike against Iran. War is the only option, says Charles Krauthammer: "Against millenarian fanaticism glorying in a cult of death, deterrence is a mere wish."

How can they be so certain? Iran, though it has sponsored

terrorists, hasn't started a war against another country for two hundred years. Iran may acquire a nuclear weapon, but they don't have one now. They are an ocean and a continent away. And what exactly is the United States supposed to do? Invade and conquer a country that has twice as many people as Iraq, and then pry their yet-to-be-developed nuclear device from their cold dead hands?

Kristol, Krauthammer, and the neoconservatives have been right about a lot. The mainstream media mocked the surge in Iraq, but the surge appears to have worked. Still, today some people want the military to:

- contain China
- transform failed states into democracies
- chase terrorists
- train foreign militaries to chase terrorists
- protect sea lanes
- keep oil cheap
- stop genocide
- protect innocent people
- protect European, Asian, and Middle Eastern states from aggression
- spread goodwill through humanitarian missions
- respond to natural disasters
- secure the Internet
- police the Mexican border

People with such an expansive—and expensive—notion of what our military should do are indignant when others express doubt. After all, it seems downright cruel to *not* try to create a better regime in

Libya . . . or protect people in Darfur . . . or topple that nasty Iranian regime . . . or . . . The list is endless, which is the troubling part.

Politicians have a hard time saying no to such noble goals. And no one wants to appear "soft on defense."

I don't know exactly where our soldiers should be, but I do know that:

- The impulse to smash the bad guys at every opportunity leads us to moves that create new bad guys, who want to kill us.
- Military intervention is always brutal, even when troops try to avoid civilian casualties.
- War tends to increase the power of government.
- Policing the world is *expensive*. How can we achieve a sustainable budget while spending $700 billion on defense?

WHAT INTUITION TEMPTS US TO BELIEVE:

We need to spend big to build democracies.

WHAT REALITY TAUGHT ME:

Government doesn't do a good job building

anything, let alone democracies.

Nation building is the worst form of central planning.

After World War II, the Marshall Plan seemed to have worked, but McFarland points out, "[W]e gave them money and *they* decided how and what to spend it on. With Afghanistan and Iraq, we spent it on stuff *we thought* they should have—and it never works. They are not grateful, we're resentful that they are not appreciative, and in the end we spend millions and have nothing to show for it, including friends."

And in the fog of war, the waste is astonishing.

In June 2004, the U.S. military loaded $12 billion in shrink-wrapped hundred-dollar bills (weighing nearly four hundred tons) onto planes headed for Iraq. That money has since disappeared. What happened to it? None of us knows. One U.S. official described Iraq as a scene "awash in $100 bills." There was pressure to dole the money out quickly to Iraqi companies and ministries that were supposed to rebuild the country. Some officials wrote checks to ghost employees and kept the money themselves. To audit the money spent, the government, according to a report prepared for the House Committee on Oversight and Government Reform, hired an obscure consulting firm that "operates out of a private home in San Diego."

Frank Willis, the U.S. official in charge of the coalition's Ministry of Transportation, told *60 Minutes* that there was so much cash flying around the office that bricks of money were called footballs. "We passed them around in little pickup games in our office." At one point, the government awarded huge contracts to most anyone who came calling. A company called Custer Battles arrived in Baghdad with no security experience. They presented a $15 million proposal to provide security for Baghdad Airport. Colonel Richard Ballard described the proposal to *60 Minutes* as "something that you and I would write over a bottle of vodka, complete with spelling and syntax errors." Custer Battles got the contract anyway.

Custer promised to provide bomb-sniffing dogs at security checkpoints. For $15 million, it supplied exactly one dog. Even that dog was not a champion bomb-sniffer. "He would be brought to the checkpoint, and he would lie down. And he would refuse to sniff the vehicles. . . . I think it was a guy with his pet, to be honest," Ballard said.

In another example of stellar nation building, $900,000 was set aside to build a farmers' market. In free societies, farmers set up their own markets. But America spent almost a million taxpayer dollars to build one in Iraq. How did the project go? Nothing got built—aside from a "concrete slab and a tin roof," according to USAID deputy mission director David Atteberry. No organic produce in sight.

One State Department official wrote in *Foreign Policy* magazine about projects he funded that he now admits were "wacky": French pastry classes that the State Department had to pay Iraqis to attend, a play about donkeys, a children's art calendar. "No idea was too bizarre, too gimmicky, or pointless for us hearts-and-minders. . . . We actually preferred handing out croissants and children's calendars to tackling tough issues like health care or civic services."

No one knows how much money has been squandered in Afghanistan. The special inspector general for reconstruction reports that $55 billion is unaccounted for. Some billions went to local warlords like Ahmad Wali Karzai, brother of the Afghani president; $200 million went for unfinished Afghan army buildings, $5 million to police buildings so poorly built that they are unusable, and so on.

One of the more infuriating stories, reported by World Bank veteran Clare Lockhart, tells how $150 million was given to a UN agency to rebuild homes in a small village destroyed by American forces. The UN personnel didn't do the work themselves, but after taking 20 percent off the top for overhead, hired a contractor. He subcontracted to another contractor, who took money for overhead, too. And so on down a chain of subcontractors, until at the end, there was only enough money to pay for some wooden beams. The beams were the wrong type—too heavy for the local homes made of mud—so in the ultimate illustration of the futility of the government's efforts, the locals used the beams for firewood—$150 million up in smoke.

When a private company loses money, it goes out of business. If money vanishes, executives might get thrown in jail. But the Pentagon loses billions and gets away with a slap on the wrist from a congressional committee—something a handful of viewers watch on C-SPAN2.

Government is clumsy and wasteful at everything it does. Why would that not be true for defense? The Pentagon, like other government departments, sometimes even spends money in deliberately wasteful ways in order to establish "need" for at least as much next year. I've heard stories of soldiers flying helicopters on pointless missions just to burn up fuel.

And military rules are just as complex and bureaucratic as any other part of government. The Defense Department's brownie recipe is twenty-six pages long:

> [S]helled walnut pieces shall be of the small piece size classification, shall be of a light color, and shall be US No. 1 of the US Standards for Shelled English Walnuts. A minimum of 90 percent, by weight, of the pieces shall pass through a 4/16 inch diameter round hole screen and no more than 1 percent, by weight, shall pass through a 2/15 inch diameter round hole screen. The shelled walnuts shall be coated with an approved food grade antioxidant and shall be of the latest season's crop. . . .

I have no cure for military inefficiency any more than I have one for inefficiency at the U.S. Postal Service, except to say that we should rely on both as little as possible.

. . .

If government cannot run profitable trains, teach kids to read, or run effective poverty programs, why should we think that it can create a democracy in, say, Afghanistan? George W. Bush, debating Al Gore in 2000, said: "I don't think our troops ought to be used for what's called nation building." Yet four years later, when asked by NBC's Tim Russert if he had changed his mind on nation building, President Bush said, "Yeah . . . we're also fighting a war so that [the Iraqis] can build a nation."

Candidate Bush—rather than President Bush—had the right idea. We have tried to build a democracy in Afghanistan for more than a decade. Are we winning hearts and minds? A 2010 poll of more than 1,600 Afghans found that just 43 percent had a favorable impression of the United States—down from 83 percent in 2005.

Nation building fails for the same reason that economic central planning fails: top-down rarely works. Europe did a terrible job of creating individual-rights-respecting regimes during the colonial period in Africa. The United States has repeatedly intervened in Latin America but seldom created regimes that think highly of us. In fact, our intervention is a reason we got petty potentates like Fidel Castro and Hugo Chávez. The dictators are lauded as *defenders* against American marauders.

The best outcomes bubble up from free decisions made by local people. They, not the planners, have more relevant information about their own lives and incentives. When they don't get the decision right, they adjust. But when central planners—be they kings, viceroys, bureaucrats, or democratically elected politicians—try to create something as complicated as a new social order, they are likely to fail.

In Afghanistan, the central planners' attempt to nation build led to PowerPoint slides like this one:

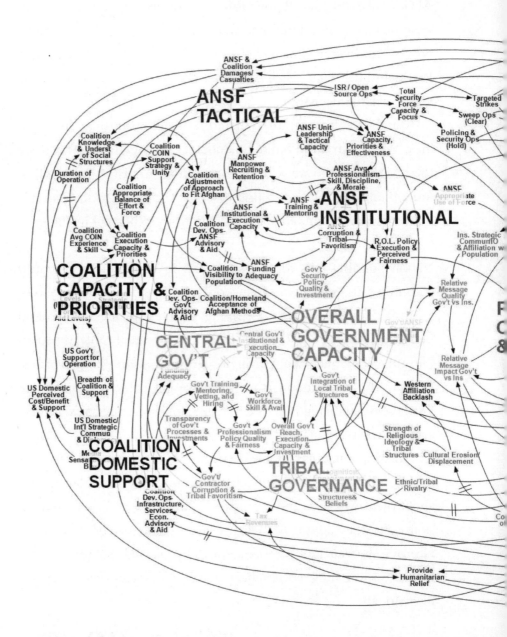

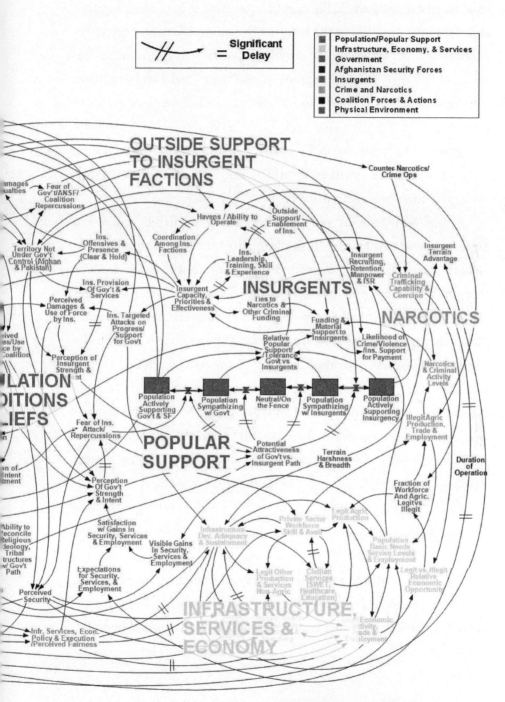

WORKING DRAFT – V3

What is the likelihood that American soldiers could understand this, let alone put a workable plan into action? When that map was leaked, it became a hit on the Internet because it illustrates the overwhelming complexity of the problem: warring tribes, competing political factions, varying degrees of education and infrastructure, uncertain loyalties, varying local customs and degrees of religiosity, etc.

When U.S. Army colonel Lawrence Sellin, serving in Afghanistan, criticized the "blinkered bureaucracy" for using PowerPoint slides like that, he was fired.

A different type of top-down planning occurred when the United States tried to reopen the Iraqi stock market. Before the invasion, the market was low-tech and chaotic. But it worked. Over many years, many individuals figured out, little by little, how to get things done. The United States sought to remake the new Iraqi market in the image of the New York Stock Exchange. It would be the most technologically advanced market in the Arab world.

They entrusted the job to a twenty-four-year-old Yale graduate named Jay Hallen, who worked in real estate. He asked his superiors, "Are you sure you want me to do this? I don't have a background in finance." They told him not to worry, that he would be project manager, and subordinates would do the finance work.

Iraqi stockbrokers begged him to reopen the exchange the way it was, but Hallen ordered supercomputers and wrote complex new regulations.

Then the supercomputers were delayed. Hallen wanted to wait for them, but pressure was strong to reopen, so they bought dry-erase boards and reopened the exchange basically as it had operated before.

According to Rajiv Chandrasekaran's book *Imperial Life in the Emerald City,* when asked what would have been different if U.S. planners hadn't intervened, an Iraqi official replied: "We would have opened months earlier."

WHAT INTUITION TEMPTS US TO BELIEVE:

Cutting military spending would betray our soldiers.

WHAT REALITY TAUGHT ME:

Our soldiers are better served if we narrow their *mission.*

The only way to spend less without threatening our troops is to rethink the military's mission. I was appalled to learn from Cato homeland security analyst Ben Friedman that apportionment of defense funds has practically been on automatic pilot since the Kennedy administration: The navy and marines get 29 percent, the air force 28, the army 27 percent. "Annual deviations are rarely ever above two percent," says Friedman.

Someone needs to make tougher decisions.

What's a reasonable goal? If the mission is to "provide for the common defense," then we should adopt a posture of *defense.* It needn't cost $749,748,000,000 to protect our shores but otherwise stay out of the wider world's affairs.

Today the United States spends nearly as much on our military as the rest of the countries in the world *combined.* Even if we cut military spending in half, we'd still spend more than any rival. One reason is that we station soldiers all over the globe, for example:

Country	Number of U.S. Troops
Germany	54,120
Japan	32,459
South Korea	27,968
United Kingdom	9,304
Italy	6,974
Greenland	134

Source: Department of Defense Base Structure Report 2009.

We built an air force base in Greenland to monitor the Soviet Union during the Cold War. What are we doing there now?

North Korea's crazy regime is a real threat to South Korea. But South Korea's economy is thirty-eight times bigger. It has the resources to protect itself. Since South Koreans know the United States protects them, they don't spend what they could. So we stay, and we pay.

Does that make us safer?

WHAT INSTINCT TELLS US:

The 9/11 attacks proves the need for a powerful Department of Homeland Security.

WHAT REALITY TAUGHT ME:

DHS excesses help terrorists win.

I live and work in Manhattan. After 9/11, I feared the next attack. My instinctive response to that fear was to want government to "do something" to keep us safe.

I watched as Congress created the Department of Homeland

Security and the Transportation Security Administration. At airports, I take off my shoes and try not to grimace as I am searched. It was worse when Saddam Hussein was still at large, because I look like him.

The government claims that its increased vigilance has protected us from other big attacks. It's possible. But I can't judge for myself. It's top secret. I have to take their word for it. The TSA spends five times what the previous screeners spent, but I have to wonder, is that security—or security theater? Sometimes it seems like TSA stands for Thousands Standing Around.

Even before they increased security spending, airline hijackings had been declining for years.

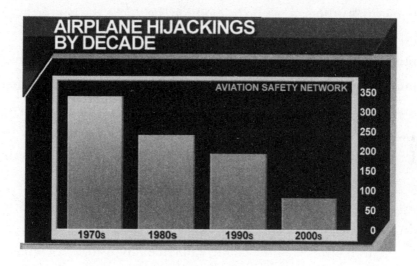

In the panic after 9/11, the Senate voted 100–0 to federalize airport security. Senator Tom Daschle said, "You can't professionalize if you don't federalize." This is the intuitive reaction to crisis. When we're scared, we assume that "federal" is "professional." But that's utter nonsense. The opposite is invariably true.

Israel and Europe once tried government-managed airport security but gave it up. They went back to hiring private contractors to do the work. Private contractors are more efficient. They can try different things. And if they fail, government can fire them.

The government never fires itself.

Before the TSA was created, American airports had private security contractors. There's no evidence that the more expensive TSA screeners are better. They may be worse. According to a leaked TSA report, when officials planted phony explosives in luggage, TSA screeners in Los Angeles missed 75 percent of them, but in San Francisco, one of the few cities allowed to have privately managed security, screeners missed only 20 percent.

Those San Francisco screeners have better incentives. Their boss knows that if they don't do a good job, he'll lose the contract. So he tries harder. The *Washington Post* reports that San Francisco's private screeners "compete in a workplace 'March Madness'–style tournament for cash prizes, some as high as $1,500. The games: finding illegal items and explosives in carry-on bags; successfully picking locks on difficult-to-open luggage; and spotting a would-be terrorist (in this case Covenant Aviation Security's president, Gerald L. Berry) on security videos."

"We have to be good," Berry said, "equal or better than the feds. So we work at it, and we incentivize."

Sixteen airports in the country opted out of using TSA screeners. When Kansas City did, officials noticed a difference.

"Unlike a government job, these contract employees can be removed immediately with poor performance, attitude, or unsuitability," said Kansas City airport director Mark VanLoh. "It shows in our passenger surveys for customer satisfaction."

That leaked TSA report concluded that those private screeners performed at "the same level or better."

In a reasonable world the Department of Homeland Security would say, "This is more proof that private sector competition is a good thing. We're disbanding the TSA, and will have private contractors compete for the business."

But we don't live in a reasonable world. We live in a big-government world.

No one knows how much money DHS has wasted. The TSA made a big fuss over its "five-level, color-coded airport Threat Condition Indicator," then dropped it, saying it provided "little practical information."

DHS spent your money on things like special boats to protect a lake in Nebraska, all-terrain vehicles for a small town in Tennessee, and security training courses in Michigan that no one attended. Of course, that happened because DHS wanted to please its bosses in Congress. Each congressman wants his district to get a cut of the loot. Government management means government waste.

The 9/11 attacks were largely a failure of government. Our so-called intelligence agencies knew nothing about the plot. The CIA, says McFarland, "for all the money we spend on it, missed all the major world-changing events: the collapse of the Soviet Union, the fall of the Shah of Iran, and the Arab Spring."

When an Arizona FBI agent suggested that his bosses check out some suspicious Middle Eastern students attending flight school, the FBI did nothing. The then Immigration and Naturalization Service, charged with keeping track of foreigners who overstay their visas, lost track of all nineteen hijackers. One INS excuse was that it had an antiquated computer system. (If only the feds had used some of the millions they spent charging Bill Gates with antitrust violations to buy his software instead!)

The private airport security screeners who worked on 9/11 did everything the Federal Aviation Administration asked them to do. The box cutters and small knives the hijackers carried were permissible under FAA rules. The FAA didn't require strong cockpit doors or allow pilots to carry guns.

Finally, part of the failure was America's interventionist foreign policy, which needlessly made enemies. As Congressman Ron Paul says, history did not begin on September 11, 2001.

Government failed on 9/11, and the politicians' response to its failures is always the same: "Give us more money and power." And we do.

WHAT INTUITION TEMPTS US TO BELIEVE:

Trust the experts.

WHAT REALITY TAUGHT ME:

Experts exaggerate their success.

Randolph Bourne, an opponent of U.S. entry into World War I, famously said, "War is the health of the state." When there is war, government grows in power.

After September 11, Senator Charles Schumer declared that the "era of a shrinking federal government is over." That was more Schumer nonsense. Government hadn't shrunk. Bill Clinton and both Bushes talked about shrinking it but didn't do it. For politicians like Schumer, a terrorist attack was another excuse to increase government's power and spend more.

This spending plays into terrorists' hands. In one videotaped message, Osama bin Laden talked about "bleeding America to the point of bankruptcy."

Fear of attacks on the United States is as much a weapon as the attacks themselves. That's the nature of terrorism. Admiral Mike Mullen, former chairman of the Joint Chiefs of Staff, recently said, "This is the most dangerous time I've seen growing up the last four decades in uniform."

The most dangerous time? More than when hundreds of Soviet nuclear missiles were pointed at us? That's absurd.

Nine-eleven was an unusually successful terror attack. But that was more than ten years ago. Even if there were a similar attack now, and every ten years, that would average about 300 Americans killed a year. Terrible, but house fires kill 2,700 per year. Heart disease, cancer, and auto accidents kill many times more Americans. We fear those things, but our brains are wired to react more strongly to the dramatic attack.

But we play into terrorists' hands when we respond with emotion rather than reason. The point of "terrorism" is to create terror and disrupt our lives. That's what happened. We fear terrorism so much that we spend billions on things that curtail our freedom but don't make a difference.

Defense was one area where I thought Democrats might cut government. But Democrats rarely cut anything. Al Gore campaigned for president vowing to spend *more* on the military than George W. Bush.

Barack Obama promised to end the war in Iraq. It was a reason his followers were so excited—Obama the peacemaker! Candidate Obama said: "I have been against it in 2002, 2003, 2004, -5, -6, -7, -8—and I will bring this war to an end in 2009! So don't be confused."

But I am confused. Two years later, Obama announced that he will bring the troops home but will keep 16,000 "embassy employees" in Iraq—and more soldiers in Afghanistan than under George W. Bush.

Many of his Republican opponents want to spend even more. Mitt Romney complains about proposals for "massive defense cuts" and says talk of cuts "flows from the conviction that if we are weak, tyrants will choose to be weak as well."

What? Who holds *that* conviction? And no one in authority has proposed "massive defense cuts." What Romney calls "massive cuts" are reductions in planned spending *increases*.

Maybe Romney was just pandering to win Republican votes. On this issue, I hope that his reputation as a flip-flopper is borne out.

WHAT INTUITION TEMPTS US TO BELIEVE:

We need to scare people so that they don't attack us.

WHAT REALITY TAUGHT ME:

It's hard to scare people who are willing to
commit suicide for their cause.

Perhaps American power really does keep bad guys in line. I'm glad that the U.S. military killed Osama bin Laden and other terrorists. I assume that is a gain for peace and security.

But I'm not even sure about that.

Crippling the leadership of terrorist organizations is a good thing, but entering Pakistan's airspace against Pakistan's wishes diminishes our safety by creating new terrorists. When we kill one alleged Taliban foot soldier, we make new enemies of his friends and family.

Given what I've learned about government, I'm not even convinced that the reported "air strikes against Al Qaeda" really find their targets. Anonymous government officials tell the media that a top Al Qaeda leader "may have been killed." Journalists then pick up the story and, eager to create drama, report it as a devastating blow to terrorist organizations. But a UN report claims that one-third of those people killed are nonmilitants.

I do *not* argue here that our military actions abroad are *the* reason we were attacked on 9/11. We were attacked by religious fanatics. But our military presence in so many countries wins the fanatics support.

WHAT INTUITION TEMPTS US TO BELIEVE:
Fight the enemy.

WHAT REALITY TAUGHT ME:
Trade with our enemies.

America can have a huge impact on the rest of the world even without deploying the military. We already do.

People call libertarians who want to shrink our military's mission "isolationists." But we are not isolationists. By all means, let us buy and sell things all over the world. Let our movies play in theaters across the world, let our rock music alarm mullahs, let neo-conservative foundations fund the overseas sales of books filled with ideas the local autocrats consider dangerous.

A new report funded by the governments of Canada, Norway, Sweden, Switzerland, and the United Kingdom says that "the level of armed conflict in Muslim countries is far lower today than it was two decades ago" and that trade is a reason. When goods cross borders, armies don't.

People credit Ronald Reagan's military buildup for the fall of the Soviet Union. His defense buildup played a part. But so did Bruce Springsteen. In 1988, 160,000 people in East Berlin sang along to "Born in the USA." Springsteen stopped his performance and told the crowd, "I came to play rock 'n' roll for you East Berliners in the hope that one day all the barriers will be torn down." A year later, the Berlin Wall came down.

Springsteen wasn't responsible, but the obvious comparison between Soviet repression and America's vibrant culture played a role. So did the dramatic success of our market economy. People in the Soviet bloc wanted what we have. Such cultural and economic influences work, and they don't kill people or increase our debt.

I don't presume to know the "right" amount to spend on national defense. But I do know that our current spending, adjusted for inflation, is greater than it was during the Cold War, when nuclear Armageddon was possible and I did "duck and cover" drills in school. Spending more than we spent during the Korean and Vietnam wars, and more than when thousands of nuclear missiles were aimed at us is . . . too much spending.

12

KEEPING NATURE EXACTLY
AS IS . . . FOREVER

WHAT INTUITION TEMPTS US TO BELIEVE:

Plants and animals exist in a state of harmony
that we disrupt at our peril.

WHAT REALITY TAUGHT ME:

The natural world is brutal and violent.

The idea that human greed destroys nature, absent restraint by government, is deeply ingrained in our culture. The world was perfect until people ruined it. We must reduce the impact of humans in any way we can. A project by a writer known as "No Impact Man" got lots of play in the press (he writes a blog where he seriously asks questions like "Is Progress Good or Bad?"). No Impact Man's goal was to live for a year "without making any net impact on the environment. In other words, no trash, no carbon emissions, no elevators, no products in packaging, no plastics, no air conditioning, no TV, no toilets . . ." Of course, his effort also resulted in book and movie deals.

For decades, nature documentaries warned us that species were going extinct because we insist on building homes, cutting down trees, and so forth. We weep for the animals, like tigers in Asia. They are being hunted into extinction.

WHAT INTUITION TEMPTS US TO BELIEVE:

To protect the tigers, ban tiger hunting.

WHAT REALITY TAUGHT ME:

To protect tigers, eat tigers.

In India, China, and Russia, there were once one hundred thousand wild tigers. Only a few thousand survive. Most were killed by poachers who sell crushed tiger bone, which is made into a paste that is thought to kill pain. Under pressure from conservationists and UN types, local governments implemented the usual solution: bans on tiger hunting and bans on sale of crushed tiger bone. That made everyone feel good. Actor Harrison Ford filmed a public-service announcement in which he says, "When the buying stops, the killing can, too. Case closed!"

But no, Indiana Jones, the case isn't closed. The ban on the sale of tiger products has been in effect for years, yet tigers still disappear.

The ban seemed like the obvious solution: if tigers are

threatened, just ban tiger hunting and the sale of its by-products. But as we've seen with drug prohibition, banning something does not make it go away. "If we continue the current approach . . . the tiger is doomed," says Terry Anderson of the Property and Environment Research Center. Anderson points out that governments have repeatedly failed to save animals by banning their sale. They've failed with the colobus monkey in West Africa, the alligator in China, and now with the tiger in Asia.

How do we save them? Here's an idea: Sell them. And eat them.

I know that sounds bizarre, but think about this: Does anyone worry about a shortage of chickens? No—because we eat chicken. Farmers have an incentive to breed them and protect them.

Millions of wild bison once roamed America—great herds that were owned by no one. Then Europeans arrived and killed bison for food and sport. No one complained, because no one "owned" the bison. By 1900, bison were almost extinct.

Then some ranchers began to fence in the bison and farm them. Only then did the rampant killing stop. Today there are again big herds in America. The difference was private ownership.

WHAT INTUITION TEMPTS US TO BELIEVE:
Public ownership is nicer than private.

WHAT REALITY TAUGHT ME:
Public ownership leads to the "tragedy of the commons."

It makes us feel good to think about sharing for the common good, but public ownership usually means that no one gives a damn.

It's why the bison were nearly eliminated.

But today, America has half a million bison because private owners—like Ted Turner—hope to make a profit off people who eat bison meat.

We don't have to eat endangered species to save them. In Africa, rhinos were disappearing because poachers killed them to get their horns, which they ground up into products they thought to be aphrodisiacs. African governments banned the products, but this did little good. A black market, with the usual official corruption, arose to service the demand for rhino horns. Government game wardens took bribes. Even when they were honest, they couldn't guard the entire rhino habitat.

"It was a complete failure," says Brian Child, who spent twenty years working to save endangered species. "Wildlife was disappearing everywhere." What finally worked, he says, was letting landowners own rhinos so they could make money from tourism. Suddenly, tribes could profit by charging Westerners fees to watch rhinos, and in some cases, hunt them. The hunting was limited because each tribe wanted to make sure it would be able to profit off rhinos the following year. With profit at stake, the rules were enforced. Every member of the tribe became a game warden because the tribe had skin in the game.

It's human nature. No government protects resources as effectively as you protect your own property. In Africa, says Anderson, once tribes had ownership rights, formerly indifferent government security guards suddenly became fierce protectors of their tribal rhinos. He asked one: " 'What happens if you catch a poacher? You kill him?' He said, 'No, we just beat them up. They go back to their village and don't ever come back.' These people don't tolerate poaching because they want to keep the animals alive. They allow hunting. They allow photography. *That* is the way to save wildlife."

American conservation groups don't like this idea. Judy Mills, of Conservation International, told me that bans are the way to go. "[A] survey we did recently in China . . . showed that ninety percent of Chinese people actually support the ban [on the sale of tiger products]."

But so what? It's nice that Chinese people *say* they support the ban, but that same poll revealed that they also consumed products *they thought contained tiger.* Mills's response to that: "The ban hasn't had a chance to work."

It hasn't had a chance to work? The ban has been in effect for three decades.

What *has* worked is letting people own and profit from the sale of exotic animals. It's worked with elephants in Zimbabwe, rhinos in southern Africa, and the bison in America. Says Anderson, "If we make animals a marketable product, they will be saved."

But to most people, environmental issues seem like a choice between cute animals living the way God intended and greedy capitalists destroying them. Instead of asking, "Would property rights create better incentives for conservation?" people ask, "Which do you love more, the animals or the capitalists?" You don't have to watch years of Ted Turner–produced *Captain Planet* cartoons to know how you're supposed to answer.

WHAT INTUITION TEMPTS US TO BELIEVE:
When it comes to a necessity like water,
government needs to intercede.

WHAT REALITY TAUGHT ME:
Government screws up water just like everything else.

Property rights would solve most of the conflicts over who gets to use the American West's limited supply of freshwater. Now bureaucrats beg people to conserve water.

Some do. Most don't. But if water were a true free-market commodity, we wouldn't have constant fights over how much to use. The price system would work that out. People would pay more for highly valued water uses, like showering and agriculture, and less for frivolous uses like playing in a sprinkler. But once a product is "free," people get mad if you put a price on it. Bolivia nearly had a revolution recently over the government's effort to privatize its water system. The government backed down and stopped contracting out the water service. Soon there were shortages.

But, hey, who cares about consequences? Government's solutions are accepted because the motives sound "nice." When regulators and activists say they do it all for "equality" and to save the bunnies, fish, and beautiful blue skies, we passively submit.

WHAT INTUITION TEMPTS US TO BELIEVE:
Environmentalists are compassionate.

WHAT REALITY TAUGHT ME:
Authoritarian environmentalists kill people.

DDT was banned by President Richard Nixon's Environmental Protection Agency, a decade after Rachel Carson's book *Silent Spring* claimed that the pesticide threatened human health and birds. Many scientists said Carson was wrong, but they didn't write as well as she did.

Overuse of DDT did threaten birds by thinning the shells of

their eggs. But, as always with chemicals, the danger was in the dose. When I was ten, bureaucrats drove trucks through residential neighborhoods spraying thick white clouds of DDT. They sprayed much larger amounts than were needed to control mosquitoes. Many of us ran toward the trucks—as if they were ice cream trucks—because we were so happy to have mosquitoes repelled. Tons of DDT were sprayed on food and people. Despite this overuse, there is no evidence that the DDT caused any injury to humans.

Nevertheless, the Carson-fueled hysteria led to DDT's suppression in Africa. American bureaucrats decreed that foreign aid could not be used to finance DDT. Instead, American foreign aid paid for much less effective antimalaria remedies, like mosquito nets, which people are supposed to install over their beds. Of course, many Africans don't have beds. And nets develop holes.

Tens of millions of people died because of the DDT ban. Some scientists call it mass murder. But they could not move the rich environmental dogmatists—who reflexively condemned all kinds of chemicals.

DDT is the best antimosquito, antimalaria pesticide known. A tiny amount of it sprayed on the walls of a hut keeps the malarial mosquito at bay for as long as six months. But thanks to a scientifically ignorant writer, the worldwide environmental movement, and politically correct bureaucrats in the United States and at the United Nations, the use of this benign chemical was discouraged, and killer mosquitoes spread death.

I don't expect apologies from the people who permitted this to happen. But I am thankful that finally, science overwhelmed the antipesticide hysterics. The World Health Organization now calls DDT the "most effective" pesticide for indoor use and supports indoor spraying of DDT and other insecticides.

Some environmental groups have finally changed their anti-DDT tune, including Greenpeace, the Environmental Defense Fund, and the Sierra Club. Greenpeace spokesman Rick Hind told the *New York Times*, "If there's nothing else and it's going to save lives, we're all for it. Nobody's dogmatic about it."

Glad they're reasonable now, but they sure *were* dogmatic. How many other unthinking green crusades cost lives—and billions of dollars—because of our vague intuition that nature is good and chemicals are bad?

WHAT INTUITION TEMPTS US TO BELIEVE:

"Going green" is smart.

WHAT REALITY TAUGHT ME:

Green energy is a scam.

Junk-science debunker Steven Milloy of the Competitive Enterprise Institute wonders what the environmentalists' reluctance to change their position on DDT says about the superficiality—the faddishness—of environmental thinking, even among brainy elites. "There are no new facts on DDT—all the relevant science about DDT safety has been available since the 1960s," Milloy says. The same people who spread DDT hysteria back then now push the global warming scare. "If they and others could be so wrong about DDT, why should we trust them now?" Good question.

Don't trust the media, either. As energy journalist Robert Bryce, author of *Power Hungry: The Myths of "Green" Energy and the Real Fuels of the Future*, points out, the media have been predicting the age of the electric car for nearly a century.

The *Washington Post*: "Prices on electric cars will continue to drop until they're within reach of the average family." That was in 1915.

The *New York Times*: "Electric is the car of tomorrow." That was in 1959.

In 1979, the *Washington Post*: "GM has an electric car breakthrough in batteries . . . makes them commercially practical."

Thirty-three years later, electric cars still are not commercially practical. We do have cars like the Chevy Volt. But such boondoggles exist only because of fat government favors, uh, I mean subsidies. Wait, no, silly me. "Investments" is the euphemism du jour. And a fairly lousy "investment" so far. Government Motors claimed a sales target of 10,000 cars for 2011, but as I write they have sold fewer than 4,000. GM sells more Suburbans in a single month than they've sold electric cars all year. Even obscure cars like the Buick Lucerne outsell the Volt.

I don't suggest that the environmentalists are crazy or even very different from me. All of us enjoy the idyllic thought of quiet, nonpolluting transportation. I've donated to conservation efforts. I often ride a bike to work. I instinctively want government to pass laws that encourage others to "go green"—ride bikes, use less energy, shrink our carbon footprint.

But reality has taught me that so much "going green" is just bunk, combined with wishful thinking.

Oil billionaire T. Boone Pickens bought TV ads saying: "I have a plan! We can unleash wind power." The Pickens website carried moving videos showing how many jobs government-subsidized windmills created in Sweetwater, Texas. I'm sure windmills have been great for Sweetwater, but that looks only at what's seen. What's *unseen* are all the people who are hurt because they were taxed to pay for the high cost of building and operating Sweetwater's wind-mills. It's the broken window fallacy at work again.

Politicians say, "America needs a national energy policy!" Bunk. We have one. It's called the free market. If and when clean energy is practical, investors will rush to fund it. For now, oil and natural gas get a much bigger return for far less effort.

Some people think that windmills can be made more efficient by creating flexible blades that employ subtleties of quantum mechanics to hit air molecules just right. Then they might reap currently impossible energy returns. I'll be delighted if that works—and if it does, taxpayers won't need to subsidize it. There will be no shortage of investors eager to put money into superwindmills.

How about solar power? Architects like the idea of solar panels, but they'll tell you that they aren't yet good for much.

I put solar panels on the roof of my house. When the sun is strong, I can take long hot showers without cost or guilt. At least I think I can. The builder tells me that it works, but I have no way of knowing whether it's the sun or the supplemental propane that heats my water.

And that's all my solar panels do: heat water. I could have in-stalled panels for electricity, but my builder said they would never pay for themselves. And the only reason my solar hot water will "pay for itself" is the "green" subsidies and tax credits that politicians thrust on me. Assuming my accountant can figure them out. And assuming he doesn't charge me *more* for figuring them out than the cost of installing and repairing the panels. But I *think* my solar pan-els will pay for themselves. So, thanks! I'm glad that you pay for my showers. It just doesn't seem like a good deal for *you*.

Obama giving out your money to solar panel makers like Solyndra wasn't a good deal for you, either. Everyone likes the idea of solar, but it's not yet efficient enough to be good for much.

Biofuels like ethanol are an even worse "green" gimmick. They have had the tragic effect of taking millions of acres of land that might have been used to produce food and devoting them instead to inefficient, tax-subsidized energy production. The unintended consequences: increased food prices and misery in the developing world. It's another example of warmhearted greens undermining one of their pet causes by unthinkingly pushing another.

Alternative Energy Sources That Survive Only Because We Subsidize Them

- Wind
- Solar
- Biofuels (like ethanol)
- Synfuels (liquid by-products of coal, gas, shale, and biofuels)
- Cold fusion research
- Geothermal

Conventional Energy Sources That Greens Want Us to Stop Using

- Wood
- Dams
- Nuclear
- Coal
- Oil
- Natural gas

WHAT INTUITION TEMPTS US TO BELIEVE:

The right laws will make America "energy independent."

WHAT REALITY TAUGHT ME:

You'd have to change the laws of physics first.

Presidents Nixon, Carter, Reagan, Bush, Clinton, Bush, and Obama all promised that if we'd elect them, they would reduce America's oil imports. None did.

It's not like they didn't try. They worked constantly, they said, to develop alternative fuels. Unfortunately, when politicians say "work constantly" what that means is that they constantly spend more of your money. Why haven't the billions of your dollars that they've "invested" yielded results?

"It's simply not possible," says Robert Bryce.

An energy reporter, Bryce used to be a left-liberal, but then, he says, "I educated myself about math and physics. I'm a liberal who was mugged by the laws of thermodynamics." I told Bryce that I thought of myself as somewhat "green" because I ride my bike to work. Bryce (kindly) let the wind out of my sails. "Let's assume you saved a gallon (a generous assumption) of oil in your commute . . . by biking to work, you save the equivalent of one drop in ten gasoline tanker trucks."

How about wind power? The media rave about how much power Denmark gets from wind. *New York Times* columnist Thomas Friedman says, "If only we could be as energy smart as Denmark."

"Friedman doesn't fundamentally understand what he's talking about," Bryce said. Denmark uses eight times more coal and twenty-five times more oil than wind.

In America, even with all the subsidies, "renewable" energy today barely makes a dent on our energy needs.

But suppose we built *more* windmills? Bryce says that to get significant amounts of energy, we would have to practically smother America in windmills. To match the output of one nuclear power plant with wind turbines "would require an area the size of Rhode Island. This is energy sprawl." To grow enough corn to produce the same amount of energy with ethanol would take twenty-four Rhode Islands. And to make solar a viable replacement for oil, we'd have to blanket huge portions of the earth with solar panels.

"The problem is very simple," Bryce said. "It's not political will. It's simple physics. Gasoline has eighty times the energy density of the best lithium ion batteries. There's no conspiracy here of big oil or big auto." Another silly documentary, *Who Killed the Electric Car?*, implied that there was. But Bryce retorts, "It's a conspiracy of physics."

Even the "energy independence" argument is silly. We do buy oil from some nasty people: dictators in Venezuela and the Middle East. But *inter*dependence is just fine.

Our biggest foreign oil suppliers are Canada and Mexico. They don't threaten us. Venezuela and Iran might, but they need oil money. If they cut us off they would hurt themselves. And we'd get their oil anyway. All the world's oil ends up in the same bathtub. The dictator sells to someone who sells to someone who sells to us. Chasing energy "independence" is pointless. Free trade is better. It makes everyone richer and more secure.

WHAT INTUITION TEMPTS US TO BELIEVE:
"Green jobs" are futuristic, so they are both an
ecological and economic advantage.

WHAT REALITY TAUGHT ME:
There are trade-offs in life, and if the market doesn't
drive your plan, the advantage is imaginary.

The human brain is torn between simple intuition and the more complex hard work of figuring out the unintended consequences of any policy. Who doesn't like thinking about trees and greenery and happy animals? Who doesn't want to see steps taken to protect those things, all else being equal? But all else is not equal. There are costs to environmental benefits. Civilization doesn't work when central planners treat each tree as if its value is infinite.

Politicians specialize in convincing you that, with their help, you can have your cake and eat it, too. The idea of a new "green economy" that is both clean and rich with jobs became popular under Bill Clinton's administration, thanks in large part to a compliant media and Vice President Al Gore. But if going green is good for business, government wouldn't have to force it on business with regulations, taxes, and subsidies.

Anyone who understands economics knew that President Obama's $2.3 billion green jobs initiative was snake oil. Obama boasted that his plan would "help close the clean-energy gap between America and other nations." But other nations have moved in the opposite direction. The American Enterprise Institute's Kenneth P. Green says that "countries are cutting these programs because they realize they aren't sustainable and they are obscenely expensive." After Spain spent billions on a green jobs program, economists at La Universidad Rey Juan Carlos found that each "green" job cost more than $750,000.

President Obama claims that if we "invest" more, "the transition to clean energy has the potential to create millions of jobs—but only if we accelerate that transition." What could make more sense? A little push from the smart politicians and—voilà!—we can have an abundance of new jobs and a cleaner, sustainable environment. It's the ultimate twofer. Except it's an illusion, because governments do not "create" jobs. "All the government can do is subsidize some industries while jacking up costs for others," writes Green. "It is destroying jobs in the conventional energy sector—and most likely in other industrial sectors—through taxes and subsidies to new green companies that will use taxpayer dollars to undercut the competition. The subsidized jobs 'created' are, by definition, less efficient uses of capital than market-created jobs."

This is good, solid economic thinking. Many years ago, Henry Hazlitt wrote in his bestseller *Economics in One Lesson*, "The art of economics consists in looking not merely at the immediate but at the longer effects of any act or policy; it consists in tracing the consequences of that policy not merely for one group but for all groups."

In judging Obama's green jobs plan, or any government initiative, you can't look just at the credit side of the ledger. Government is unable to give without first taking away. Inevitably, more is taken away because the government substitutes force for free exchange. Instead of a process driven by consumers weighing their preferences, we get one imposed by politicians' grand social designs, what Hayek called "the fatal conceit." The green schemes haven't created many jobs, but they have succeeded in making energy cost more.

Of course, some who push "green jobs" *want* the price of energy to rise. Then we might live in smaller homes, drive less, and burn fewer fossil fuels. But if the environmental lobby wants Americans to be poorer, it ought to come clean about that.

Once you decide nature is inherently harmonious—not to mention healthy, moral, and beautiful—the reasons to restrict human activity are endless. Every time we move or breathe, we alter the environment in some way. Some environmentalists won't be satisfied until our carbon footprint is reduced to zero, no animal is inconvenienced, not one more inch of the earth's surface is disturbed.

Of course, that would require abolishing civilization, but if humanity's impact on nature is an evil, abolishing us wouldn't be so bad. The group Earth First! used to have the slogan "Back to the Pleistocene!" Many greens—not to mention their friends among animal rights activists—think that agriculture was a big mistake and things started going downhill about ten thousand years ago.

Most of us don't think civilization is evil—we work hard to keep it going and make it better. But we worry so much about what environmentalists say that we passively submit to green demands. Most of us don't have the time to do complicated calculations about the economic trade-offs. It's easier to just recycle something, buy a Prius, and donate to the Environmental Defense Fund.

WHAT INTUITION TEMPTS US TO BELIEVE:

To save the planet, recycle and go "green."

WHAT REALITY TAUGHT ME:

The planet won't notice.

Today, people put up with amazing intrusions in the name of environmentalism. There are a million petty regulations mandating surtaxes on gas, separation of garbage into multiple recycling bins, special lightbulbs, taxes on plastic bags, and so on.

Yet these things are of so little ecological consequence that the earth will never notice. Many are done to make people who care about such things feel good.

Environmentalists are so desperate to "do something" to save the earth that they look for rituals that make them feel cleansed. People recycle obsessively, buy carbon "offsets," and buy products with seals that label them "green." This has gotten so ridiculous that even environmentalists object. Heather Rogers, despite working for a progressive think tank, wrote a book called *Green Gone Wrong*.

Rogers scoffs at Al Gore's claim that by buying carbon offsets, he cancels emissions he creates flying around the world giving lectures on global warming. "Carbon offsets can't do that," she says. "A tree-planting project takes ten, twenty, 100 years . . . Or a 'carbon neutral' power plant. Does the power plant get built? . . . [I went to] a carbon neutral power plant, and what's happening there is . . . trees are being cut down in order to fuel that plant!" The tree-burning power plant is nonetheless considered a carbon offset.

Rogers believes in organic farming but sees scams. "I went to South America and researched a large-scale organic farm there. They're deforesting in order to expand their organic cropland. You know, again, this is not what people have in mind when they see the seal on the products that they buy."

Once you start thinking about environmental issues in terms of costs as well as benefits, you think differently about the threat of global warming. So many people say, "It couldn't hurt to err on the safe side." But the cost of that error is enormous. In 2008, Al Gore said he hoped that America would produce "100 percent of our electricity from renewable energy and truly clean carbon-free sources within ten years." But the UN climate action plan he supports would reduce human energy use by about a quarter. That's not something you do by weather-stripping houses and changing lightbulbs. Think about it: energy consumption means, essentially, *everything* humans do. If something unintended suddenly reduced energy production by a quarter, we'd consider it one of the greatest disasters of all times.

Americans narcissistically imagine that coercing our neighbors into buying a Prius or using compact fluorescent lightbulbs will materially change carbon output, but it won't. Americans are the biggest energy consumers now, but as billions of once desperately poor people in China and India acquire wealth, they too want cars and air-conditioning. Soon they will consume amounts of energy comparable to what we do (and that's great). The shape of our lightbulbs is a pittance in comparison.

WHAT INTUITION TEMPTS US TO BELIEVE:
We must address global warming now!

WHAT REALITY TAUGHT ME:
Devote resources where you get the most bang for the buck.

Bjorn Lomborg is a left-wing statistics professor who started out very green—but now calls himself "the skeptical environmentalist" because he thinks greens have been bad at prioritizing environmental proposals.

Lomborg believes that global warming is a threat. So do I, but I don't know that it's a big threat.

Humans do churn out increasing amounts of greenhouse gases. These gases probably warm the earth, although it's not clear by how much, or whether a warmer planet might also bring positive benefits.

We need to ask ourselves whether the cost of trying to do something about greenhouse gases now is worth the benefits—especially when we could spend the money on so many other things. On my show, Lomborg said what politicians want to do now "is incredibly costly and yet will do virtually nothing against global warming, even one hundred years from now. That's not smart. That's simply wasting money. It's something that we do to make ourselves feel good, but they won't actually solve the problem."

Lomborg asked eight top economists, including five Nobel Prize winners, to answer the question: What are the best ways to advance global welfare? After working on this for two years, the economists came up with thirty ways to improve the world. Addressing global warming was near the bottom of the list.

At the top, with biggest payoff for the smallest effort, were simple things like micronutrient supplements for the world's poor children. Less exciting than global warming—with no corporate villains to hate—but a more immediate problem with a more obvious solution.

"Half the world's population lack not just food but micronutrients. Essentially a vitamin pill," Lomborg says. "We could make half the world smarter and stronger physically by spending a couple hundred million dollars, not billion, *million* dollars every year. There's great potential to do an enormous amount of good at very low cost. Yet we don't do it because it's not sexy."

I'm particularly fond of item #2 on the economists' list—right below #1 (micronutrient supplementation) and right above #3 and #4 (micronutrient fortification and childhood immunizations). Number 2 is free trade, key to spurring innovation and creating wealth. Contrary to the rural-idyllic dream of going back to living like hunter-gatherers—or like hippies on an organic farm—wealth makes it ever easier to cope with (and go on worrying about) all environmental problems.

13

BUDGET INSANITY

They spend us into oblivion, and we are complicit. We're like alcoholics who know we have a problem, know we've got to do something about it, but just can't stop from getting one last fix. It's always "one more infrastructure bill" or "this jobs plan" will jump-start the economy, and then we'll kick our spending addiction once and for all.

But we don't stop spending.

Here's a graph of America's spending from the Congressional Budget Office:

This includes everything: war, Medicare, Social Security, discretionary spending—the whole enchilada, adjusted for inflation. As the graph shows, for most of the history of America, government was—by today's standards—tiny. Government grew during World Wars I and II but then shrank again.

Then came Lyndon Johnson's Great Society and the promise that government would cure poverty. Spending has gone straight up ever since. It will grow worse when my peers and I retire and make Social Security and Medicare explode. This is not sustainable.

So what should we do?

WHAT INTUITION TEMPTS US TO BELIEVE:

Tax the rich!

WHAT REALITY TAUGHT ME:

The rich don't have enough. Really.

Progressives say, if you're so worried about the deficit, raise taxes! There do seem to be lots of rich people around, squandering money. On my show, David Callahan of the group Demos put it this way: "Wealthy Americans who have done so well in the past decade should help get us out."

But it's a fantasy to imagine that raising taxes on the rich will solve our deficit problem. If the IRS grabbed 100 percent of income over $1 million, the take would be just $616 billion. That's only a third of this year's deficit. Our national debt would continue to explode.

It's the spending, stupid.

Also, even if you could balance the budget by taxing the rich, it wouldn't be right. Progressives say it's wrong for the rich to be "given" more money. The *New York Times* ran a cartoon that showed Uncle Sam handing money to a fat cat. But that has it backward. Money earned belongs to those who earn it, not to government. Lower taxes are not a handout.

Progressives want to take more money from some—by force—and spend much of it on programs that have repeatedly failed. It sounds less noble when plainly stated.

That's the moral side of the matter. There's a practical side, too. Taxes discourage wealth creation.

WHAT INTUITION TEMPTS US TO BELIEVE:
Higher tax rates bring in more money.

WHAT REALITY TAUGHT ME:
Higher taxes kill the golden geese.

Even if you think government will spend tax money more usefully than money left in private hands, there is a limit to how much government can tax before people just hide their money or flee. My $616 billion assumption above is absurd. Rich people wouldn't work if government took all their money.

Progressives say they just want "some" of it. They claim a small increase in tax rates won't stop producers from producing. But some would stop. When the top marginal rate was 90 percent, actor Ronald Reagan worked just half the year. As soon as he made enough money such that every additional dollar was taxed at 90 percent, he just stopped working and went off to ride horses. Reagan later said that woke him up to the damage that high taxes impose.

Maryland created a special "tax on the rich" that legislators said would bring in $106 million. Instead, the state *lost* $257 million. "It reminds me of Charlie Brown," former Maryland governor Robert Ehrlich told me. "Charlie Brown was always surprised when Lucy pulled the football away. They're always surprised in Washington and state capitols when the dollars never come in." Some of Maryland's rich just left the state. "They're out of here. These people aren't stupid."

When New York state hiked its income tax on millionaires, billionaire Tom Golisano moved to Florida, which has no personal income tax. "[M]y personal income tax last year would've been $13,800 a day," he said. "Would you like to write a check for $13,800 a day to a state government, as opposed to moving to another state?"

Even Donald Trump, who gets so much wrong, gets this one right. He says of rich people, "They're international people. Whether they live here or live in a place like Switzerland doesn't really matter to them."

I thought that economist Art Laffer had permanently debunked the tax-the-rich fantasy years ago, when at a lunch with Don Rumsfeld and Dick Cheney, he drew a curve on a napkin that charted the way tax revenues stop rising when tax rates get too high: "People don't work to pay taxes," he said. "They'll change where they earn their income, how they earn their income, when they receive the income. They'll change all of those things to minimize taxes."

We can see that looking at tax receipts over time. Before 1963, when Reagan was riding his horse, every single dollar after $400,000 (in today's dollars) was taxed at more than 90 percent. Revenues the government got from that equaled about 18 percent of gross domestic product. Then the top rate was lowered to 70 percent, then to 50 percent, and then to as low as 30 percent, before it was raised back to 40 percent in the 1990s. Despite those sharp changes, the chart below shows that tax revenue seldom exceeded 20 percent or fell below 17 percent of GDP.

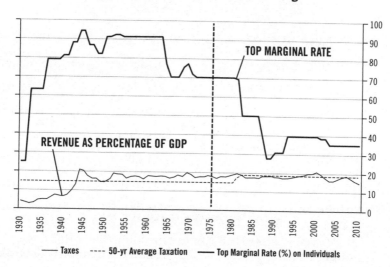

Reality Isn't Negotiable: *The Government Can't Raise More than 19% in Taxes for Long*

TOP MARGINAL RATE

REVENUE AS PERCENTAGE OF GDP

—— Taxes   ---- 50-yr Average Taxation   —— Top Marginal Rate (%) on Individuals

As Laffer says, people adjust their activities to the tax burden.

Worse, higher taxes give rich people and politicians more reasons to collude. The rich make contributions to political campaigns, and politicians pay the rich back by giving them tax loopholes.

The loopholes complicate the tax code and create work for tax specialists like my accountant Bob. I pay Bob because I can't begin to figure out my taxes. I don't *want* to give money to Bob. But our loophole-ridden tax system is now so complex that today most Americans pay someone like Bob.

That's a big loss to America. All that money and creative energy we spend trying to figure out taxes might have gone to build homes, make music, cure cancer, or . . . who knows what.

Taxes were once simple. Just over a century ago, government funded itself with tariffs and excise taxes. It didn't violate our privacy by asking us how much we made or how many dependents we have. But in 1913, politicians wanted more loot, so they created an income tax. At first, they took just 1 percent of rich people's incomes. Anyone who made less than $400,000 (in today's dollars) paid no income tax.

What began in effect as a tax on the rich is now a tax on the middle class.

And progressives want more.

WHAT INTUITION TEMPTS US TO BELIEVE:
The budget is complicated, so we should leave it to the experts.

WHAT REALITY TAUGHT ME:
If it's so complicated, we should stop doing things this way.

Our brains don't cope well with huge numbers. Anthropologists say we can keep track of about a hundred friends. Most prehistoric communities were probably around that size.

As individuals, we're hard-pressed to keep track of our own finances. Yet we trust strangers—in state capitals and in Washington, D.C.—to spend almost half our money. I suspect it's not really a contradiction. Perhaps because many people know that they can barely balance their own checkbooks, they are more eager to pass responsibility on to others. It's natural to think about how big and complicated the budget is and conclude: I can't even wrap my head around it, so I have no choice but to leave it to the "best and brightest." Government does such big things (I have a hard time imagining building a sewage treatment system myself), so it must have experts who know how to figure these things out. Let them worry about it.

But here's the secret: government isn't up to the task, either. It's a fatal conceit to think that any group of people can possibly command the sort of information necessary to "run" an economy. Even if they had good incentives, no group of experts could possibly efficiently manage a $4 trillion operation with 4 million employees.

Worse, the people who run the government face bad incentives. After all, they promote their own careers by giving your money to their friends. It's foolish to hope the politicians will be brilliant and moral and do the right thing—especially when they have countless other things to worry about, like looking important and getting reelected.

Once you drop the assumption that the government "experts" are selfless, altruistic supermen (unlike us greedy scum in the private sector) and start thinking of politicians and bureaucrats as selfish interest groups in their own right, their behavior becomes easier to explain, as do chronic government problems like waste, bribery, corruption, regional favoritism, bailouts for the politically connected, and so on.

WHAT INTUITION TEMPTS US TO BELIEVE:
Soon politicians will wise up and come up with a
reasonable budget so America won't go broke.

WHAT REALITY TAUGHT ME:
The government's budget has little to do with bookkeeping,
cost-benefit analysis, reality, or even sanity.

In early 2011, with the newly Republican House of Representatives drunk on Tea Party fervor and the federal government facing a $14 trillion debt, a fierce-seeming battle was fought in Congress. The fight culminated in a deal that we were told included "the biggest budget cuts in history!" Democrats and their media cheerleaders complained that basic services were being gutted. Republicans congratulated themselves for their frugality. But this fuss turned out to be about cuts that amounted only to roughly 1 percent of the federal budget. Apparently, even when faced with fiscal ruin, 1 percent is the most anyone can bear to shrink government. Worse, when the details of the plan came out, what was touted as $30 billion in cuts ended up being only $30 *million*—and might even lead to a slight *increase* in spending.

Given that government does *so* much that is harmful, it's amazing how hard it is to get anyone to agree on even tiny cuts. Even the threat of going bankrupt can't scare politicians into reining government in.

• • •

Politicians promise to balance the budget by using "common sense." They will get rid of what is wasteful, redundant, or unnecessary. There is, in fact, plenty that is wasteful and unnecessary, but politicians have promised to cut that for years. It never happens. It's just in the nature of the beast. Centrally planned monopolies always do things that are wasteful, redundant, and unnecessary.

Americans tell pollsters that they want cuts in foreign aid. But foreign aid makes up less than 1 percent of our spending. People get mad at me for wanting to cut the U.S Education Department, and subsidies for Amtrak, NPR, and ethanol. But even if we did all that, it would barely delay our coming bankruptcy.

Federal spending is on automatic pilot to grow and bankrupt us largely because of entitlements: Social Security and Medicare. Why the heck do they call them "entitlements"? Are we entitled to the money? We think we are. Congress says we are. But the programs are totally unsustainable.

And it's our fault.

When FDR started Social Security, most people didn't even live to age 65, let alone to today's average of 78. We also want all the cool new stuff that modern medicine invents: anticholesterol drugs, hip replacements, better diagnostic tests. And my peers and I don't want to pay for most of it, because we've been trained by government to expect that once we're old, we're entitled to these things for free, or nearly free. We paid into Social Security and Medicare for our entire working lives and damn it, we're entitled to get our money back!

Few of us realize, though, that most of us get back up to *three times* what we paid in, and that our selfish sense of entitlement will ruin American much faster than foreign aid, subsidies for NPR, or foreign wars ever will.

• • •

For all the things President George W. Bush got wrong, he made an impressive effort to tell Americans why it would be good to partially privatize Social Security. He toured the country and spoke on the topic in nearly every state (if only he were a better speaker). But most Republicans didn't back him, even though they controlled both houses of Congress. They were afraid that they'd lose elderly votes. Wimping out on Social Security reform didn't help them much. They lost both houses of Congress in 2006 anyway.

Even some Tea Party activists, to the delight of their left-wing critics, are confused when it comes to Medicare. They say they object to the growth of government, but opinion polls suggested that much of the "town hall" fervor directed against the Democrats in 2009 and 2010 was fueled by fear of Medicare *cuts*, not fear of America going broke *because* of Medicare.

Politicians have promised Social Security and Medicare recipients an impossible $46 *trillion* more than will exist. And that doesn't include the other big programs: Medicaid, the hungry military-industrial complex discussed in chapter 11, corporate welfare like farm subsidies, and paying interest on our debt.

We're basically toast.

WHAT INTUITION TEMPTS US TO BELIEVE:
Moderation and bipartisanship would help
politicians "make the tough decisions."

WHAT REALITY TAUGHT ME:
People who recommend tough decisions are called "radicals."

Republican senator Tom Coburn of Oklahoma has stoked outrage by listing ridiculous, wasteful projects—in much the same way the late senator William Proxmire of Wisconsin used to give out a "Golden Fleece Award." Coburn ridicules items like the half-million dollars spent by the U.S. Forest Service to repair windows on a visitor center that's been closed since 2007, $2 million spent studying how ants talk, and $700,000 for interactive dance-instruction software.

I have disagreements with Coburn because he is a social conservative—he wants to ban things like drugs and sex work. But I have to love him because he goes after his colleagues' sacred cows.

His staffers find dubious spending even at noble-sounding institutions like the National Science Foundation. It spent tax money on a laundry-folding robot. I might enjoy a laundry-folding robot, but since America is on the road to bankruptcy, we robot fans should pay for this stuff ourselves.

Of course, even if Coburn killed all the projects on his "wasteful" list, that would barely touch our debt. That's why it's great that House budget chairman Paul Ryan surprised Washington with a serious proposal. His "Roadmap to Prosperity" had the head-in-the-sand crowd horrified. A *Washington Post* columnist called his plan "radical . . . irresponsible . . . extreme."

Ryan's Roadmap offers some good things: less spending than President Obama wants, repeal of ObamaCare, an end to corporate welfare, a path to a balanced budget. It would make the social safety net sustainable.

Ryan's move even inspired President Obama to say he'd come out with his own deficit plan, although his plan turned out to be less of a plan and more of a list of talking points. No specific cuts, just more talk of "goals." And of course he would "raise revenues." That's another euphemism for more taxes. With all that doublespeak, no wonder cameras caught Vice President Biden sleeping during Obama's speech.

The left characterized the Ryan plan as a coldhearted attempt to kill senior citizens—one ad depicted Ryan pushing an old woman off a cliff. But Ryan isn't an anarchist, or even a libertarian. All Ryan suggested was $6.2 trillion in cuts over the next ten years—not, sadly, cuts from what government spends today, but from what President Obama wanted to spend. Spending over the next decade would actually increase by about a trillion dollars under Ryan's plan.

The Republican Study Committee proposed bigger cuts—ones that would actually end the deficit in eight years. Ryan's plan wouldn't balance the budget for, maybe, fifty years. The RSC plan raises the Social Security retirement age to sixty-seven and sells 5 percent of government lands. Good ideas. It would also reduce the federal workforce by 15 percent (Ryan's figure is 10 percent). That's a start. But they talk about reducing federal employment by "attrition." That's cowardly. They should fire the worst workers, the way private sector managers do.

Also, neither Ryan nor the RSC really addresses "defense." There's nothing in either plan that asks what the military's mission should be, or even what the role of government should be. Ryan and the RSC don't kill off any departments. They just cut most things a little—assuming that almost everything government does, it *should* do. That's not management. When Ronald Reagan ran for president, he said he would close the education and energy departments. He didn't, and they've only grown. Now, even Republicans rarely propose closing them. The monster in Washington just grows.

Today, the federal government spends 25 percent of gross domestic product. Ryan would get it down to 20 percent. That's what

Mitt Romney's promising now. But when Bill Clinton left office, the feds spent 18 percent. Would it really be so painful to go back to 1990s levels of spending?

Senator Rand Paul of Kentucky offered a better plan. He'd balance the budget in five years by cutting $4 trillion—or 20 percent—off the Congressional Budget Office's baseline.

"Congressman Ryan . . . is trying to do the right thing, but his plan will add eight trillion dollars to the debt," Paul told me. "We need to do something much more dramatic, or I think we're in for a world of hurt."

He'd get rid of whole departments, like Education, Energy, Housing and Urban Development, and Commerce. He'd also reduce military spending.

"The inconvenient truth for conservatives is you cannot balance the budget if you eliminate [only] nonmilitary spending. . . . I do believe in a strong national defense . . . but not all military spending is sacred and not all military spending is well spent."

His father, presidential candidate Ron Paul, proposed similar cuts. During a CNN debate, he said he'd cut a trillion dollars "right now." He was largely ignored.

WHAT INTUITION TEMPTS US TO BELIEVE:

Getting experts together to make cuts might do the trick.

WHAT REALITY TAUGHT ME:

Even the hypothetical plans of most experts are pretty wimpy.

The so-called congressional Super Committee failed to agree on budget cuts. If they can't get the job done, can anyone?

Pete Peterson made $2.8 billion doing investment deals. Then he retired and started spending his money to warn people about the deficit.

Last year his foundation gave $1.2 million to six think tanks to write budget proposals. The money went to two conservative groups, the American Enterprise Institute and the Heritage Foundation; three liberal ones, the Center for American Progress, Economic Policy Institute, and Roosevelt Institute Campus Network; and the Bipartisan Policy Center. On my show, representatives from most of these think tanks summarized their proposals, and I had the audience pick its favorite. We called it a "Battle of the Budgets." The winner would get one of the Emmys I'd won during my days as a consumer reporter.

Some of the liberal budget plans were ridiculous. They *increased* spending. The Heritage plan was the only one that actually balanced the budget: Heritage did that by raising the eligibility age for Social Security and Medicare to sixty-eight and phasing out benefits for people making over $110,000 a year.

My fiscally conservative studio audience voted for that plan. Stuart Butler, who coauthored the Heritage budget, actually seemed happy to take home the Emmy statue. I can't imagine why. (Emmys are silly awards that the liberal media give to people who confirm their anticapitalist attitudes. I won nineteen Emmys before I moved to Fox. I don't win them anymore.) The day after Butler's victory, the chairman of the pompously titled National Academy of Television Arts & Sciences, the group that awards Emmys, called my office to inform me that the Emmys are not my property. They are "property of the Academy." I must not give any away.

This just makes me more eager to give my Emmys away. Want one? Make me an offer.

The Heritage budget may have been the wisest choice among the six, but as a libertarian, I was underwhelmed by all the proposals. Our government spends almost $4 trillion a year—we need to eliminate entire departments. Even Heritage didn't do that. Both Heritage and AEI left military spending alone. None of these think tanks made the tougher decisions.

So I will.

Central planners shriek that without big government, planes will crash, trains, parks, and Big Bird will disappear. None of it is true.

Here are my cuts. For starters:

- *Eliminate the Small Business Administration.*
- *Repeal the Davis-Bacon rules*, under which the government must pay fat union-set wages to workers on federal construction projects.
- *Eliminate foreign aid.*

I hear the complaints already: All foreign aid? That would increase suffering! The Small Business Administration? Some companies would never begin! End Davis-Bacon? Workers will suffer! The arguments are specious, but people believe them, and the lobbying against such cuts would be ferocious. But they are absolutely necessary if we hope to have a future where the truly needy are helped. So far, I've saved $37.6 billion.

Uh-oh. Cutting $37 billion barely touches the deficit. We must cut much more. Let's eliminate whole departments:

- *Department of Education.* Kill it and we'd save $106.9 billion. (I rely here on the Cato Institute's budget numbers—available at DownsizingGovernment.org.) We don't need a *federal* education department. Spending $106.9 billion did nothing to improve learning. Education is a state responsibility.

- *Department of Housing and Urban Development:* $60.8 billion more. They build horrible housing projects and then blow them up.
- *Who needs the Energy Department?* If wind or solar power is practical, private investors will rush to invest. The joy of private investment is that if they waste billions on boondoggles like Solyndra, they waste only their own money, not yours. Private dollars, not the whims of political appointees, should determine energy investments.

We're up to $293.3 billion in cuts. A good start, but our deficit, as a write, is $1.4 trillion. We must go further.

- *Agriculture subsidies cost us $33 billion a year.* Get rid of them. They raise food prices and distort the economy.
- *End the war on drugs.* It doesn't stop drug abuse, and it turns out to be a subsidy for thugs (chapter 10). Harvard economist Jeffrey Miron estimates that the war costs the government $41 billion, and that's only a fraction of the war's total cost to society.
- Let's eliminate NASA, Fannie and Freddie, and the departments Commerce, Interior, and Labor (except for twenty-six weeks of unemployment benefits).
- Privatize the Army Corps of Engineers, the TSA, and the U.S. Postal Service. Lease the coastal plain of the Arctic National Wildlife Refuge. Eliminate federal flood insurance, the Corporation for National and Community Service, the Federal

Communications Commission, the National Endowment for the Arts, and the National Endowment for the Humanities. But that's still not enough.

To get rid of the rest of the CBO's projected deficit, we must attack "untouchable" parts of the budget:

- *Social Security.* Cato's plan to raise the retirement age and index benefits to inflation would save $85.7 billion. Heritage says cutting benefits for the richest retirees would save another $170 billion. I'd like to save more by privatizing Social Security, but my progressive friends would scream, so for this calculation, I'll leave privatization out.
- *Medicare and Medicaid.* Did you know that the Department of Health and Human Services runs four hundred separate subsidy programs? It's crazy. Medicare and Medicaid are the biggest budget busters. I'll take the Cato Institute's suggested cuts. That saves $441 billion.
- *Defense.* We currently spend $721 billion on defense. That's about one-fifth of our budget. I want to support our troops, but we could do that *and* save money if the administration shrank the military's *mission* to its most important role: protecting us and our borders (chapter 11). I propose cutting defense spending to $243 billion. That's still twice what China, the country with the next most expensive military, spends.

That gets us to some $200 billion in surplus!

But we don't even need to cut that much.

We could *grow* our way out of debt if Congress simply froze spending at today's levels. That would balance the budget by 2017. If they limited spending growth to just 2 percent per year, they'd balance the budget by 2020.

But they won't do even that.

WHAT INTUITION TEMPTS US TO BELIEVE:

Politicians just need to "get serious" about the debt.

WHAT REALITY TAUGHT ME:

The incentives to ignore debt won't go away.

It's often been observed that Americans vote for politicians in their own districts who promise to spend more—to bring home the pork—but then vote for fiscally cautious-sounding presidential candidates who promise (however falsely) that they'll stop the crazy spending. This makes sense from a selfish perspective. Americans know that America can't sustain current levels of spending, but everyone wants his region (or cause) to get the biggest slice of the pie. The projects we're most familiar with influence our thinking.

You may think (correctly) that government spending billions on dozens of job training programs is wasted—but you vividly remember how hard your own county was hit by the economic downturn, so a grant for regions just like yours somehow isn't so crazy. You'll make *just one exception* to your overall desire for tight control of the budget. . . .

It doesn't mean you're a bad person. But neither does it mean we should embrace the hypocrisy. Remember, the real tragedy is that *every* dime spent by the government is likely (not certain, but likely) to be spent less efficiently than the private sector would spend it. That means a net loss for society every time the government spends anything. The last thing we should do is look for excuses for it to spend on pet projects.

But given that voters usually reward politicians who bring home the bacon, what possible mechanism could stop the process?

Some partial remedies include urging the populace to be more vigilant (most people would rather watch *American Idol*), urging the press to point out wasteful items (in most media, that happens only when the pork is silly enough to entertain), urging the government to take a newfound interest in efficiency (pretty much impossible), a line-item veto (not a bad idea, though presidents can also use it to strike out budget *cuts*), and just electing better politicians.

That final suggestion doesn't hurt, of course—that's the basis of democracy. It's a reason that so many voters gravitated toward Tea Party politicians who promise to shrink government. But even those politicians are not to be trusted once they are in office. Arch-libertarian Ayn Rand voted for Franklin Delano Roosevelt the first time he ran for president, because FDR supported repealing Prohibition (a good move that actually happened in the first year of his presidency) and because the Democratic platform at the time vowed to shrink the government by about a quarter! That part didn't happen.

One promising-sounding idea that both candidate Obama and Senator Coburn agreed upon before Obama became president was increased "transparency." We'd have "Google government," that is, a detailed, searchable online budget that in theory allows any citizen to log on and see exactly how every dime is spent. That's a good step, and I hope enterprising reporters use it to ferret out boondoggles— but the sad truth is, much of the budget is entitlements (which most politicians fear touching), and the rest makes for extremely boring reading. You won't find an item called Pilot Project for Oppressing

Common People While Spending Huge Amounts on Holiday Parties and New Office Furniture. You find references to road resurfacing projects—but in most cases, you won't have the slightest idea whether the amount allocated makes sense, nor how it's actually spent on the ground.

It's depressing writing this. We're going broke, most reform plans are insufficient, the few that are sufficient are derided as radical, and few politicians will say anything serious about entitlements.

But there is some good news—some role models. A few other democracies have actually managed to make cuts. They said, "Yes, we can!"—and meant it.

They may not be where you expect.

CONCLUSION

THERE OUGHT *NOT* TO BE A LAW

I am a libertarian in part because I see the false choice offered by both the political left and right: government control of the economy—or government control of our personal lives.

People on the far left and right think of themselves as freedom lovers. The left thinks government can eliminate inequality and help the poor. The right thinks government control can diminish self-destructive behavior and make Americans more virtuous. Instinct tells us that if "our side" just beats the "other side" once and for all, things will get better. I say we're best off if neither side attempts to advance its agenda via government.

Let both *argue* about things like drug use and poverty programs, but let no one put anyone else in jail, unless that other person steals or attacks someone. Let no one forcibly take more than a minimum amount of property from people to fund public goods like national defense and a limited safety net. When in doubt, leave it out—or rather, leave it to the market and other voluntary institutions.

But this is not how most people think. Most people see a world full of problems that can be solved by wisely applied laws. They assume it's just the laziness, stupidity, or indifference of politicians that prevents the problems from being addressed. But government is force, and government is inefficient. The inefficient use of force creates more problems than it solves.

I'd rather government *didn't* try to address most of life's problems.

People tend to believe that "government can!" How do I get them to see the countless things that government can't do—but free individuals can?

COLLAPSE AND CONSTITUTIONALISM

Even the collapse of the Soviet Union, caused by the appalling results of central planning, didn't shock the world into abandoning big government. Europe began talking about some sort of "market socialism." Politicians in the United States dreamed of a "third way" between capitalism and socialism, and of "managed capitalism"—where politicians often replace the invisible hand. You'd think the Cold War was a tie instead of a forfeit.

Bill Clinton responded by pushing HillaryCare, a big tax hike, and an economic stimulus package that reeked of industrial planning. When the public rejected his overreach and handed control of Congress to Newt Gingrich and the Republicans, Clinton seemed to get the message. He famously said, "The era of big government is over." My jaw dropped when I heard that. Now even a Democratic president recognizes the horrors of big government! Or if not, at least the public is now so angry about command and control that opportunistic politicians like Clinton feel they must show restraint! I didn't even know that either party recognized that we were in an "era of big government." Now they do, so it's over!

Boy, was I wrong.

Congress did pass welfare reform, and kept new spending initiatives relatively small, but my optimism was ludicrous, as I should have known from my vantage point in the mainstream media. At the time I was at ABC, where anchor Peter Jennings called that 1994 vote a "tantrum" by "two-year-olds." Most of my coworkers demanded bigger government. In journalism, emotion rules. My colleagues' intuition told them that next time, central planning would work.

The newly empowered Republicans believed that, too. Soon Newt Gingrich was talking about "preserving" Medicare and Social Security, subsidizing laptop computers for the poor, and doubling spending on the National Institutes of Health. He's still at it. During his presidential campaign, Newt defended ethanol subsidies and called for more spending on Alzheimer's research. No matter how big government gets, some Republicans are eager for *more*.

George W. Bush ran for president promising a "lean" government and no more attempts at nation building. Once elected, he decided America ought to build a "freedom society" in Iraq, create a new $50-billion-per-year prescription drug entitlement, and expand the already bloated Education Department by creating a largely useless bureaucracy called No Child Left Behind. Under Bush, Republicans *doubled* discretionary spending (the greatest increase since LBJ's Great Society), expanded the drug war, and hired ninety thousand new regulators.

Bush's increases in regulation didn't mollify the media's demand for still more. Instead, when the housing bubble collapsed, there was endless commentary about irresponsible "deregulation." It's just intuitive: Is there a problem? More regulation is the answer!

In 2008, the mainstream media announced that a new Messiah was at hand—a magic politician—one so wise and articulate that he would bring us together and solve America's problems. The earth would heal and the waters would stop rising. Just thinking about it sent chills up my leg. . . .

OBAMA

But within the first year of Obama's administration, something changed, just a little: unemployment stayed high despite spending big enough to bankrupt all our children. That, plus ObamaCare, fueled new anger—and the Tea Party.

One Tea Party solution to the problem of excessive government is the Constitution. This was exciting! People held up copies at rallies. I'd never seen that. Would people now reembrace the Constitution as a guide to government? The Constitution does explicitly state which functions the federal government is to have and strongly implied that it should have no others. Aside from courts, coinage, the mail, defense, and the conduct of foreign policy, there isn't much government to be found in the Constitution. If people embraced the Constitution, that would be great!

But I was fooled again. Maybe I was too optimistic because I now worked at Fox Business Network, where for the first time in my career I was surrounded by smart people who understood the harm done by big government. They got it! They debated constitutional limits! Listening to them and to the new freshmen in

Congress after the Tea Party–influenced 2010 elections, I let myself believe that a new era of limited government had dawned.

Wrong again.

Within months, the new "fiscally conservative" Republicans had voted to preserve farm subsidies, vowed to "protect" Medicare, and cringed when Congressman Ryan proposed his relatively timid deficit reduction plan.

Despite talk about the Constitution and Obama's overreach, the intuition-guided march toward more central planning and "free stuff from government" continues.

Perhaps, as the deficit worsens and interest rates rise, it will take riots—like those under way now in Greece—to wake people up to the fact that no, government can't.

The good news is there is still time to turn things around before life gets that bad. Other countries did it—including one nearby that might surprise you.

CANADA

As I write this, the United States has fallen to ninth place on the Economic Freedom list compiled by the Heritage Foundation and the *Wall Street Journal*. That means we fell behind Hong Kong, Singapore, Australia, New Zealand, Switzerland, Canada . . .

Wait, what? Canada? What's Canada doing atop a list of free countries? Canada is that socialist country with government health care!

But it turns out that Canada is less socialist these days.

Twenty years ago, Canada faced a debt crisis very similar to ours. Canada's debt to investors was 67 percent of GDP (America's today is 70 percent). Canada's finance minister said, "We are in debt up to our eyeballs. That can't be sustained."

The value of the Canadian dollar had fallen to just 72 American cents. The *Wall Street Journal* called it "the peso of the north." Moody's put Canada's debt on a credit watch. Sound familiar?

The problem, says economist David R. Henderson, a Canadian who now lives in the United States, was that Canada's government safety net was more like a hammock. "When I grew up in Canada, people who went on unemployment insurance were said to go in the 'pogey.' Some young people worked for eight weeks and then played hockey for the rest of the year."

No more. Now Canada's unemployment insurance is funded by an individual worker's contribution and pegged to workers' salaries instead of government subsidies. The rest of the Canadian welfare state was pared down. Canada cut federal spending from 17.5 percent of GDP to 11.3 percent.

This wasn't merely a cut in the growth of spending, that favorite trick of U.S. congressional committees. These were actual reductions in spending. "If a cabinet minister wanted a smaller cut in one program, he had to come up with a bigger cut in another," says Henderson.

All but one of Canada's twenty-two federal departments experienced real cuts: agriculture was cut 22 percent; fisheries, 27 percent; natural resources, almost 50 percent.

Canada did also raise taxes slightly, but spending was cut six times more. It happened quietly, without riots or protests from unions, probably because a liberal government imposed the cuts, and liberals didn't want to criticize their own. The result of the cuts was that Canada ran budget surpluses, and its debt gradually went down. Now Canada's debt is less than 30 percent of GDP, and the Canadian dollar is worth as much as the American dollar.

The supposedly "painful" cuts created more gain than pain. "The economy boomed," Henderson says. That shouldn't surprise anyone. "Think about what government does. Government wastes most of what it spends, and so just cutting government and having that money in the hands of people means it's going to be used more valuably."

Canada fired government workers, but unemployment didn't increase. It dropped from 12 percent to 6 percent. Today Canada's unemployment is still well below America's.

"We should learn from Canada's experience," Henderson says. "Government is so wasteful. There's so much to cut, without causing much real pain—in fact, *not* causing pain, but helping your economy grow, helping people become better off."

Henderson adds, "We need to move more quickly than the Canadians did. Unfortunately, we're moving more slowly."

Are we moving at all?

When Republicans won control of the House in 2010, Speaker John Boehner said he and his fellow Republicans wanted to make big cuts. When he was sworn in, he declared, "Our spending has caught up with us. . . . No longer can we kick the can down the road." But when NBC anchorman Brian Williams asked him to name a program "we could do without," he said, "I don't think I have one off the top of my head."

The Republican leader didn't yet know what he wanted to cut? I don't know which explanation is worse—not having a list or not having the courage to talk about it.

Eventually, Republicans said they'd start by cutting $100 billion. The media were aghast. Liberals wailed about "draconian" cuts. I thought: they live in an alternate universe. Congress planned to spend almost $4 trillion: $100 billion is just 2.5 percent of that. Firms in the private sector make bigger cuts all the time.

But governments almost never make such cuts. All that union protest and shrieking fuss in Wisconsin happened without Governor Scott Walker proposing to fire *anyone*.

We need to make real decisions about which workers pull their weight, and what our priorities are. Politicians will have to learn that there is no budget line labeled "waste." If our representatives plan to create a sustainable budget, they must ax entire programs.

I'm not confident they have it in them. They're politicians, after all. I'm reminded of one "tough conservative," former senator Spencer Abraham. He once sponsored a bill to abolish the Department of Energy. Good for him! He was right. The department should be abolished. Transfer its nuclear weapons responsibilities to the Defense Department and kill the corporate welfare it gives to politically favored solar panel makers. Senator Abraham saw the waste and wanted to end it. But then George W. Bush appointed him to head the department. Suddenly he changed his mind.

"Yeah, real quick," he told me on my show. "I changed it shortly after being asked to serve. It was very clear to me that we weren't ever going to abolish the department. There wasn't enough support for that, and the next best thing was to be in charge of it and try to change the way it operated so that at least the American taxpayers got their money's worth."

It would be nice if they got their money's worth—but I doubt that they did. On Abraham's watch, the department's budget increased by 20 percent. He funded a money-losing solar panel project that cost $147 million.

As the Who sang: "Meet the new boss, same as the old boss."

A BRIGHT SPOT IN THE UNITED STATES: PUERTO RICO

But not every boss is hopeless. You know about the budget-cutting efforts of New Jersey's Chris Christie, Wisconsin's Scott Walker, Florida's Rick Scott, Ohio's John Kasich, Michigan's Rick Snyder, etc. But you may not know about Luis Fortuño, governor of Puerto Rico.

Two years ago, Fortuño cut spending much more than any state governor. He fired seventeen thousand government workers. In return, union members held noisy demonstrations outside Fortuño's house. They fought with police. They called him a fascist. Fortuño stood firm.

Fortuño had to make the cuts because Puerto Rico's economy was a mess. "Not just a mess. We didn't have enough money to meet our first payroll." Fortuño's predecessors grew Puerto Rico's government to the point that government employed one out of every three workers (the U.S. mainland average is about one in seven). Puerto Rico was broke. So the new conservative majority, the first in Puerto Rico in forty years, finally cut spending.

What was cut? "Everything." Fortuño told me, "I started with my own salary." The protesters said he should raise taxes instead. "Our taxes were as high as they could be, actually much higher than most of the country. So what we've done is the opposite." Fortuño reduced corporate taxes from 35 percent to 25 percent. He reduced individual income taxes. He privatized government agencies.

"Bring in the private sector," says Fortuño. "They will do a better job. They will do it cheaper."

Fortuño's cuts haven't made him popular. He may save Puerto Rico's economy, but most voters don't yet understand that it's a good thing when fewer people work for the state. It's just not intuitive.

Fortuño's advice for other governors: "Do what you need to do swiftly, like when you take off a Band-Aid. Just do it. And move on to better things." President Ronald Reagan and Michigan governor John Engler did that. They eventually came to be appreciated for the economic booms that followed the cuts. But when they made the cuts, they were harshly criticized.

Maybe Fortuño too will eventually be hailed as a hero. Although people don't understand economics, sometimes they notice results.

The invisible hand works. Around the world, free markets have helped more than a billion people escape "absolute poverty"—living on one dollar a day, or less—since I started reporting.

But once they escape, most instinctively turn to government to "fix" their remaining problems.

RUNNING OUT OF TIME

Economics is complicated. That's one more reason to be grateful for the Constitution: In its relative simplicity, its rules keep government within bounds, so that we need to engage in elaborate number-crunching to try to prove that the bureaucrats' pet programs will bring us to financial ruin.

Some Tea Party activists understand that, and it's one reason why they call for a return to constitutional, limited government. But to get the majority of America to wake up, it may take mounting evidence of crisis. The next crisis after Greece will probably be elsewhere in Europe or in Japan. The population in those places is "graying"—the number of young workers shrinking relative to retirees in need of support—faster than in America. Watching their crises, we will get an advance look at the financial poison that we foist on America's young people.

But I'm not sure voters will pay attention. If Americans didn't learn the folly of central planning from the collapse of the Soviet

Union and the stagnation of socialist economies around the world, they may not learn about the danger of unsustainable budgets from bankruptcy in Greece, Spain, or Japan. Maybe it will take events closer to home. That's why I have mixed feelings when I read about the stupid decisions made by legislatures in California, Illinois, and Connecticut. All three states' politicians pander to unions, and their citizens will suffer for it. But maybe they are "useful idiots." Maybe it will take the economic implosion of California, Connecticut, or Illinois to wake people up.

It is unfortunate that the United States, a nation founded on more libertarian principles than most other countries, now seems incapable of admitting that government has gotten too big. One "problem" is that we've had things so good for so long that most of us simply don't believe, in our guts, that government controls can strangle the golden goose. Overseas, where people see the contrast between good and bad policies more starkly, they sometimes understand the need to make changes before we do. East Asian countries embraced markets and flourished. Sweden and Germany recently liberalized their labor markets and saw their economies improve. Even in the statist nations of Africa, there are growing numbers of free-market activists critical of intrusive governments—and of the foreign aid that helps prop them up.

Again, the enemy here is human intuition. Amid the dazzling bounty of the marketplace, it's easy to take the benefits of markets for granted.

I can go to a foreign country, stick a piece of plastic in the wall, and cash will come out. I can give that same piece of plastic to a stranger who doesn't even speak my language—and he'll rent me a car for a week. When I get home, Visa or MasterCard will send me the accounting—correct to the penny. That's capitalism! I just take it for granted.

Government, by contrast, can't even count votes accurately.

Yet whenever there are problems, people turn to government. Despite the central planners' long record of failure, politicians promise that this time they will "fix" health care, education, the uncertainty of old age, etc., and people believe. Few of us like to think that the government that sits atop us, taking credit for everything, could really be all that rotten. And look at all the good things around us! What, besides our unique government, could have brought us such plenty?

But it's not from $3.8 trillion in spending, eighty thousand new pages of regulations—or democracy—that we get wonderful options like flexible contact lenses, Google, cell phones, increasing life spans, and so much food that even poor people are fat. We get that from limited government and free markets. Government gets credit for the good times even when it does little to bring them about.

All our potential achievements could be imperiled if we do not soon wake up to the fact that big government impedes rather than creates.

The great twentieth-century libertarian H. L. Mencken lamented, "A government at bottom is nothing more than a group of men, and as a practical matter most of them are inferior men. . . . Yet these nonentities, by the intellectual laziness of men in general . . . are generally obeyed as a matter of duty [and] assumed to have a kind of wisdom that is superior to ordinary wisdom."

There is nothing that government can do that we cannot do better as free individuals—and as groups of individuals, working together voluntarily, not at the point of a gun or under threat of a fine.

Without big government, our possibilities are limitless.

NOTES

INTRODUCTION: IS THERE ANYTHING GOVERNMENT CAN'T DO? WELL . . .

1   Congress has only a 12 percent approval rating: Tarrance Group and Lake Research Partners, Battleground Poll 2012 (XLV), Study #13161, Field Dates November 6–9, 2011.

2   "rise of the oceans began to slow and our planet began to heal": Barack Obama, speech in St. Paul, MN, June 23, 2008.

2   "the curious task of economics": F. A. Hayek, *The Fatal Conceit: The Errors of Socialism* (Chicago: University of Chicago Press, 1988).

5   "We are all socialists now!": Jon Meacham, "We Are All Socialists Now," *Newsweek*, February 6, 2009.

5   stimulus jobs: David Leonhardt, "Judging Stimulus by Job Data Reveals Success," *New York Times*, February 16, 2010.

5   can't let GM or Chrysler go bankrupt: David Rogers and Mike Allen, "Bush announces $17.4 billion auto bailout," Politico.com, December 19, 2008.

5   "We've got a responsibility to help them make ends meet": "Obama delivers remarks on jobless benefits: Speech transcript," *Washington Post*, July 19, 2010.

6   Regulation could prevent that: Frank Newport, "Banks, Businesses, and Bailouts," Gallup.com, April 19, 2010.

7   instincts that evolved when we lived in small tribes: Hayek, *The Fatal Conceit*.

8 suck the life out of the local economy: Dennis Coates and Brad R. Humphreys, "The Stadium Gambit and Local Economic Development," *Regulation* 23, no. 2 (2000).

8 Living-wage laws: N. Gregory Mankiw, "The Cost of a 'Living Wage,'" *Boston Globe*, June 24, 2001.

8 help people escape greedy landlords: Robert J. Schiller, "Mom, Apple Pie, and Mortgages," *New York Times*, March 6, 2010.

9 Government's "green" subsidies suck money: Drew Thornley, *Energy & The Environment: Myths & Facts* (New York: Manhattan Institute, 2009).

9 In 2001, Jesus topped the list. In 2009, it was Barack Obama: Dan Froomkin, "Bigger Than Jesus?" *Washington Post*, February 19, 2009.

10 "Generations to come will benefit": R. W. Apple, "Edmund S. Muskie, 81, Dies; Maine Senator and a Power on the National Scene," *New York Times*, March 27, 1996.

10 Ted Kennedy died: John M. Broder, "Social Causes Defined Kennedy, Even at the End of a 46-Year Career in the Senate," *New York Times*, August 26, 2009.

10 "More than any other single person of this age": "The Nobel Peace Prize 1970: Norman Borlaug: Award Ceremony Speech," Nobel Prize.org.

11 "I've taken on tougher guys than this": Ed O'Keefe, "McCain and Obama's New Economic Ads," *Washington Post*, September 17, 2008.

12 "government scientists later concluded that the Corvair": This was the widely reported conclusion of a 1972 National Highway Traffic Safety Administration report conducted by Texas A&M University.

13 "Corporate power lies behind nearly every major problem": Michael Marx and Marjorie Kelly, "Who Will Rule?" *YES!* July 29, 2007.

14 Now the company spends millions on lobbying: Jonathan D. Salant and Jeff Bliss, "Google Follows Microsoft Playbook in Boosting Lobbying Spending," Bloomberg.com, October 21, 2011.

CHAPTER 1: "FIXING" THE ECONOMY

21 "The consensus is": Barack Obama interview, *60 Minutes*, CBS, November 16, 2008.

22 paper clip and trades his way up to a house: Kyle Macdonald, OneRed Paperclip.blogspot.com.

NOTES

22 "save or create" 3.5 million jobs: President Barack Obama, remarks at signing of American Recovery And Reinvestment Act, Denver, CO, February 17, 2009.

23 government had to "jump-start" the economy: Roger Runningen, "Obama Says Jobs Proposal Would 'Jump Start' Economic Growth," Bloomberg.com, September 26, 2011.

23 "Companies are sitting on billions of dollars": Neil Irwin, "With consumers slow to spend, businesses are slow to hire," *Washington Post*, August 21, 2010.

23 "regime uncertainty": Robert Higgs, "Regime Uncertainty: Why the Great Depression Lasted So Long and Why Prosperity Resumed After the War," *Independent Review* 1, no. 4 (Spring 1997).

24 "Pyramid-building, earthquakes, even wars": John Maynard Keynes, *General Theory of Employment, Interest, and Money* (London: Palgrave Macmillan, 1936).

25 "opportunity for a real boom economy in Haiti": Carolyn Lochhead, "Pelosi: Earthquake a chance for 'fresh start' in Haiti," *San Francisco Chronicle*, January 15, 2010.

25 if "space aliens were planning to attack": Paul Krugman interview, *Fareed Zakaria GPS*, CNN, August 14, 2011.

25 "broken window fallacy": Frédéric Bastiat, "That Which Is Seen, and That Which Is Not Seen," 1850.

26 "unofficial jobs creation act": Eric Dash, "Feasting on Paperwork," *New York Times*, September 8, 2011.

27 the New Deal failed: Amity Shlaes, *The Forgotten Man: A New History of the Great Depression* (New York: Harper, 2007).

28 Canadians have a higher rate of home ownership: Alex J. Pollock, "Why Canada Avoided a Mortgage Meltdown," *Wall Street Journal*, March 19, 2010.

29 "It is private capital that is at risk": Franklin D. Raines, "An Open Letter from Frank Raines," April 2004.

29 "stark reminder of the failures": Glen Johnson, "McCain says government 'forced' to bail out AIG," Associated Press, September 17, 2008.

31 pro-bailout columns: Vincent Reinhart, "Secretary Paulson Makes the Right Call," *Wall Street Journal*, September 16, 2008.

31 "Don't Just Do Something, Stand There": Russell Roberts, "Don't Just Do Something, Stand There," *Wall Street Journal*, October 31, 2008.

33 "the reason for FDR's limited short-run success": Paul Krugman, "Franklin Delano Obama?" *New York Times*, November 10, 2008.

34 "There is no disagreement": President Barack Obama, news conference, January 9, 2009.

35 *Fortune* magazine said Serious was "booming": "Serious Windows," *Fortune*, June 8, 2009.

35 *Inc.* magazine did a cover story: Leigh Buchanan, "How to Build a Great Company: Entrepreneur of the Year: Kevin Surace of Serious Materials," *Inc.*, December 2009/January 2010.

35 And why do I mention only the *vice* president?: "Vice President Joe Biden Visits Serious Materials," press release, Serious Materials, April 27, 2009.

35 Rachel Maddow: "One More Thing: Economic Stimulus in Action," *Rachel Maddow Show*, MSNBC, March 2, 2009.

35 Cathy Zoi: Steven Thomma, "Obama energy official has ties to firms that stand to benefit," McClatchy Newspapers, April 26, 2010.

38 "[i]ndustry support of regulation is not rare at all": Bruce Yandle, "We Want to Be Regulated," *Freeman* 60, no. 1 (January/February 2010).

39 alpaca boom a speculative bubble: Tina L. Saitone and Richard J. Sexton. "Alpaca Lies? Speculative Bubbles in Agriculture: Why They Happen and How to Recognize Them," *Applied Economic Perspectives and Policy* 29, no. 2 (2007).

40 National Research Council: National Research Council (Division on Engineering and Physical Sciences) et al., *Transitions to Alternative Transportation Technologies* (Washington, DC: National Academies Press, 2009).

41 Henry Hazlitt adapts: Henry Hazlitt, *Economics in One Lesson* (New York: Harper & Brothers, 1946).

41 "Manufacturing plants have added shifts": "Cash for Clunkers Wraps Up with Nearly 700,000 car sales and increased fuel efficiency, U.S. Transportation Secretary LaHood declares program 'wildly successful,' " press release, U.S. Department of Transportation, August 26, 2009.

42 price of used cars rose $1,800: "Money Guzzler: The Downside of Cash for Clunkers," *Chicago Tribune*, September 22, 2010.

43 leaked documents showed that the Marlins were profitable: Jeff Passan, "Marlin's Profits Came at Taxpayer Expense," Yahoo Sports, August 24, 2010.

43 Pataki complained: Kelly Payeur, "Board rejects Jets stadium," LegislativeGazette.com, June 13, 2005.

44 "go line by line through the federal budget": "Remarks of President Barack Obama—as Prepared for Delivery, Address to Joint Session of Congress," February 24, 2009.

CHAPTER 2: MAKING LIFE FAIR

48 "theory of justice": John Rawls, *A Theory of Justice* (Cambridge, MA: Belknap, 1971).

48 Michael Moore took this thinking to its intuitive conclusion: Michael Moore interview by Laura Flanders, GRITtv.org, February 28, 2011.

49 Fannie Mae and Freddie Mac: Peter J. Wallison, "Opposing view: Fannie, Freddie caused financial crisis," *USA Today*, November 25, 2011.

51 Today residents of Hong Kong are almost as wealthy as Americans: $46,000 per capita in Hong Kong vs. $48,000 per capita in the U.S.

54 "It well appeared that famine must still ensue the next year": Henry Hazlitt, "Private Enterprise Regained: Communism Failed in Plymouth Bay Colony, Too," reprinted in *Freeman* 54, no. 9 (November 2004).

60 "[R]esource-users frequently develop sophisticated": Royal Swedish Academy of Sciences, "The Sveriges Riksbank Prize in Economic Sciences in Memory of Alfred Nobel 2009: Elinor Ostrom, Oliver E. Williamson," press release, Royal Swedish Academy of Sciences, October 12, 2009.

61 *Governing the Commons*: Elinor Ostrom, *Governing the Commons: The Evolution of Institutions for Collective Action* (Cambridge: Cambridge University Press, 1990).

61 Reporter Louis Uchitelle: Louis Uchitelle, "Two Americans Are Awarded Nobel Prize in Economics," *New York Times*, October 12, 2009.

61 Jim Scott's book *Seeing Like a State*: James C. Scott, *Seeing Like a State: How Certain Schemes to Improve the Human Condition Have Failed* (New Haven, CT: Yale University Press, 1998).

CHAPTER 3: KEEPING BUSINESS HONEST

67 Members of New York's City Council: Gail Robinson, "Unions Flex Their Political Muscles," GothamGazette.com, October 12, 2009.

68 One claimed that he had to take off a year and a half: Tom Namako, "A load of bull spit! Months off for spat-on drivers," *New York Post*, May 25, 2010.

69 they still manage to lose money every year: "Transportation 101: What's up with the MTA?" Tri-State Transportation Campaign, TSTC.org, accessed December 2, 2011.

71 As economist Thomas DiLorenzo notes: Thomas J. DiLorenzo, "The Myth of Natural Monopoly," *Review of Austrian Economics* 9, no. 2 (1996).

71 Naomi Klein, wrote a book titled *No Logo*: Naomi Klein, *No Logo: Taking Aim at the Brand Bullies* (Toronto: Picador, 2000).

72 "secret diners": See for example RestaurantSolutions.org.

72 "Hello, E. Coli": Jonathan Cohn, "Bye Bye, Big Bird: Hello, E. Coli," *New Republic*, February 12, 2011.

74 Las Vegas's anticompetitive licensing rules: "IJ Wins Court Victory Vindicating Economic Liberty for Las Vegas Limo Operators: Clutter v. State of Nevada," IJ.org, accessed November 15, 2011.

74 Vegas cab and limousine businesses give "substantial" donations: Dylan Scott, "Woodbury leads all candidates in fundraising for Boulder City election," *Las Vegas Sun*, April 2, 2011.

78 David Price spent six months in a Kansas jail: Steve Fry, "Price Freed from Jail," *Topeka Capital-Journal*, February 23, 2010.

79 a rule called the precautionary principle: "Precautionary Principle—FAQs," Science & Environmental Health, SEHN.org, accessed October 20, 2011.

79 "Never do anything for the first time": Ron Bailey, "Making the Future Safe," *Reason*, July 2, 2003.

82 "a race to the bottom": Senator Sherrod Brown, *Congress from the Inside: Observations from the Majority and the Minority* (Kent, OH: Kent State University Press, 2004).

CHAPTER 4: IMPROVING LIFE FOR WORKERS

84 things like outlaw any wage below $7.25 an hour: U.S. Department of Labor, "Minimum Wage Laws in the States—January 1, 2011," DOL.gov.

85 Before regulation, deaths dropped just as fast: W. Kip Viscusi, *Risk by Choice: Regulating Health and Safety in the Workplace* (Cambridge, MA: Harvard University Press, 1983).

86 "Toward a Marginally Improved Society!": Robert Higgs, *Crisis and Leviathan: Critical Episodes in the Growth of American Government* (New York: Oxford University Press, 1989).

87 Then he could remind Gorbachev: Kenneth T. Walsh, "Ronald Reagan 1911–2004," *U.S. News & World Report*, June 6, 2004.

89 from the union to the candidate who promised: Daniel DiSalvo, "The Trouble with Public Sector Unions," *National Affairs*, Fall 2010.

91 A Heritage Foundation study concluded: James Sherk, "Inflated Federal Pay: How Americans Are Overtaxed to Overpay the Civil Service," Heritage.org, July 7, 2010.

91 Chris Edwards of the Cato: Chris Edwards, "Federal Pay Continues Rapid Ascent," Cato-at-Liberty.org, August 24, 2009.

91 *USA Today* did a comparison of jobs: Dennis Cauchon, "Federal pay ahead of private industry," *USA Today*, March 8, 2010.

92 ninety-five percent of American workers make *more* than the minimum wage: U.S. Bureau of Labor Statistics, "Characteristics of Minimum Wage Workers: 2010," BLS.gov, February 25, 2011.

93 union membership has fallen to only 8 percent of private sector jobs: Steven Greenhouse, "Labor's Decline and Wage Inequality," Economix.blogs, NYTimes.com, August 4, 2011.

94 even 61 percent of Tea Party sympathizers: John Harwood, "53% in US Say Free Trade Hurts Nation: NBC/WSJ Poll," CNBC.com, September 28, 2010.

95 American companies that outsourced jobs also hired: "Outsourced Jobs Become Midterm Election Issue," NPR, *Morning Edition*, October 29, 2010.

96 "start sending a message that somehow we're just": John Nichols, "Is Obama Forgetting About Main Street?" http://www.dailymail.co.uk/news/article-1134608/Obama-backs-Buy-America-EU-warns-start-global-trade-war.html.

96 "consistent with U.S. obligations under international agreements": "The American Recovery and Reinvestment Act (ARRA)," Canada International.gc.ca, June 6, 2011.

96 "Beggar-thy-neighbor policies create more beggars": Burton G. Malkiel, "Congress Wants a Trade War," *Wall Street Journal*, February 5, 2009.

101 After the ADA passed, that number dropped to 48.9: M. J. Field, and A. M. Jette, eds., *The Future of Disability in America: Institute of Medicine (U.S.) Committee on Disability* (Washington, DC: National Academies Press, 2007).

102 They sued Chipotle Mexican Grill: David Goldman, "The 'Chipotle Experience'—A Substitute Experience Violates the ADA," Wendel .com (website of Wendel Rosen Black & Dean LLP), accessed September 9, 2011.

102 Basketball Town, in Rancho Cordova, California: Melody Gutierrez, "Basketball Town a long shot: Legal morass may doom facility despite offer of help for disabled," *Sacramento Bee*, October 3, 2007.

103 *New York* magazine called the ensuing controversy: Peter Hellman, "Toilet Wars," *New York*, May 3, 1993.

104 51 percent of Republican voters favored increasing: Arthur Delaney, "Two-Thirds of Americans Support Raising Minimum Wage: Poll," HuffingtonPost.com, May 25, 2011.

104 "They'll be shouting, Olé!": Rob Scherer and Carla Murphy, "Minimum wage goes up. Do workers care?" *Christian Science Monitor*, July 24, 2009.

105 As economist Don Boudreaux puts it: Donald Boudreaux, letter to the *Wall Street Journal*, June 19, 2008.

108 "Take This Internship and Shove It": Anya Kamenetz, "Take This Internship and Shove It," *New York Times*, May 30, 2006.

CHAPTER 5: FIXING HEALTH CARE

111 WellPoint, Humana, and Cigna got out of the child-only business: Michael F. Cannon, "Six Months Later . . . ," *Washington Times*, September 23, 2010.

111 Principal Financial stopped offering health insurance altogether: Avery Johnson, "Principal Financial Quits Writing Health-Care Policies," *Wall Street Journal*, October 1, 2010.

111 The largest group that got an exemption?: Charles Hurt and Yoav Gonen, "Teachers union gets a pass on ObamaCare rule," *New York Post*, October 8, 2010.

113 relationship between income and health is greater in Canada: June E. O'Neill and Dave M. O'Neill, "Health Status, Health Care and Inequality: Canada vs. the U.S.," National Bureau of Economic Research Working Paper No. 13429 (September 2007).

113 The British National Health Service: Randeep Ramesh, "NHS waiting times soar as doctors blames cuts in hospital budgets," *Guardian*, August 18, 2011.

114 "My baby with Down syndrome": Sarah Palin, "Statement on the Current Health Care Debate," Sarah Palin's Facebook page, http://www.facebook.com/note.php?note_id=113851103434, August 7, 2009.

114 "trying to bring about government-run health care": Lynn Sweet, "Obama says his 'public option' is not 'government run' healthcare," *Chicago Sun-Times*, June 16, 2009.

115 Canadians say they can't find a family doctor: John J. Walters, "Great Quotes About Socialized Medicine," MDPolicy.org, January 20, 2011.

119 an otherwise interesting *New Yorker* article on health-care costs: Atul Gawande, "The Cost Conundrum," *New Yorker*, June 1, 2009.

119 "rationally to comprehend its own limitations": F. A. Hayek, *The Counter-Revolution of Science: Studies in the Abuse of Reason* (Indianapolis: Liberty Fund, 1980).

120 one of the first hospitals in America: Christopher Little, "Detroit Medical Center Awarded 2009 Top Innovator Award for . . . Using Barcodes," The Loftware Blog, April 20, 2009.

121 doctor now spends 14 percent of his income on insurance paperwork: David Fisher, "Why Is Health Insurance So Expensive?" About.com, February 12, 2009.

127 "The disparity between women and men": Senator John Kerry, "Kerry Introduces Legislation to End Gender Disparity in Individual Health Insurance Market," press release, May 5, 2009.

130 Steven Horwitz's First Law of Political Economy: Steven Horwitz, "Have Pro-Deregulation Economists Been Bought?" TheFreeman Online.org, October 7, 2010.

133 73 percent of Republicans and 92 percent of Democrats: "4/18 McClatchy-Marist Poll," MaristPoll.Marist.edu, April 18, 2011.

CHAPTER 6: THE ASSAULT ON FOOD

136 it slightly decreases your "good cholesterol" level: Kathleen Meister, *Trans Fatty Acids and Heart Disease* (New York: American Council on Science and Health, 2006).

137 Felix Ortiz proposed a ban on the use of *any* salt: Andy Newman, "Pass the Salt Ban?" Cityroom.blogs, NYTimes.com, March 10, 2010.

137 The *Washington Post* described the FDA's anti-salt push: Lyndsey Layton, "FDA plans to limit amount of salt allowed in processed food for health reasons," *Washington Post*, April 20, 2010.

138 people who ate low-salt diets were *more* likely to die: Hillel W. Cohen and Michael H. Alderman, "Sodium, blood pressure, and cardiovascular disease," *Current Opinion in Cardiology* 22, no. 4 (July 2007).

138 "no single universal prescription for sodium intake": Michael H. Alderman, "Salt, Blood Pressure, and Human Health," *Hypertension* 36 (2000).

138 "revenue enhancement": Annette Nellen, "New York Proposal for Non-Diet Soda Tax," 21stCenturyTaxation.blogspot.com, December 18, 2008.

139 Politicians in Illinois passed a 6 percent tax on candy: Matt Bartosik, "Chicago Braces for Candy and Alcohol Tax Hike," NBCChicago.com, September 1, 2009.

141 As the *Los Angeles Times* reported in 2010: P. J. Huffstutter, "Raw-food raid highlights a hunger," *Los Angeles Times*, July 25, 2010.

143 about half of new chemicals fail to get EPA approval: *America's War on "Carcinogens": Reassessing the Use of Animal Tests to Predict Human Cancer Risk* (New York: American Council on Science and Health, 2005).

144 "Some early animal studies produced results": Richard Sharpe, "Hidden Danger in Baby Bottles?" *Sun*, December 5, 2011.

149 "another fossil-fuel machine": Michael Pollan, "Power Steer," *New York Times Magazine*, March 31, 2002.

CHAPTER 7: CREATING A RISK-FREE WORLD

157 Centers for Disease Control and Prevention found no good: Robert A. Hahn, Oleg O. Bilukha, Alex Crosby, et al., "First Reports Evaluating the Effectiveness of Strategies for Preventing Violence: Firearms Laws," *MMWR* 52 (RR14), October 3, 2003.

158 "We're never going to get a gun control law": Barbara Walters, *The View*, ABC, April 18, 2007.

158 a day trader's shooting rampage in Atlanta: "Suicide of Atlanta shooting suspect ends unspeakable day," CNN.com, July 29, 1999.

158 the very next day in a suburb of Atlanta: "Would-Be Assailant Thwarted in Georgia," Reuters, August 3, 1999.

159 crime fell by an average 10 percent: John R. Lott, *More Guns, Less Crime* (Chicago: University of Chicago Press, 2000).

160 D.C. mayor Adrian Fenty predicted: "Gun ruling to spark legal battles nationwide," MSNBC.MSN.com, June 26, 2008.

160 "If they come in here, break the door open, I can't do nothing": Ariane de Vogue, "Supreme Court Weighs Chicago's Strict Gun Ban," ABCNews.go.com, March 2, 2009.

161 describes some of the absurd things that happen: Paul Rosenzweig and Brian W. Walsh, *One Nation Under Arrest: How Crazy Laws, Rogue Prosecutors, and Activist Judges Threaten Your Liberty* (Washington, DC: Heritage Foundation, 2010).

163 Americans legally bet a hundred million dollars *every day*: John W., "A Blinding Look at the City of Lights," OnlineCasinoReports.com, October 19, 2007.

164 Texas police once raided a branch of Veterans of Foreign Wars: "Texas Close 'Em: Cops Raid Poker Games," Reason.TV (accessed October 3, 2011).

167 flood insurance now insures 5.5 million homes: FEMA, "Resources: Flood Facts," FloodSmart.gov, November 14, 2011.

170 They save fifteen thousand lives a year: National Highway Traffic Safety Administration, "Lives Saved Calculations for Seat Belts and Frontal Air Bags," DOT HS 811 206 (December 2009).

171 It's called the Peltzman Effect: Paul G. Specht, "The Peltzman Effect: Do Safety Regulations Increase Unsafe Behavior," *Journal of SH&E Research* 4, no. 3 (Fall 2007).

CHAPTER 8: MAKING SURE NO ONE GETS OFFENDED

178 Such laws allowed the Canadian Human Rights Commission: John Jalsevac, "Two Years and $100,000 Later: Ezra Levant Complaint Dismissed by Human Rights Commission," ArpaCanada.ca, August 7, 2008.

178 Human Rights Commission debated hate speech charges: "Rights commission dismisses complaint against Maclean's," CBC.ca, June 28, 2008.

178 A Washington State bagel store owner was fined: William R. Maurer, "Blowing a Hole in the First Amendment," IJ.org, October 2003.

183 Alien and Sedition Acts: Constitutional Rights Foundation, "The Alien and Sedition Acts: Defining American Freedom," CRF-USA .org (accessed August 22, 2011).

184 "strikes at the heart of democracy": Editorial, "The Court's Blow to Democracy," *New York Times*, January 21, 2010.

184 "threatens to undermine the integrity of elected institutions": Editorial, "The Supreme Court removes important limits on campaign finance," *Washington Post*, January 22, 2010.

184 Nat Hentoff put it in the title of his book: Nat Hentoff, *Free Speech for Me—But Not for Thee: How the American Left and Right Relentlessly Censor Each Other* (New York: Perennial, 1993).

185 "Corporations are people": Serafin Gomez, "Mitt Romney at Iowa State Fair," http://politics.blogs.foxnews.com/2011/08/11/romney -confronts-hecklers-hard-iowa.

185 One government lawyer: Benjamin Barr, "Will S.G. correct the government's book banning mistake?" CampaignFreedom.org, September 17, 2009.

CHAPTER 9: EDUCATING CHILDREN

190 "have literally been cutting for five, six, seven years in a row": Gail Connelly, "A Conversation with Secretary of Education Arne Duncan," *Principal*, November/December 2010.

191 "MBA-style thinking": Jim Epstein and Michelle Fields, "What We Saw at the Save Our Schools Rally in Washington, DC," Reason.TV, July 30, 2011.

193 Albert Shanker: "Teachers Unions Made Their Bed, Must Lie in It," *Meridian [MS] Star*, August 13, 1985.

193 But today American teachers average more than $50,000: Matthew DiCarlo and Nate Johnson, "Survey & Analysis of Teacher Salary Trends, 2007," American Federation of Teachers.

200 "identifying the bottom 10 percent of employees": Jack Welch with Suzy Welch, *Winning* (New York: HarperBusiness, 2005).

203 "If I wanted to find a great public school for Malia and Sasha": David Jackson, "Obama: 'D.C. public schools are struggling,'" *USA Today*, September 28, 2010.

204 "Children in public schools generally performed as well or better": *Comparing Private Schools and Public School Using Hierarchical Linear Modeling*, U.S. Department of Education, NCES 2006–461.

205 In 2010, the Department of Education came out with the results: *The Evaluation of Charter School Impacts: Final Report*, National Center for Educational Evaluation and Regional Assistance, 2010.

208 the U.S. Department of Health and Human Services found: Press Release: "Head Start Children Not Adequately Prepared for School, HHS Report Concludes," U.S. Department of Health and Human Services, June 9, 2003.

CHAPTER 10: THE WAR ON DRUGS: BECAUSE ALCOHOL PROHIBITION WORKED SO WELL . . .

220 "individuals whose actions are in clear and unambiguous": David W. Ogden, "Memorandum for Selected United States Attorneys on Investigations and Prosecutions in States Authorizing the Medical Use of Marijuana," U.S. Department of Justice, October 19, 2009.

221 But the State Department called their spraying a big success!: Garry Leech, "State Department Report Delivers a False Positive," Colombia Journal.org, April 24, 2004.

222 "The crowd went silent at his call to legalize hard drugs": Page Six, "The Lesser Evil," *New York Post*, May 21, 2008.

223 The National Institutes of Health found: *Epidemiologic Trends in Drug Abuse*, National Institute on Drug Abuse, January 2008.

224 as Jacob Sullum points out in the book *Saying Yes*: Jacob Sullum, *Saying Yes* (New York: Tarcher, 2004).

CHAPTER 11: WARS TO END WAR

234 I read the Natan Sharansky book that Bush kept next to his bed: Natan Sharansky, *The Case for Democracy: The Power of Freedom to Overcome Tyranny and Terror* (New York: PublicAffairs, 2004).

235 The *Wall Street Journal* editorializes with such certainty: Review & Outlook, "The 9/11 Decade," September 10, 2011.

235 "Bomb bomb Iran": Don Gonyea, "Jesting, McCain Sings: 'Bomb, Bomb, Bomb' Iran," NPR.org, April 20, 2007.

235 Smart defense hawks like Bill Kristol say: Jamie Fly and William Kristol, "A Period of Consequences," *Weekly Standard*, June 21, 2010.

235 "Against millenarian fanaticism": Charles Krauthammer, "The Tehran Calculus," *Washington Post*, September 15, 2006.

238 "awash in $100 bills": David Pallister, "How the U.S. sent $12bn in cash to Iraq: And watched it vanish," *Guardian*, February 7, 2007.

238 so much cash flying around the office: "Billions Wasted in Iraq?" segment of *60 Minutes*, CBS, February 12, 2006.

239 a play about donkeys: Peter Van Buren, "Checkbook Diplomacy," *Foreign Policy*, September 29, 2011.

239 One of the more infuriating stories: Clare Lockart et al., transcript of Session II of a Council on Foreign Relations Symposium on Afghanistan, Pakistan, and U.S. National Security, April 21, 2009, Washington, DC.

245 According to Rajiv Chandrasekaran's book: Rajiv Chandrasekaran, *Imperial Life in the Emerald City: Inside Iraq's Green Zone* (New York: Knopf Doubleday, 2007).

248 "compete in a workplace 'March Madness'"–style: Derek Kravitz, "As outrage over screenings rises, sites consider replacing TSA," *Washington Post*, December 31, 2011.

CHAPTER 12: KEEPING NATURE EXACTLY AS IS . . . FOREVER

260 *Silent Spring*: Rachel Carson, *Silent Spring* (Boston: Houghton Mifflin, 1962).

262 "If there's nothing else and it's going to save lives": Nicholas D. Kristof, "It's Time to Spray DDT," *New York Times*, January 8, 2005.

262 the media have been predicting the age of the electric car: Robert Bryce, *Power Hungry: The Myths of "Green" Energy and the Real Fuels of the Future* (New York: PublicAffairs, 2011).

263 We do have cars like the Chevy Volt: Mark Modica, "Chevy Volt Sales Disappoint," National Legal and Policy Center, NLPC.org, December 5, 2011.

266 "If only we could be as energy smart as Denmark.": Thomas Friedman, "Flush with Energy," *New York Times*, August 9, 2008.

269 Henry Hazlitt wrote in his bestseller: Henry Hazlitt, *Economics in One Lesson: The Shortest and Surest Way to Understand Basic Economics* (New York: Three Rivers Press, 1988).

271 *Green Gone Wrong*: Heather Rogers, *Green Gone Wrong: How Our Economy Is Undermining the Environmental Revolution* (New York: Scribner, 2010).

272 "100 percent of our electricity from renewable energy": "Al Gore's Speech on Renewable Energy," NPR.org, July 17, 2008.

CHAPTER 13: BUDGET INSANITY

275 Budget estimates from CBO, American Enterprise Institute, Heritage Foundation, Center for American Progress, Economic Policy Institute, Roosevelt Institute Campus Network, Bipartisan Policy Center, and Cato Institute.

CONCLUSION: THERE OUGHT *NOT* TO BE A LAW

299 vowed to "protect" Medicare, and cringed: Naftali Bendavid and Jonathan Weisman, "Medicare Revamp Exposes Division Within the GOP," *Wall Street Journal*, May 17, 2011.

299 the United States has fallen to ninth place: Heritage Foundation/*Wall Street Journal*, "Index of Economic Freedom World Rankings: Top Ten of 2011," Heritage.org.

300 Now Canada's debt is less than 30 percent of GDP: *National Post* Staff, "WTF: The federal budget and Canadian debt," *National Post*, March 21, 2011.

303 finally cut spending: Greg Allen, "As Puerto Rican Economy Lags, Some Question Cuts," *All Things Considered*, NPR, September 26, 2011.

ACKNOWLEDGMENTS

In his book *The Rational Optimist*, British journalist Matt Ridley writes about "ideas having sex." That concept intrigued me, so I asked him to explain it on my FBN show. Ridley argues that life improves because "ideas mate and produce combinations of different ideas . . . just as genes recombine and produce new genes . . . that's what causes innovation."

That made sense to me, and made me realize that it is also the process that created this book. Television is a collaborative business. For my TV shows, I get to harvest the best ideas of my six-person staff, Fox's researchers in its "Brain Room," and the libertarian economists who understood these issues long before I did.

So I am grateful to all of you, especially Todd Seavey, Sheldon Richman, Don Boudreaux, David Boaz, Andrew Coulson, Michael Cannon, and Ilan Zechory. I took your ideas and combined them into the arguments in this book.

I especially thank Executive Producer Kristi Kendall for working so hard to organize my TV show, and this book, and make my work possible.

Many chapters are based on research and writing done by Kendall and Fox producers Patrick McMenamin, Maxim Lott,

Andrew Kirell, Mike Ricci, Tim Silfies, Frank Mastropolo, and Nate Chaffetz.

My wonderful assistant, Alexandra Martin, did research and allowed me to write the book by organizing my life.

I'm indebted to my liberal friends, Alan Meyers, Joe Sibilia, Joe Simonetti, Kevin McKean, Jim Floyd, Mark Smith, and Miriam Cukier for passionately arguing your incorrect positions so that I could better see that you are wrong and I am right.

I'm indebted to my brother, Tom, who, despite being much smarter than I, only belatedly came around to appreciate the wisdom of Hayek, Smith, Von Mises, and his little brother.

I thank Andrea Rich of StosselintheClassroom.org, because you convert the ideas in this book into videos that teachers use to teach high school students about markets.

I thank my interns, whose ideas and research were mated into passages of *No, They Can't*, especially Charles Cougar, Andrew Lundeen, Arielle Mellen, and Tracy Oppenheimer.

I thank my book agent, Mel Berger, for your quick responses, editor Mitchell Ivers for your thoughtful comments, and Richard Leibner and Carole Cooper for preventing me from throwing away my TV career in fits of anger at my bosses at ABC.

Finally, I'm grateful to Threshold publisher Louise Burke, Eric Strauss, and Laur, Max, and Zena Partha for the many things you did that make this book possible.

All your ideas met, had sex, and then produced the better (I hope) ideas that are in these pages.

Of course, what if some of our ideas were dumb? Ridley had an answer for that: "Lots of people in a room talking to each other, however stupid they are, can achieve a lot more than clever people."